AF216077

Ballet

THE ESSENTIAL GUIDE TO TECHNIQUE AND CREATIVE PRACTICE

Ballet

THE ESSENTIAL GUIDE TO TECHNIQUE AND CREATIVE PRACTICE

EDITED BY

JENNIFER JACKSON

THE CROWOOD PRESS

First published in 2021 by
The Crowood Press Ltd
Ramsbury, Marlborough
Wiltshire SN8 2HR

enquiries@crowood.com

www.crowood.com

This impression 2026

© Jennifer Jackson and contributors 2021

All rights reserved. No part of this publication may be reproduced or transmitted in any form or by any means, electronic or mechanical, including photocopy, recording, or any information storage and retrieval system, without permission in writing from the publishers.

British Library Cataloguing-in-Publication Data
A catalogue record for this book is available from the British Library.

For product safety-related questions contact productsafety@crowood.com

ISBN 978 1 78500 830 6

Picture credits/copyright
Frontispiece: Isabela Coracy and Mthuthuzeli November in Cathy Marston's *The Suit* for Ballet Black. Photography by ASH.
Front cover: Johan Persson.
Back cover: Nicholas Espinosa.

The images on the following pages have been sourced from The Royal Ballet School Special Collections by kind permission: p.22; p.25; p.26; p.27; p.29 (right); p.30; p.31 (left and right); p.32 (left and right); p.33; p.34; p.37; p.38; p.39; p.40; p.44 (bottom); p.45; p.46 (top and bottom); p.47; p.48; p.50; p.51; p.52; p.53; p.55; p.76; p.99; p.100; p.155.

The archives of The Royal Ballet School have accrued since its founding in 1926 and are available to researchers. Over 700 items can be accessed via the School's website. Descriptions of the Special Collections are available on the Jisc Archives Hub (formerly the Joint Information Systems Committee (JISC)) research network.

ASH (Arnaud Stephenson & Amber Hunt): p.98; p.178; p.181; p.183 (bottom); p.185; p.186; p.187 (top and bottom). **Patrick Baldwin:** p.44 (top). **Baron:** p.48. **Annie Bloomfield:** p.121 (left and right); p.126; p.127; p.132; p.134 (left and right). **Deirdre Chapman:** p.196 (top); p.207. **Rachel Cherry, Royal Ballet School:** p.20; p.94 (top). **Nicholas Espinosa:** p.56; p.58; p.60; p.62; p.63 (top and bottom); p.64; p.65; p.66 (top and bottom); p.70; p.71; p.73; p.74; p.75; p.80; p.81; p.82; p.83; p.86; p.87; p.89 (bottom); p.90; p.91; p.92. **Claudia Evans:** p.120 (left and right); p.122 (left and right); p.123 (left and right); p.129 (left and right); p.130 (top and bottom); p.131; p.138 (top and bottom); p.139. **Alex Fine:** p.159. **Felix Fonteyn:** p.49. **Gerschel:** p.46 (top). **Sean Goldthorpe:** p.172; p.177. **Gregory Heisler:** p.115. **Adrian Hobbs:** p.158; p.160; p.162; p.163 (bottom); p.165; p.166. **Rachel Hollings, Royal Opera House:** p.188; p.190; p.202; p.205; p.208. **Emma Kauldhar:** p.174 (top); p.176. **Robin Kent:** p.169. **Tristram Kenton, Royal Ballet School:** p.12; p.94 (bottom). **Ewa Krasucka:** p.154; p.157. **Lipnitzski:** p.47. **Nigel Norrington/ArenaPAL:** p.105. **Sasha Onyshchenko:** p.168. **Mikael Örtenheim:** p.170. **Johan Persson:** p.78; p.106; p.111; p.116; p.143; p.145; p.150; p.212. **Martin Pyne:** p.209. **Graham Read:** p.104. **Sasha (Alexander Stewart):** p.99. **Frank Sharman:** p.50. **Brian Slater:** p.21; p.174 (bottom). **Leslie Spatt:** p.108. **Gavin Sutherland:** p.183 (top). **Martha Swope:** p.55. **Andrej Uspenski, Royal Ballet School:** p.18 (left and right); p.88. **Andrej Uspenski, Royal Opera House:** p.9; p.89 (top); p.95; p.102; p.114; p.182; p.196 (bottom); p.197; p.198; p.200; p.201; p.210. **Filip van Roe:** p.163 (top). **Dorothy Wilding:** p.25.

Illustrations
Sally Geeve: p.14 (top and bottom). **Adrian Hobbs:** p.17. **Gregory Mislin, The Royal Ballet:** p.204. **Susan Tyler:** p.119; p.125; p.136.

Typeset by Simon and Sons

Cover design by Maggie Mellett

Printed and bound in India by Thomson Press India Pvt. Ltd.

CONTENTS

DEDICATION AND ACKNOWLEDGEMENTS

FOR ROGER TULLY (1928–2020) IN LOVING MEMORY

This book emerges from what has been a hugely stimulating process in the company of wonderful colleagues. It is a great privilege to have worked with them all and to have learnt so much along the way. There are many people to thank for their generosity, support and commitment to making this book happen and for thought-provoking conversations and exchange.

Very special thanks to Adrian Hobbs for his support throughout, for feedback, for his tireless work on the images to prepare them for publication and for post-production on photographs in Chapters 3, 4 and 6.

Thanks also to the authors of each chapter for their stamina, the stimulation of our numerous exchanges and for their excellent contributions.

Nicholas Espinosa for his photographic expertise and huge generosity, providing practical resources for the photoshoots.

Susie Crow for her insightful reading and help at each stage, and taking time away from her own (PhD) writing project; Kate Flatt, Nicholas Minns and Angela Wilson for reading, excellent suggestions and feedback on the final drafts.

Anna Meadmore and Rachel Hollings for going out of their way to help with gathering photographs. Kevin O'Hare (Royal Ballet), Ruby Wolk (Learning and Participation, Royal Opera House), Christopher Powney and Mark Annear (Royal Ballet School), Nicholas Espinosa (London Studio Centre), Aakesh Odedra and Leantwoproductions for authorizing the permission to use their photographs.

All the artists and interviewees who contributed their invaluable thoughts in conversations and in written responses to our questions during research for the book.

Sally Geeve, Adrian Hobbs and Susan Tyler for illustrations.

I am especially grateful to Lavinia Exham and the following photographers for their generosity and for giving permission for the use of their work. They are:

Adrian Hobbs, Alex Fine, Andrej Uspenski, Annie Bloomfield, Arnaud Stephenson & Amber Hunt (ASH), Brian Slater, Claudia Evans, Emma Kauldhar, Ewa Krasucka, Filip van Roe, Graham Read, Gregory Heisler, Johan Persson, Leslie Spatt, Martin Pyne, Mikael Örtenheim, Patrick Baldwin, Rachel Cherry, Rachel Hollings, Robin Kent, Sasha Onyshchenko and Sean Goldthorpe.

The dancers for their great good humour and time in the photoshoots:

Abbie Hollis, Abigail Everard, Angela Wilson, Anita Feerick, Denilson Almedia, Lauren Everard, Mark Coates, Laura Bratek, Madeleine Smith, Montanna Springer, Oona Landgrebe, Regan Wilson, Ryan Hine, Serafina Barbieri and Zoe Arshamian.

CONTRIBUTING AUTHORS

Mark Annear is Head of Training and Access at The Royal Ballet School. Since performing with The Australian Ballet, Mark has worked extensively in vocational dance training for thirty years. He lectured at West Australian Academy of Performing Arts, was a senior classical teacher, then head of senior school and academic studies at the Australian Ballet School.

Karen Berry has had a diverse career in dance, including performing, researching, choreographing, teaching and developing dance syllabi, and courses for students and teachers. She currently works as a peripatetic teacher and Teacher Training Manager at The Royal Ballet School in London, whilst continuing to teach at Danscentre in Aberdeen.

Ginny Brown is chief executive of the Imperial Society of Teachers of Dancing (ISTD). Ginny started her career as a ballet teacher, specializing in introducing ballet to new audiences. She worked for the education departments of several UK companies before being invited to establish the Dance Partnership and Access Programme at The Royal Ballet School.

Deirdre Chapman danced professionally with San Francisco Ballet, Rambert Dance Company, and The Royal Ballet. She has a teaching diploma from The Royal Ballet School, and an MA in dance anthropology. She currently works to assist and re-stage ballets by choreographers, including: Kim Brandstrup, Kurt Jooss, Cathy Marston, Crystal Pite, Hofesh Shechter and Pam Tanowitz, and teaches vocational and professional ballet and contemporary classes.

Stephanie De'Ath has studied dancers' health throughout her professional dance training, and developed this interest at Trinity Laban in an MSc in dance science, later qualifying as a soft-tissue therapist from North London School of Sports Massage (NLSSM). Stephanie has been a lecturer in dance science at UK universities and vocational dance colleges and is now Head of Student Welfare at London Studio Centre and a dance-specialist soft-tissue therapist.

Laura Erwin's interest in experiential anatomy and somatic practices began when studying dance at Middlesex University and London Contemporary Dance School. After working freelance as a dance performer and teacher she qualified in STOTT Pilates and now works as Head of Dance Science at London Studio Centre.

Jennifer Jackson is a former soloist with The Royal Ballet, lecturer at University of Surrey and choreography tutor at The Royal Ballet School. She is currently Artistic Director of London Studio Centre's Images Ballet Company. She is published in academic books and professional dance journals, and her commissioned choreography includes works for ballet companies and vocational schools.

Nicola Katrak is of English-Pakistani parentage and began ballet lessons in Kent, before joining The Royal Ballet School where teachers included Joan Lawson, Pauline Wadsworth, Nancy Kilgour, Pamela May and Eileen Ward. Dancing with Sadler's Wells Royal Ballet (1975–88), her principal roles included

Lise, Giselle, Aurora and Swanilda. She was the first SWRB artist in education before returning to The Royal Ballet School, where she currently teaches.

Anna Meadmore graduated from The Royal Ballet School Teachers' Training Course, later joining the staff as dance history teacher and archivist. She contributed to the school's focus on style series of masterclasses (2012–13), which has informed her chapter in this book. Anna co-edited *Robert Helpmann: the Many Faces of a Theatrical Dynamo* (Dance Books, 2018) with Richard Allen Cave.

Nicholas Minns received his BA in architecture at Cambridge before training as a dancer at the Rambert School of Ballet and with Roger Tully in London. He performed with Les Grands Ballets Canadiens in Montreal and now writes about dance on his blog: writingaboutdance.com.

Jonathan Still has been a company pianist for English National Ballet and Ballett der Deutschen Oper, Berlin, and music development manager for the Royal Academy of Dance. He has an MA in music education from UCL Institute of Education, where he is also completing a PhD.

Side stage at 'Beginnners'.

INTRODUCTION
Jennifer Jackson

This book gathers together the experience, knowledge and wisdom of ballet practitioners: dancers, choreographers, teachers and scholars, all experts in their field. They have written this for you, the dancer, who has a serious interest and feeling for ballet, and who wants to know more.

It is a guide to knowledge – the knowledge that will encourage you to grow as an artist, to explore what is good practice, to reflect on your experience and to ask questions.

It tells you from where the art form comes, in order to help you know where you might take it, while developing a healthy dynamic relationship with the subject of your curiosity and passion.

It will be of benefit to teachers, who are also dancers and remain curious about engaging with new resources and ideas. It aims to educate in ballet (as in the Latin word *educere)* 'to lead out' from you, the person who dances.

Each chapter focuses on an aspect of ballet as a performing art with traditions of training, and creative and performance practices, spanning almost four centuries. You can read any of the chapters separately, and together they outline a journey you might make today from the underpinning principles of ballet, through an appreciation of different styles and schooling, into the studio for practice in class, outside class, in choreography and rehearsals.

Chapter 1 reveals ways in which ballet is both extraordinary and accessible, how the geometry underpinning the aesthetic is rooted in natural physical law and is fundamental to the human body. In Chapter 2, the social nature of ballet as a performing art is highlighted, as you tour its rich history of oral transmission between peoples and nations over time. People make art! You learn that style and schooling emerge through the creative activity of dancers, teachers and choreographers. The next three chapters offer perspectives on practical dance training in the ballet class and for the serious vocational student. Common to all is an emphasis on attention to the fundamentals of technique, your own sense of engagement and potential for growth. The principles, rules and vocabulary are a framework for exploration, for discovery and for developing good, disciplined and truthful practice. The dance science in Chapter 6 supports your practical study with analysis of the anatomy of key postures and movements in ballet technique, and advice on nutrition and lifestyle. Moving outwards from the individual dancer's practice to focus on creating and collaborating, Chapter 7 opens up the craft of choreography through the voices of choreographers at different stages of their careers. Chapter 8 focuses on a ballet musician's insight into the diverse ways in which music is a vital component in both ballet choreography and class. Chapter 9 considers what is best practice in the rehearsal studio, where ballets are prepared for the stage, and the Conclusion invites you to reflect on what leads the dancer back to class.

Your teachers are your essential guides in your dance journey. Knowing what has influenced an artist can help locate their practice and your understanding of their views. My own experience, and that of several of the authors, has been shaped by study and careers with The Royal Ballet School and Company. Amongst my early teachers, Eileen Ward showed me that with attentive practice according to the rules, transformation happens. Her little saying 'do it for YOURself' encouraged the essential responsibility that you take as the dancer for your learning and lifestyle. Anya Grinstead inspired me in the 'dance' and flow of movement, passing on the wisdom of her teacher Audrey de Vos. Piers Beaumont helped me to find the courage and imaginative tools to meet the demands of performing principal roles. As a mature dancer I had the good fortune to work with another great teacher, Roger Tully, who studied with Kathleen Crofton, one of Anna Pavlova's dancers, and later a ballet mistress with American Ballet Theatre in the 1960s. In Tully I found a radical and subtle guide to unlocking individual potential and learning through practical experience of the essential principles. His emphasis on research and discovery of the initiation of movement, and the play of opposition around the aplomb, re-awakened my curiosity and revolutionized my thinking and practice. I also learnt that practising without a mirror shifts attention away from a two-dimensional body image toward sensation and feeling, and the multi-dimensional 'dance'. He expressed big ideas in simple but pithy phrases that led to deeper engagement – 'the dynamic of movement is in the opposition', 'you have the ideal body for your own dance' and 'your dance refines your ideal body'. You will encounter his 'voice' and thoughts in several chapters.

Your experience of choreography and performing is also your essential guide to growing in knowledge and understanding. It is useful to think of being in relationship with ballet and, like any relationship, it is dynamic and changes with experience over time. You often make big leaps when you are in unfamiliar territory – intellectually, emotionally or physically – where you are on the edge of your known abilities; for example, in workshop or performance. The energy of performing is a part of every time you dance – even in class.

As a dancer today, you are both an artist and an athlete. Chapter 6 points you toward a wealth of sport and dance science research that has boosted knowledge of the athletic aspects of practice. The remaining chapters lean toward supporting your artistic growth, for which there is little research and no 'how to' manual. Use the book to encourage, provoke and feed your 'own dance', and to pursue your dream. Remember that in ballet, you have a language for some fundamentals of the human condition in your everyday practice. Each person's journey and relationship with ballet as a performing art is complex and unique, with rich discoveries on the way. Look deeply and be in no hurry. The art form itself – its principles, vocabulary and repertoire – is your essential guide.

Marianna Tsembenhoi and James Large, Royal Ballet (Upper) School students performing *Sea Interludes* by Andrew McNicol at the Royal Opera House.

CHAPTER 1

FOUNDING PRINCIPLES OF CLASSICAL BALLET
Ginny Brown

Ballet is one of the most popular dance styles in the world. There are ballet companies based in most major cities, principal ballet dancers have become household names and each week millions of children learn ballet at local dance schools. The spectacle of ballet, with its super-human skill and extraordinary synthesis of aural and visual splendour, offers entertainment and escape. But a deeper attraction, I believe, is that the underlying classical principles of ballet are based on the laws of nature and the human form. So when we watch or perform ballet, the harmony of the shape and movement feels intuitively 'right'.

Yet with its highly specialized technique and long history, ballet can appear inaccessible and difficult to understand. The physical challenges take time and perseverance to master, and its codified language requires specialist study. Therefore, ballet is often perceived as an elite activity – traditionally only enjoyed by those who have spent years learning about the art form and who have been able to pay for the privilege! But this need not be the case. The beauty of ballet is that the classical principles, at its heart, are fundamentally connected to our natural human movement potential. These classical principles, which underpin both the codified technique and the ballet repertoire, can provide an understandable entry point into this complex and physically demanding dance style. By exploring these foundations, this chapter aims to inspire the experienced dancer and teacher to reconnect with the fundamental principles that shape the art form, as well as offering a starting point from which inexperienced dancers can understand, embody and enjoy the classicism of ballet.

CLASSICAL PRINCIPLES

Like all classical art forms, ballet draws on the classical ideals of balance, harmony and proportion. These qualities are found throughout nature, including in the human body, which is naturally vertical, symmetrical and balanced. Therefore, when learning or teaching ballet it is liberating to remember that, whilst the technical movement may be challenging to master, it is also firmly rooted in the natural design of our bodies.

The Golden Section

These classical principles can be described by a set of geometric proportions known as the Golden Section or the Divine Proportion. Mathematically, the Golden Section proposes a particular relationship between the parts and the whole, and is most easily understood when illustrated as a straight line.

This straight line is divided approximately into three-fifths and two-fifths. This same proportion can be found in our own bodies and relates to the famous Fibonacci series of numbers.[1] For example, try measuring the length of your body from

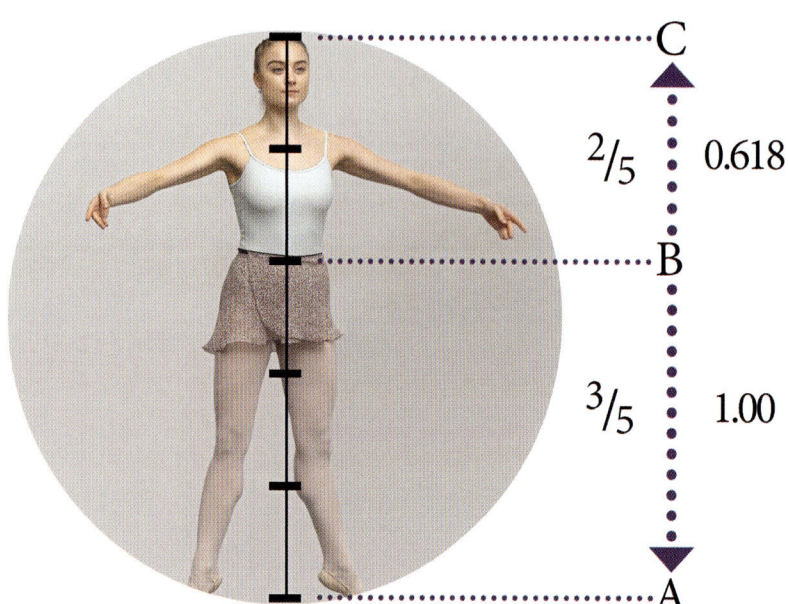

C

$^2/_5$ 0.618

B

$^3/_5$ 1.00

A

The whole (AC: 1.618) to the longer (AB: 1) as the longer (AB: 1) is to the shorter (BC: 0.618).

Using these proportions, a rectangle can be drawn with ever decreasing segments. A golden spiral is formed by connecting the rectangles.

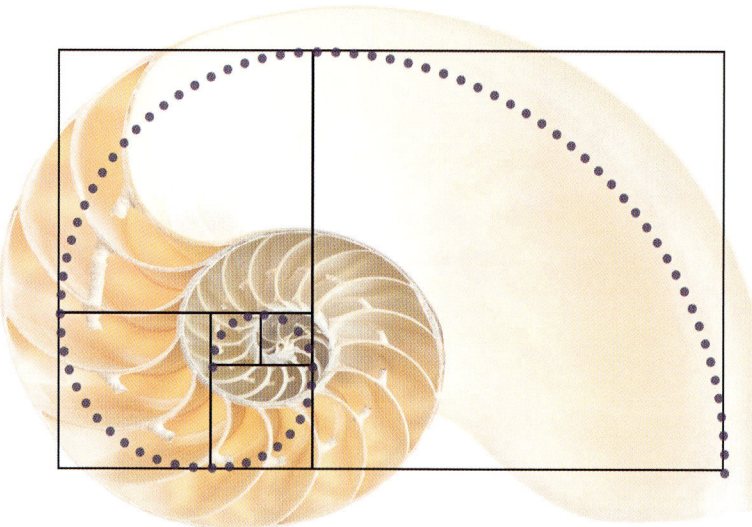

head to feet (AC). Then measure the length from your navel to feet (AB) and from navel to head (BC). You should find that the proportions broadly match those of the illustrated line (the length from head to navel is approximately two-fifths of your total height and the length from navel to feet is approximately three-fifths).

Patterns in Nature

These proportions give rise to a series of shapes and dynamics that appear throughout nature from the uncurling of a leaf, to the spiral of a galaxy. They form principles of harmony that have been acknowledged as fundamental truths. They are reflected in the proportions of our bodies – not only in the ratio of one body part to another, but in whorls of hair, our fingerprints and in the spiral of the inner ear canal. These proportions have also been used by architects to produce buildings of outstanding beauty: from the pyramids of Egypt, to the Parthenon in Athens, European Gothic cathedrals and even modern buildings, such as the Gherkin in London.[2] So let's consider how ballet employs these principles of balance, harmony and logical order to shape the design of the body and its movement through time and space.

Geometric Patterns

Leonardo da Vinci illustrated this, the first known treatise on the Divine Proportion, by Luca Piacolli. Da Vinci's drawing depicts the perfect proportions of the human body. The man's body is symmetrical either side of the vertical axis. The figure is

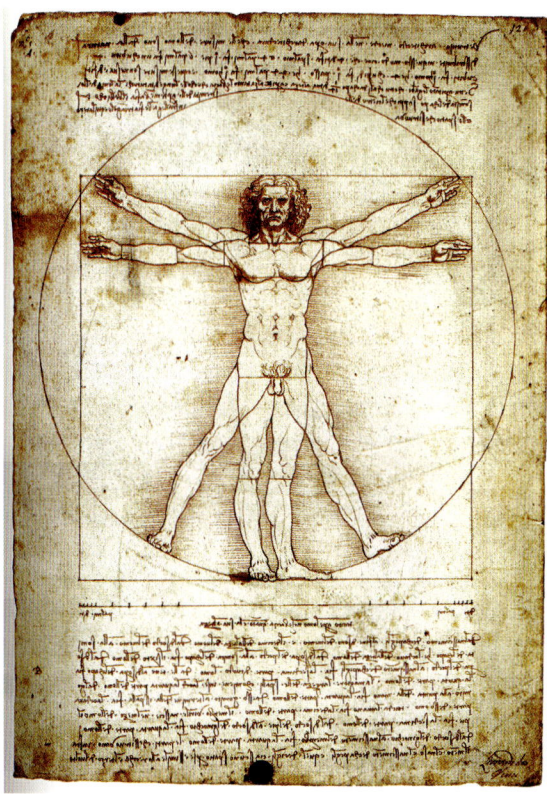

Vitruvian Man, one of Leonardo da Vinci's most famous drawings, depicts the perfect proportions of the human body.

inscribed within a circle and a square – the fundamental geometric patterns that inform classical ballet. All the movements that your body performs in ballet take place within an imaginary circle (your kinesphere) and in relation to an imaginary square (the dancer's square).

HISTORICAL CONTEXT

Ballet's interest in the classical principles of refining and formalizing natural patterns into geometric designs can be traced right back to its inception. Ballet began in the Renaissance, in the French and Italian courts of the sixteenth and seventeenth centuries, where dancing was considered a noble skill for royalty and courtiers. These court dances drew inspiration from local folk dance – the dance of the people – which, in turn, reflected patterns in nature, such as circling, spirals, opening and closing, advancing and retreating. This connection to nature can be traced through ballet's history – in the earthly scenes of Romantic ballets, the stylized character dances of Petipa's classical ballets and in the pagan ritual portrayed in Nijinsky's revolutionary *Rite of Spring*.

Verticality

Ballet begins with one of the unique features of the human body – our verticality. Standing still, we can sense a straight line running vertically through the body – from the centre of the head, through the torso and down between the two feet. This imaginary vertical line allows you to feel your weight in relation to gravity and so remain balanced and 'centred' (*en place*). This concept is so fundamental to ballet that moving up and down the vertical 'plumb line' (aplomb) is the first thing a ballet dancer practices every day in the form of *plié* (to bend). A distinctive feature of ballet is how the dancer then utilizes this verticality to resist gravity in order to balance, spin and leap.

HISTORICAL CONTEXT

From the early flowering of ballet at the court of the French King Louis XIV, upright stance (with feet firmly planted on the ground but head reaching toward the heavens) was employed to create an illusion of divine presence. Use of the vertical 'plumb line' was then refined and extended during the romantic ballet period to create the illusion of ethereal, weightless creatures. Advances in technical skill enabled the dancer to perform sustained balances, resulted in the development of *pirouettes* (turns), slow, graceful *adage* movements, such as *arabesques*, and higher elevation and the introduction of pointework (the female dancer balancing on the tips of her toes). Classical ballet's *pas de deux* (duet) then took the dancer's verticality to spectacular new heights. The ballerina's pointework evolved into a technical feat, the male dancer performed soaring leaps and together they created impressive lifts, virtuoso turns and extraordinary balances.[3]

Turn Out

In order to create a wider range of movement, the ballet dancer rotates the arms and legs outwards around their imaginary vertical axis. This twisting action of the opposing muscles, which are activated in rotation, creates spirals in the body and results in the turned out positions of the legs and feet. Five formal, outwardly rotated, positions create the start and end of every movement in ballet. This outward rotation also enables the dancer to extend their limbs well beyond the usual anatomical limit. The combination of verticality and outward rotation leads to movements on horizontal and vertical planes, and particularly to movements of the legs directed to the front, side and back. This pattern is formalized as *en croix* (in the shape of a cross), which is practised in the second

exercise of ballet class – *battements tendus* (leg stretches).[4]

By connecting the points of the cross, the limbs trace circular patterns – *en dehors* (outwards, with a feeling of moving away from the centre of the body) and *en dedans* (inwards, with a feeling of moving toward the centre of the body). These circular movements of the arms and legs trace the three-dimensional periphery of the kinesphere, resulting in twisting spirals and movements that open and close – mirroring natural rhythms, such as breathing. Movements *en dehors* and *en dedans* are practised in ballet class as *ronds de jambe* (circles with the leg) and *ports de bras* (movements with the arms). Spinning around the vertical axis is then utilized later in the class in the performance of *pirouettes*.

The line of aplomb implies a centre or still point from which movement may move out, to which it will return and which will be present throughout. 'En-dehors', 'En-dedans', 'En place'*: the outward movement, the inward movement, and being in place; these are the three great expressions of the classical dance.*[5]

Choreographers often use these opening and closing movements to create light and shade in the dance; to portray emotion, mood and meaning. For the dancer, the feeling that is evoked when you take time to experience these geometries is personal to you – so the principles of *en dehors*, *en dedans*, *en place* and *en croix* are also 'tools' for exploring expression.[6]

Spatial Orientation

Use of geometry extends beyond the individual body, to the placement of the dancer in space. First conceived as a vehicle for royal presentation, all the movements of early ballet were orientated frontally – toward the king. As ballet moved into the theatre, this frontal arrangement naturally leant itself to theatrical presentation to an audience. Therefore, all

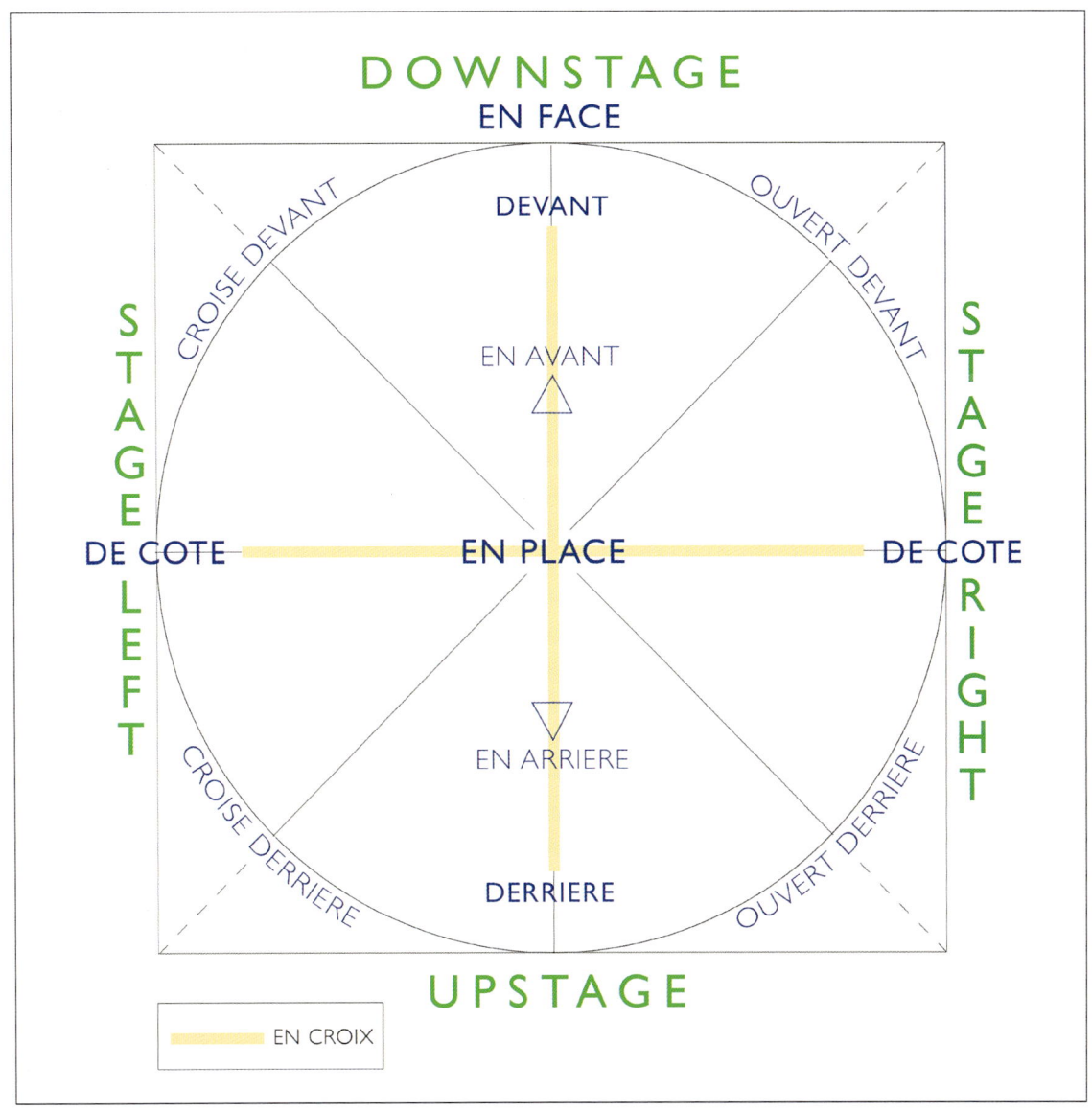

The dancer's square showing the combination of body design (*en croix*) and direction in space. (Note: the accents on French capitalized letters are omitted here.)

movement relates to *en face* (the front), where the audience is sitting.

In order to achieve uniform use of the space, each dancer orientates themselves within an imaginary dancer's square. For example, when the dancer is asked to face the downstage corner, they turn 45 degrees to face the corner of their imaginary square. In this way, the direction of each dancer's movement is precisely the same. This combination of clear body design and precise use of direction ensures the movement of the dancer is legible to the audience, even at the back of the largest auditorium.

Each movement is precisely orientated in space making the form legible even at a distance. Yu Hang, Royal Ballet (Upper) School student, as Aurora in *Aurora's Wedding* staged by Anthony Dowell from Marius Petipa's *The Sleeping Beauty* at the Royal Opera House, London.

The power of the dancers' connection is illustrated through their shared body design. Rimi Nakano and Eric Pinto Cata, Royal Ballet (Lower) School students dancing in *Pulcinella Suite* by Mark Annear.

Patterns in Space

By projecting the line of movement and energy beyond the bounds of the kinesphere, the dancer's movement radiates out into the external stage space. The geometric shapes performed in the body are reflected in travelling patterns as the dancer moves through the space – along diagonal lines; standing centre stage; crossing from stage right to stage left; advancing and retreating; and travelling in a circle.

These movement patterns are further magnified by sharing spatial design with a partner or group. For example, when the principal dancers perform a classical *pas de deux* (duet), their powerful connection is portrayed through shared body designs and travelling pathways, which connect across the stage space to create a strong sense of unity and harmony. Equally, group patterning of the *corps de ballet* (the main body of dancers) is used to magnify and reflect the movement and emotion of the individual dancer, enabling a large group of dancers to move as one body.

In these ways, ballet draws on the classical principles of harmony and proportion to recreate the dancer as a work of geometry and beauty. Not only does the human body incorporate the geometry of the Golden Section, this natural geometry is emphasized to present the dancer in an idealized form. In the next chapter, which looks at the historic roots of ballet, you can discover how the desire for human expression and interest in representing the human form as 'ideal' has driven the development of the ballet as an art form.

BALLET TODAY

An Evolving Art Form

Today ballet reaches across the globe and can best be defined by its diversity. Its versatile technique, based on universal principles of harmony and proportion, lends it a timeless quality that speaks to the human experience at a fundamental level. This has enabled ballet to continue to evolve and adapt to changing fashions, aesthetics and interests, and modern-day choreographers to draw on ballet's rich vocabulary to portray complex narrative, abstract movement and nuanced atmosphere. However, the rapid development of diverse dance styles has challenged ballet's aesthetic, offering antidotes to its formal, codified structure. In particular, the American and European modern dance movements (known as contemporary dance in the UK) emphasize self-expression and movement that isn't bound by historic convention – making it attractive for choreographers who are interested in creating dances that resonate with their audiences. Creative contemporary dance has also become the basis for teaching dance in UK state schools, providing young people with methods to create, perform and appreciate dance without the need to first master the physical skills of ballet technique. As a result, some have questioned the continued relevance of ballet and the strength of its connection with today's society.

Yet each week millions of children learn ballet at dance schools in their local communities, and adult classes are increasingly popular. These ballet classes are often supported by carefully constructed, progressive syllabi that introduce the classical principles outlined in this chapter through a series of technical training exercises. Achievement of each syllabus level is formally acknowledged through participation in a practical graded examination. This method of teaching ballet has proved so popular that UK teaching societies, such as the Imperial Society of Teachers of Dancing (ISTD) and the Royal Academy of Dance (RAD) now operate worldwide. In 2019, these two organizations alone delivered over 300,000 ballet exams – illustrating both the enduring popularity of ballet and its ability to transcend both geographic and cultural divides. However, despite the popularity of such classes, their cost and availability inevitably presents a barrier that prevents many from participating in this beautiful art form.

Engaging New Audiences

The need for classical art forms to evolve and capture the spirit of the age is a common theme across all the performing arts. In ballet, this has led to questions about who learns and performs ballet, and who has access to watch performances. Housed in some of the country's finest cultural institutions, and attracting significant public funding, ballet is an important element of national identity. However, for it to remain so, young people (who will form tomorrow's society) must have opportunities to learn about, and participate in, ballet's rich cultural heritage. This necessitates overcoming a number of economic and cultural obstacles associated with cost and who feels welcome in ballet spaces. For instance, ballet is frequently perceived as the preserve of the female, mainly white, middle classes and thereby out of step with our culturally diverse twenty-first century society.

Over the past thirty years, ballet institutions have worked hard to overcome these barriers. In the UK, all funded professional ballet companies have a remit to engage new audiences, which they typically achieve through participatory learning opportunities linked to their repertoire. Much of this activity is focused toward schoolchildren but, increasingly, companies are expanding their work to engage with adults and older people.

Whilst such participatory activity is often short term in nature, there are some notable long-term training initiatives. A prime example is the Royal Opera House's *Chance to Dance* programme, which is designed to broaden the diversity of those who learn ballet in the hope that this will be reflected in the future composition of companies like The Royal Ballet. *Chance to Dance* works with primary schools in lower socio-economic and ethnically diverse communities. Each year, children are introduced to ballet through specially designed demonstrations and practical workshops in their schools. Those identified as having a particular talent for ballet are then offered free weekly ballet classes in their local community. Some of these children have gone on to train at leading vocational ballet schools and some have now entered the profession as ballet dancers.

Likewise, the UK's Centres for Advanced Training provide pre-vocational training for young people who demonstrate talent for dance, but may not have previously had an opportunity for sustained technical dance training. This government-funded scheme provides training in a range of dance disciplines for young people between the ages of eleven and eighteen years, and ballet is typically viewed as an important foundation technique.

At a professional level, ballet companies such as Dance Theater of Harlem in New York and, more recently, the UK's Ballet Black, actively profile ballet dancers from ethnic minorities. In doing so, they are successfully challenging and dismantling the historic cultural norm of ballet as an art form performed by predominantly white dancers for largely white audiences.

The Future of Development of Ballet

In turn, these initiatives induct new audiences into the world of ballet, providing accessible opportunities for a broader cross-section of society to learn about its history, vocabulary and aesthetic values. Enabling a wider range of people to participate in, influence and contribute to the development of the art form is essential to the future societal relevance of ballet.[7] Such initiatives have led some practitioners to rethink the way in which ballet is introduced and taught – focusing on ballet's classical movement principles as a springboard for stimulating curiosity and for allowing the dancer a sense of self-discovery, rather than viewing

Royal Opera House Chance to Dance students learn *ports de bras*.

ballet as a set of knowledge and physical skills to be imposed. This methodology has been used in ground-breaking projects initiated by The Royal Ballet School, which partnered highly skilled vocational ballet school students with young people who learn dance in state school settings. Transcending their differing skills and experiences, these students worked together to explore ballet's classical principles creatively, and to use these as a catalyst from which to make and perform original dance pieces. By employing creative exploration and composition, both vocational and state school students developed a deeper understanding of the art form and the confidence to utilize this knowledge in their own choreographies.[8] Such initiatives illustrate that when young people from varied backgrounds have authentic opportunities to engage in,

and contribute to, ballet as active participants, the art form has the potential to transcend cultural and social divides.

Throughout its history, ballet's enduring appeal has been its ability to embody classical principles and, in doing so, to transform the human body into an ideal form. This remains as relevant today as in the past. Ballet's confident upright stance and expansive use of space is empowering – as is the possibility of physically and creatively engaging with its classical heritage. Those who learn, choreograph, teach and perform ballet are its lifeblood – responsible for safeguarding the future of this beautiful art form and ensuring that it remains connected to the past, relevant to the present and accessible to our changing society. You, the practitioner, are the future.

Young dancers draw inspiration from the use of line and symmetry in classical ballet as a stimulus for creative exploration. Royal Ballet School aDvANCE Project rehearsal.

Dress and Vanity Fair

FASHIONS · THE STAGE · SOCIETY · SPORTS · THE FINE ARTS

Mme. Pavlova in "Le Cygne"

CHAPTER 2

BALLET STYLES AND SCHOOLING: SHARED ROOTS, DIFFERENT CULTURES
Anna Meadmore

The distinctive training and performance traditions of each of the world's principal styles, or 'schools', of classical ballet have emerged through a combination of cultural and historic influences. The older Italian, French, Danish and Russian schools were established during the eighteenth century, while the younger English and American schools formed much later, in the early part of the twentieth century. In spite of their different foundation stories, they share the same roots in the Italian Renaissance, over five hundred years ago.

Like most forms of human expression, dance has its origins in communal activity; three types of social dancing gave rise to the historical development of classical ballet:

- Traditional folk dances, with their roots in ancient rural life and rituals.
- Aristocratic court dances of the Renaissance, whose origins lay in popular country dances, as well as military and religious pageantry.
- Social dances of the aspiring middle-classes, adapted from both folk and courtly dances.

All dance forms display the unique stylistic characteristics of different peoples and countries, and these can also be seen in their national styles of ballet. In Chapter 1, we identified the essential 'classical' principles that underpin all ballet training. Here, we trace the cultural origins of those principles and discover who shaped them, in order to see how distinctive 'schools' of ballet emerged over time.

WHAT IS MEANT BY A 'STYLE' OR 'SCHOOL' OF CLASSICAL BALLET?

Many elements contribute to the formation of different schooling and performance styles. Fundamental to all dance, including classical ballet, is the instrument itself: the dancer's moving body. The interplay between physique and technical training, or 'schooling', is central to stylistic variation. The demands of particular choreographers and repertoires also shape balletic style, as do the unique attributes of specific dancers. Musicality profoundly informs the distinctive movement and dynamic qualities that are embedded within different ballet traditions. National cultural approaches to theatre and dance influence not only the content and presentation of ballets, but also the different venues and audiences for ballet around the world.

OPPOSITE: **Anna Pavlova (1881–1931)** in *Le Cygne* or *The Dying Swan.* **Pavlova's world tours caught the public imagination and she became an international celebrity; her slender legs and arched feet established a new aesthetic for ballet.**

KEY ELEMENTS OF STYLE

As you read this chapter, consider how these key elements of ballet performance compare across the world: how do they reveal stylistic differences? Can you locate them within your own dance study?

- Whole body: alignment, placement and carriage.
- Limbs, head and eyes: lines, levels, extensions.
- Legs and feet: articulation on floor/in air.
- Head, limbs, hands and eyes: gesture and detail.
- Dynamics: contrast, quality and musicality.
- Body in space: jumps, turns and directions.
- Stage space: floor patterns and travelling.
- Social and cultural norms: ideals and customs.
- Artistic traditions: music, literature, drama and design.
- Theatrical traditions: performance venues and values.
- Cultural context: political and economic.

THE ITALIAN SCHOOL: HISTORY AND STYLISTIC FEATURES

Ballet in Italy: a History of Regional Politics and Patronage

In the early fifteenth century, Italy was a patchwork of city states, with rival princedoms, dukedoms and hugely wealthy families, all competing to attract the finest musicians, painters, poets, philosophers and engineers to their palaces and courts.[9]

Such intensive patronage of the arts and sciences led to an extraordinary period of creativity, later called the Renaissance (a 'rebirth' of classical ideals), in which ballet originated. Each of Italy's splendid regional courts required the services of a dancing master; as a result, ballet developed in several major cities and not as a centralized national school.

THE ORIGIN OF THE WORD 'BALLET' CAN BE TRACED TO AROUND 1400

The earliest known European dance manual pre-dated the advent of printing: *De arte saltandi et choreas ducendi* (On the Art of Dancing and Conducting Dances) was written by Domenico da Piacenza (birthdate unknown; died *c*.1476). Called 'the King of the Art', he was dancing master to the powerful d'Este family of Ferrara. Domenico made the significant distinction between a *danza* and a *ballo*: a *danza* has a regular rhythm throughout, while a *ballo* has varied rhythms. *Balli*, the plural of *ballo*, were also called '*balletti*'; in France, this became '*balet*', or '*ballet*'.

Classical Ballet: A Product of the Italian Renaissance

The role of dancing master was important to Italy's ruling dynasties, who often used dance to display their family's wealth and talents: in 1455, ten-year-old Ippolita Sforza danced at a family wedding in Milan, and Isabella d'Este was just six when she first performed in public. The girls' own marriage prospects partly depended on how well they presented themselves – not only in outward appearance but, more interestingly, because people thought that 'the character of everyone is made known by the dance'.[10] This significant idea was introduced by the dancing master, Guglielmo Ebreo of Pesaro (1420–84). He published his theories in around 1463, which recognized dance as an innate human activity requiring specialist study.

Guglielmo served Lorenzo de Medici (1449–92), the remarkable ruler of Florence, known as Lorenzo the Magnificent. He was a true 'Renaissance man' – poet, politician, patron and military leader. In high Italian style, he developed a tradition of elaborate processions featuring music, costume and dancing; these were displays of the prince's wealth, status and power.

They became known as *trionfi* (or triumphs) and were extremely successful forms of propaganda – designed to entertain, amaze and impress.

'Dinner Ballets': Widely Copied in Renaissance Europe

Dinner ballets originated in fifteenth-century Italy, later becoming fashionable among the European nobility as the influence of the Renaissance spread. They consisted of dance interludes, called 'entries', which punctuated lengthy and highly elaborate banquets. In France, the opening course to a meal is still called an *entrée*. Other Italian dance forms originated in the lively folk dances and street theatre that flourished in the *piazzas* outside the palace walls.

THE *TARANTELLA*: ICONIC FOLK DANCE FROM SOUTHERN ITALY

Legend says it may be danced to overcome the poisonous bite of a spider. Depending on where it is performed, it is also a shepherd's or courtship dance: 'At Sicilian weddings the guests dance the tarantella in honour of the newly-weds. The various figures show in mime the usual actions of greeting, discord, flight, forgiveness, and the final kiss.'[11] The use of narrative gesture in this and other peasant dances of Italy – together with quick footwork, vivacious upper body movements and buoyant jumps – undoubtedly informed the Italian balletic style.

Commedia dell'Arte characters appear in many ballets: Lydia Lopokova as Mariuccia the Maid, in Léonide Massine's *The Good-Humoured Ladies* (1917).

Commedia dell'Arte: Theatre of the People

This popular form of comic mime rippled out across the European continent between the mid-fifteenth to eighteenth centuries. Also called the 'Comedy of Masks', its origins were in ancient Italian carnival traditions – professional entertainers representing universal characters (crafty servants, foolish doctors, forlorn lovers and so on) improvised lively and daring acrobatic scenes, in which actions were more significant than words. *Commedia* established a vigorous tradition of story-telling conveyed through movement and gesture.[12]

Italian Court Ballet: Developments in Story-Telling and Technique

There were similar developments in the dignified setting of the Italian courts, where the *ballo* increasingly took the form of a narrative dance suggesting emotion; in one called *Gelosia*, the men constantly changed partners, while the women responded with mimed indications of 'jealousy'.[13] Fabritio Caroso (dates vary: c.1526–1605) was a ballet master based in Milan. In 1581 he published *Il Ballarino* (The Male Dancer), followed by a similar text for the female dancer in 1600. These manuals described up to seventy-four different steps demanding considerable technical facility.

Ballerini Milanesi del 1580. che danzano la gagliarda, cavati dall'Opera di Cesare de'Negri Celebre Maestro e scrittore di Ballo in Milano. Cagnoni

Two male *ballerini* in 1580, performing *La Gagliarda* (or 'Galliard') at the Milan Opera, then directed by renowned ballet master Cesare Negri; during the same period, the Italian *galliard* became a favourite dance at the Court of Queen Elizabeth I in England.

Milan: a Major Choreographic Centre of Europe

By the late sixteenth century, Milan's predominance as a centre of choreographic development was rivalled only by the court of France. Attracted by French spending-power, a steady tide of ballet masters flowed north from Italy, including Balthazar de Beaujoyeulx (originally Baldassarino de Beljiojoso). He emigrated to Paris in 1555 and was appointed to the court of Catherine de Medici, Queen of France (the great-grand-daughter of Lorenzo the Magnificent).

Italian Designers: Spectacle and the Proscenium Stage

Changing political and cultural trends in Italy meant that ballet moved from the sphere of courtly entertainment to that of the professional theatre – retaining its palatial scale. During the seventeenth century, Italian architects and engineers led European innovation in theatre design. Giacomo Torelli (1608–78) established the proscenium arch as a frame for spectacular performances in which elaborate sets were moved by complex stage machinery. From 1640, Torelli worked in Venice and, from 1645, at the court of Louis XIV of France.[14]

Italian 'Founding Fathers' of European Romantic Ballet

During the eighteenth and nineteenth centuries, several generations of brilliant Italian dancers, choreographers, teachers and musicians gravitated toward the opera houses of Europe and Russia. First among these were the dancing dynasties of the Vestris, Viganò and Taglioni families; the Cecchettis continued this legacy into the twentieth century.

Italian-born Carlotta Grisi (1819–99) trained at La Scala, Milan; she created the title role in the original production of *Giselle* (1841), becoming a great star of the Paris Opera.

ENRICO CECCHETTI: VIRTUOSITY AND VERSATILITY

Enrico Cecchetti (1850–1928) was born in a theatre dressing-room, to parents who were dancers. Cecchetti excelled in both classical and mime roles, studying under Giovanni Lepris, who had himself been taught by Carlo Blasis. Expanding upon their teachings, Cecchetti became a highly influential ballet master in St. Petersburg (1892–1902), then taught for the Diaghilev Ballets Russes (1909–18), opened his own studio in London (1918–23) and, finally, returned home to teach at La Scala, Milan.

Cecchetti's teaching emphasized musicality and artistry, alongside evidence-based analysis, which applied 'scientific' logic and understanding to natural anatomy. In 1922, a wish to perpetuate his approach led to the founding of the Cecchetti Society in London, and the publication of *A Manual of Classical Theatrical Dancing (Cecchetti Method)*. This set out his training exercises as recorded by a former pupil, Stanislas Idzikowsky, and the writer, Cyril Beaumont; the maestro himself gave final approval.

The Italian School: Embodied in the Cecchetti Method

Cecchetti was one of the most significant teachers in ballet history; a product of La Scala, Milan, he refined and structured the historic Italian School. During Cecchetti's long career, he taught many great dancers and teachers of the early twentieth century; through them, his teaching profoundly influenced the emerging national ballets of England and America.

The first fully documented French court ballet *Le Ballet Comique de la Reine* or *The Queen's Drama-Ballet* (1581), was created by an Italian, Balthazar de Beaujoyeulx.

CHARACTERISTICS OF THE ITALIAN (CECCHETTI) SCHOOL

- Quick, lively and 'clean' footwork.
- Strong and buoyant jumps.
- Multiple turns and *pirouettes.*
- Expressive, clearly defined *ports de bras.*
- *Épaulement* and deep bends in the torso.
- Close coordination of eyes, head, torso and limbs.
- Off-balance movement and recovery (*renversé*).
- Characterization, gesture and narrative mime.
- Vivacious, dynamic quality.
- Body positions delineated by a proscenium stage.

THE FRENCH SCHOOL: HISTORY AND STYLISTIC FEATURES

French Classical Ballet: a Noble Art with a Serious Purpose

French ballet had its roots in Italy, in the Milanese tradition of grand-scale court entertainments introduced to France by Catherine de Medici (1519–89). During her reign, French *ballet de cour* (court ballet) developed 'a formal discipline and design, derived from the desire to make dance and music a measure of the order of the universe… it was a breathtaking ambition, and one that never really died in ballet'.[15]

FRENCH *BALLET DE COUR* AND BALLET TERMINOLOGY

Inspired by the European Renaissance, court ballets were modelled on the classical Greek dramas of the ancient world: they combined music, poetry and song; elaborate stage designs and costumes; drama and satire – and they reflected social and political interests.[16]

In seventeenth-century France, this creative synthesis of form and aspiration became highly developed and codified under the patronage of Louis XIV. As a result, the terminology of classical ballet became firmly established in French, and remains so to this day.

Dance: Among the French Academies of Arts and Sciences

Under Louis XIII (1601–43), Cardinal Richelieu established prestigious 'academies' as centres of excellence designed to enhance the reputation of France in Europe. Louis XIV succeeded his father to the throne and, in 1661, he founded the world's first ballet school, *L'Académie Royale de Danse*, dedicated to the unique 'language' of court ballet.

This was followed in 1669 by *L'Académie Royale de Musique* (later known as The Paris Opera), to which the King's favourite ballet composer, Jean-Baptiste Lully, attached a new school teaching dancing and musicianship to aspiring professionals.

As ballet vocabulary expanded, increasing levels of technical complexity demanded more specialist dance training and, in 1713, Lully's School was renamed *L'école de Danse*. Now called the Paris Opera Ballet School, it represents 350 continuous years of schooling in the French style.

Louis XIV (1638–1715)

Louis was an excellent dancer, and his youthful performances as Apollo, god of the Sun and of the Arts, were stunningly successful acts of propaganda; throughout his 72-year reign, Louis XIV would be known as *le Roi Soleil* (the Sun King). His mastery of mind and body was much admired – the

Le Ballet de la Nuit or *Ballet of the Night* (1653), was performed over 13 hours, ending at dawn when the teenage King Louis XIV appeared as the rising Sun, wearing golden armour and a diamond headdress.

Petipa's *The Sleeping Beauty* (1890) was originally inspired by Louis XIV's Court at Versailles; this splendid costume for Prince Charming was designed by Léon Bakst (Diaghilev revival, 1921).

monarch displayed his majesty through dancing, bringing a grandeur to ballet, which it still retains.

Of equal importance was the brilliant virtuosity that entered ballet vocabulary through the acrobatics of hired performers, whose comic or 'grotesque' interludes livened up the more stately proceedings of the amateur nobility. As Louis XIV became older and he stopped dancing in public, the emphasis shifted toward the professional performer.

JEAN-BAPTISE LULLY (1632–87)

Lully was Florentine by birth; like many of his contemporaries, he was both a dancer and violinist. Court composer to Louis XIV by the age of twenty, his comic antics would make the young King cry with laughter. Lully assumed charge of the *Académie Royale de Musique* in 1672; moving the *Opéra* away from Court to the Palais Royal, he opened it up to the burgeoning middle-classes, and introduced female dancers to the French stage.

Lully was noted for creative collaborations with Pierre Beauchamps, and the playwrights Racine and Molière – and also for his temper. Accidentally stabbing himself in the foot with his conductor's baton in a fit of rage, he subsequently died from gangrene.

PIERRE BEAUCHAMPS (DATES VARY: 1631/36–1705)

Beauchamps came from a French family of dancers and musicians. A professional violinist and dancer in the 'noble' style, he was Louis XIV's personal dancing master for over twenty years, becoming 'superintendent of the King's ballets' (or royal choreographer).

In *The Dancing Master* (a manual published in Paris, 1725) Pierre Rameau claimed that Beauchamps was first to codify the five positions in ballet. Beauchamps also created a system of dance notation; it was published in 1700 by his former student Raoul-Auger Feuillet, whom Beauchamps unsuccessfully sued for plagiarism.

Paris Opera stars Françoise Prévost (*c*.1680–1741) and Claude Ballon (1671–1744) in *Les Scythes*; both were pioneers of *ballet d'action* in the early eighteenth century.

Ballet d'Action or 'Story Ballet'

The eighteenth century saw a movement for creative reform in ballet, known as *ballet d'action*, which became widespread in Europe through the work of the Franco-Swiss ballet master, Jean-Georges Noverre (1727–1810). He thought choreography, music and costume should be less formulaic, telling a story with more natural expression. Even so, until the French Revolution of 1789 finally swept away

the 'old order' (or *ancien régime*), the new ideas of *ballet d'action* were resisted by the state-run Paris Opera.

French Romantic Ballet: New Themes and Iconography

After the revolution, ballet in France successfully embraced the innovations of *ballet d'action*, while retaining its strong academic foundations in *danse*

Marie-Anne de Cupis de Camargo (1710–70), known as the first *prima ballerina*, joined the Paris Opera in 1726 and reformed female ballet technique; shortening her skirts and later removing heels from her shoes, she performed steps of elevation previously danced only by men.

Marie Sallé (1707–56) was the first renowned female dancer-choreographer, making her Paris Opera debut in 1727; she created and appeared in *Pygmalion* (London, 1734), dancing in a simple muslin tunic, with sandals and loose hair, in contrast to the wide skirts fashionable at the time.

d'école (or 'schooled' dance). The Paris Opera duly became the focal point of the romantic ballet movement during the nineteenth century.

Surviving ballets from this era, especially *La Sylphide* (1832) and *Giselle* (1841), show how new narrative themes reflected great social change, and the interests of an increasingly middle-class audience. They presented exotic and idealized versions of village life – but also of women, who were often depicted as supernatural creatures.

Through the romantic Ballet in France emerged the feminine counterbalance to the masculine ideal of the *danseur noble*, which had been dominant for centuries. The new female iconography of pointe-work and tutus, with its emphasis on ethereality and lightness, had a great impact on the technical and stylistic development of the French School. A seemingly effortless grace disguised women's increasing virtuosity, and their prominence in supported adage further evolved balletic line and limb extensions.[17]

Marie Taglioni (1804–84) created the title role in *La Sylphide* (1832); Taglioni embodied a new feminine ideal in ballet.

'Supported *adage*', or *pas de deux*, depicted in *The Corsair* (Drury Lane, London, 1844), which predated Joseph Mazilier's more famous Paris Opera production of 1856.

CHARACTERISTICS OF THE FRENCH SCHOOL

- Precision, coordination and control.
- Verticality and extended line (enhanced by pointework).
- Harmonious and elegant presentation.
- *Ballon* (an elastic, suspended jump).
- Effortless grace and beauty.
- Ambition to reconcile the earthly and spiritual.
- 'Godlike' men and 'supernatural' women.
- Aristocratic grandeur: masculine ideal of the *danseur noble*.
- Ethereal lightness: feminine ideal of the *ballerina*.
- Exotic, idealized representations of peasant life.
- Aesthetic costumes, reflecting high fashion.
- Architectural use of space: design, pattern and scale.

THE DANISH SCHOOL: HISTORY AND STYLISTIC FEATURES

Origins of a National Ballet in Denmark

The first Danish court ballet was performed in 1634, modelled on both French *ballet de cour* and English court masques. Two decades later, Queen Sophie Amalie, an enthusiastic ballet patron, employed a Frenchman, Daniel Pilloy, as 'court dance instructor'. He founded a celebrated theatrical dynasty in his adopted country.

In 1726, another French ballet master, Jean-Baptiste Landé (birthdate unknown; d.1748), was appointed to Denmark's new Lille Grønnegade Theatre, which had developed its own form of comedy-ballets. Landé was a significant figure; he later journeyed to St. Petersburg, where he established Russia's Imperial Ballet School.

1771: Founding of Denmark's State Ballet School

The early flourishings of Danish ballet suffered setbacks imposed by strict Lutheran Protestantism but, in 1771, a ballet school was at last founded at the Court Theatre. It was led by Pierre Laurent, another French ballet master to settle in Denmark.

In 1775, Vincenzo Galeotti (1733–1816) came to Copenhagen and opened a second ballet school, which eventually succeeded Laurent's as the official state conservatory. Galeotti was an Italian-trained dancer and ballet master, and a champion of *ballet d'action*. Galeotti became a Danish citizen and worked for over 40 years at the Royal Theatre; his output of nearly fifty major ballets ensured that the expressive principles of *ballet d'action* became firmly established in Denmark.

Anna Margarethe Schall (1775–1852) gained fame throughout Europe in the title role of *Nina* (1802), a Danish 'pantomime ballet' created for her by Vincenzo Galeotti.

Nineteenth Century: Danish Ballet 'Democracy'

Denmark became a constitutional monarchy in 1849, the result of intellectual, rather than violent, revolution. As a result, a uniquely 'democratic' style of ballet emerged during this period: the Danes' lingering mistrust of class privilege meant that grandeur and formality were avoided onstage.

Denmark's definitive choreographer, August Bournonville, made ballets about 'middling citizens (with a few trolls, elves and sylphides), not about royals… nor even about nobles and commoners (in contrast to *Giselle*)'. The heroes and heroines of his ballets – namely, James and Effy (*La Sylphide* 1836 version), Gennaro and Teresina (*Napoli* 1842), Ove and Hilda (*A Folk Tale* 1854) – 'are all more or less equal socially'.[18]

AUGUST BOURNONVILLE (1805–79): AUTHOR OF THE DANISH SCHOOL

The Danish School is so closely associated with Bournonville's legacy that it is identified as the Bournonville School – in the same way that Cecchetti's teaching is thought of as the Italian School.

Bournonville's theatrical outlook was international: his mother was Swedish and his father came from a family of French dancers. At home in Copenhagen, Bournonville was taught by his father, Antoine, and the Italian Galeotti. While working in Paris, he studied under Pierre Gardel, Jean-François Coulon and Auguste Vestris.

Bournonville's career coincided with the rise of the romantic *ballerina* in Europe, when female virtuosity largely eclipsed that of men. In Denmark, however, Bournonville maintained parity between men and women in his teaching and choreography.

Auguste Vestris (1760–1842) and 'the New School'
[See references to Vestris in English School]

Bournonville trained with Vestris for two intensive years (1826–28). The technical and stylistic innovations of the period were consolidated in Vestris' teaching, which Bournonville called 'the new school'. Bournonville also danced at the Paris Opera and became Marie Taglioni's favourite partner; he was, in turn, inspired by her exquisite style.

Valdemar Price (1836–1908) as Gennaro in Bournonville's signature work *Napoli* (1842), which tells the colourful tale of a fisherman and his bride.

Danish Ballet: the Age of Bournonville (1830–79)

In 1830, Bournonville became ballet master of the Royal Theatre in Copenhagen, introducing Vestris' teaching reforms. Galeotti's works had become outdated and standards were in decline, so Bournonville set about creating a new repertoire. His ballets brimmed with fresh, bright dancing and lively gestural 'dialogue' in Denmark's native tradition.

CREATING A BOURNONVILLE-BASED TRAINING

In 1893, Hans Beck (1861–1952) began teaching a new generation of dancers who had never worked with Bournonville. He decided to organize the master's work into a syllabus designed to pass on Bournonville's choreographic style. Beck named some original combinations of steps after the older dancers who remembered them; he also created enchaînements from the Bournonville repertoire. In this way, he recorded around 200 exercises, arranging them into six classes named after the days of the week.

Vera Volkova (1904–75): Modernizing Training in Denmark

[see the photograph of Volkova with Margot Fonteyn in the English School]

Born in St. Petersburg, Volkova had studied with Agrippina Vaganova at Akim Volynsky's Russian Choreographic School. During the 1940s, she was a highly influential teacher in London, before becoming principal teacher and artistic adviser to the Royal Danish Ballet School and Company (1951–75).

Volkova's devoted student, Erik Bruhn, trained at the Royal Danish School from the age of nine. He recognized that exclusive immersion in the Bournonville tradition 'developed fine performers for one specific style', but with limited versatility.

Bruhn wrote that Volkova had modernized training in Denmark by 'developing dancers with a greater range, who are more adaptable to the various styles of contemporary choreographers'.[19]

CHARACTERISTICS OF THE DANISH (BOURNONVILLE) SCHOOL

- Understated virtuosity.
- Bright, articulate lower leg and foot work.
- Contrasting jumps: skimming the floor or bounding upward.
- Contained and rounded ports de bras.
- Subtle épaulement and eyeline.
- Shifts between 'tilting' and verticality.
- Equal emphasis on men and women.
- Open and generous presentation to the audience.
- Manners are modest, direct, honest and charming.
- Lively gestural 'dialogue' between characters.
- 'Democratic' communities with few hierarchies.
- Colourful depictions of middle-class life and fantasy worlds.

THE RUSSIAN SCHOOL: HISTORY AND STYLISTIC FEATURES

Russian Classical Ballet: Rooted in Ancient Popular Dance Forms

In 1788, a visitor to Russia observed that the beauty of Russian national dances lay not just in their accomplished steps, 'but in the fact that the head, trunk, arms – in other words the whole of the body – participate in the dance'. The special flowing cantilena (or 'singing') qualities of Russian folk dances may be traced to ancient circle dances, known as khorovods, usually performed to slow-paced songs.[20]

Design by Alexandre Benois for Mikhail Fokine's *Petrushka* (1911); set in old St. Petersburg's Shrovetide Fair, the ballet features contrasting styles of Russian folk dance.

Russia's earliest professional dancers were acrobatic entertainers called *skomorokhi*. These troupes of men and women often resided on the great estates of princes and boyars; their art was depicted in frescoes of the eleventh century, such as the one to be found in St. Sophia Cathedral in Kiev. This illustrates the different types of dancing that already existed in Russia: the languid *pliasati* and the fiery *skakati*.[21]

It could be argued that these contrasting dynamic qualities remain embedded in Russian ballet: for instance, in the difference between the aristocratic, lyrical Mariinsky style of St. Petersburg, and the expansive 'attack' of the Bolshoi Ballet in Moscow; or even in the dual role of Odette/Odile in *Swan Lake*.

Origins of the Imperial Theatres

In 1673, Tsar Alexei (r.1645–76) founded a court Drama Theatre; his youngest son, later known as Peter 'the Great' (r.1682–1725), established a Theatre Room in the Kremlin. Tsar Peter also introduced compulsory social 'assemblies' featuring European ballroom dances; despite strong Church disapproval, dancing thus became respectable in Russia.

In 1736, the Empress Anna Ianovna (r.1730–40) patronized Russia's first professional ballet: over 100 performers appeared in the finalé to an opera by Francesco Araja, *La Forza dell'Amore e dell'Odio* or 'The Force of Love and Hate'. These were military school cadet officers, prepared over two years by the ballet master, Jean-Baptiste Landé. There had long been a connection between the arts of fencing and ballet in Western courts; these complementary skills were now adopted in Russia.[22]

1738: Founding of the Imperial Ballet School, St. Petersburg

Jean-Baptiste Landé had danced in Paris and Dresden before becoming the royal dancing master in Stockholm, then Denmark. Arriving in St. Petersburg in 1734, he sought imperial approval for a professional school to train dancers for court performances. In 1738, the Empress Anna allowed Landé's school to be installed in a wing of the Hermitage Palace.

RUSSIAN 'SERF THEATRES'

The first intake of twenty-four pupils at the Imperial Ballet School were the children of palace servants; this followed a long tradition of 'serf' dancers who worked in private theatres owned by rich landowners. Serfs were labourers bound in service to the estates where they were born – a feudal system only abolished in Russia during the 1860s. Some serf theatres competed in scale with court productions, and continued to provide talent for the imperial theatres well into the nineteenth century; a profoundly 'native aspect' of ballet in Russia, which was otherwise an 'imported, urban and court art'.[23]

1766: The Imperial Theatres Become a State System

Catherine the Great (r.1762–96) created a central directorate to manage the imperial theatres and their affiliated schools through state funding. In Russia, this system became 'so deeply entrenched that it outlasted any single form of government'.[24]

Charles-Louis Didelot (1767–1837): *Ballet d'Action* in Russia

Generous subsidies attracted leading ballet masters from Austria, Italy and France to St. Petersburg, where they introduced the expressive reforms of *ballet d'action* during the second half of the eighteenth century. Most significant among them was Charles-Louis Didelot, a dancer, teacher and choreographer schooled in the French tradition. His principal teachers were Jean Dauberval, original creator of *La Fille mal Gardée* (1789), Auguste Vestris, master of the revitalized French School, and Noverre himself.

Didelot founded St. Petersburg's great balletic style by combining French academicism and expressive reforms with the innate facility of the Russians themselves. Although he was fiercely demanding of

Marie Taglioni as Flore in Didelot's *Flore et Zéphyre* (1831 revival). Between 1837 and 1842, Taglioni was St. Petersburg's *prima ballerina*; her 'spiritual' dancing greatly influenced the Russian School.

his dancers, the Russian poet, Alexander Pushkin, said 'there was more poetry to be found in Didelot's ballets than in all the French literature of the time'.[25] Didelot is credited with many key innovations: simpler costumes, flesh-coloured tights and early experiments with pointework.

DIDELOT: EARLY BALLET ROMANTICISM AND *BALLET BLANC*

Didelot anticipated many reforms of the romantic era: from his *Flore et Zéphyre* (1796) through to *La Sylphide* (1832) and *Giselle* (1841), 'an uninterrupted line of development of the *ballet blanc* can be traced directly to Petipa and Ivanov's *Swan Lake* [1895]'.[26] The term *ballet blanc* refers to the 'white acts' in ballets when ranks of women, all dressed in white, dance on a moonlit stage.

St. Petersburg Imports the Paris Opera Tradition

During the nineteenth century, many artists of the French romantic ballet came to St. Petersburg. Jules Perrot (1810–92), who co-created *Giselle* with Jean Coralli in 1841, became chief ballet master of the Imperial Theatre from 1851 to 1858. Another Frenchman, Arthur Saint-Léon (1821–70), succeeded Perrot from 1859 to 1870. Both were highly musical and accomplished choreographers, and greatly influenced their successor, Marius Petipa, who served under them both.[27]

Voyage en Russie (1858) was a travel account by the renowned poet and ballet writer, Théophile Gautier; he wrote that ballet was highly regarded in Russia, where elaborate stories and plentiful dancing 'made Russian ballet a self-sufficient art, in no way dependent on opera or any other kind of spectacle'.[28] This contrasted with the deteriorating situation in France, where ballet was viewed as secondary entertainment to the opera and artistic

Caricature of Marius Petipa, holding a banner inscribed '[St.] Petersburg Ballet', drawn by Nicolai and Serge Legat c.1900.

standards were of less interest than arranging stage-door liaisons with 'ballet girls'.

Marius Petipa (1818–1910): Principal Creator of Russian Classical Ballet

Born in Marseilles, Petipa had been a student of Auguste Vestris in Paris. He joined the Russian Imperial Theatre as a dancer in 1847, officially becoming second ballet master in 1863, and succeeding Saint-Léon as first ballet master from 1870 to 1905.[29] Petipa choreographed more than sixty works over many decades in Russia, combining influences from France, Italy, Spain and Russia to create beautiful and finely crafted ballets, many of which still dominate the international repertoire.

PETIPA'S MARIINSKY BALLETS: THE IMPERIAL RUSSIAN 'CLASSICAL CANON'

Under Petipa, ballet moved from its romantic era into a new age of classicism. Petipa's works are known throughout the world as *the* ballet 'classics'. They transformed ballet from 'an art dominated by foreigners and identified with the West into a Russian national expression'.[30]

Petipa's musical and inventive use of the academic ballet vocabulary, together with his mastery of choreographic structure, remain the benchmark of classical ballet. He achieved a harmonious balance between the elements that comprise a ballet: music, movement, design and *libretto* (story). Petipa's legacy underpinned the twentieth-century evolution of modern ballet, through Diaghilev's Ballets Russes (1909–29), and the subsequent formation of national ballets in Britain, the Americas, Canada and Australia.

In 1890, Marius Petipa created *The Sleeping Beauty*, his first and greatest collaboration with the composer, Pyotr Tchaikovsky; this was followed by *The Nutcracker* (1892) and *Swan Lake* (1895), both made with his assistant, Lev Ivanov. Other Petipa ballets still widely performed include *Don Quixote* (1871), *La Bayadère* (1877) and *Raymonda* (1898). Petipa also revived key works from the French repertoire, which survive in his versions, including *Paquita* (1846; Petipa 1881) and *Giselle* (1841; Petipa 1884).

Lev Ivanov (1834–1901)

Lev Ivanov was Petipa's close assistant for sixteen years. After being somewhat overlooked, Ivanov is now recognized for his breathtakingly beautiful choreography for the 'white acts' (II and IV) of *Swan Lake*; he also choreographed most of *The Nutcracker*, with its kaleidoscopic 'Dance of the Snowflakes', because Petipa was unwell at the time.

Christian Johansson (1817–1903): Development of the Russian School

Johansson was in charge of training at the Imperial School, while Petipa oversaw the ballet at the Mariinsky Theatre, 'and their word in their respective departments was absolute'.[31] Born in Stockholm, Johansson had studied with Bournonville in Copenhagen, inheriting through the Danish master the legacy of Vestris' teaching. Following a career

Pierina Legnani as Odette in the original Petipa–Ivanov production of *Swan Lake* (1895).

of twenty-eight years as a principal dancer in St. Petersburg, Johansson was appointed chief ballet master at the Imperial Theatre School in 1869, a position he held until his death thirty-four years later.

Nicolai Legat (1869–1937)

Nicolai Legat was Johansson's devoted pupil, becoming his assistant and succeeding him as teacher of the graduate 'class of perfection' in 1905. Legat recalled that Johansson rejected any idea of 'mechanical' dancing; his classes were filled instead with 'versatility, ingenuity and variety'.[32]

ECLECTICISM OF THE RUSSIAN SCHOOL

The 'Russian' school of dancing is an eclectic school – the French, the Scandinavian [the Danish], the Italian – all welded into an artistic whole by the genius of the Russian people... it lives in our bodies and in our hearts.[33]

Italians Conquer St. Petersburg: 'Divine Virginia' and Signor Cecchetti

In 1885, the vivacious Italian *ballerina*, Virginia Zucchi, appeared in St. Petersburg in a *ballet-féerie* (fairy ballet) spectacular. She was a dancer-actress rather than a technician, but the Italian dancers who followed her to Russia won popularity with their brilliant technical accomplishments, particularly in *pirouettes* and pointework.

Enrico Cecchetti's virtuosity greatly increased the prestige of the male dancer in Russia. In the original *Sleeping Beauty* (1890) he displayed dazzling versatility by creating the roles of Carabosse – a major mimed part – *and* the classically demanding Bluebird. His compatriot, Carlotta Brianza, created the *ballerina* role of Aurora. Cecchetti became an important ballet master at the Imperial School (1892–1902), introducing elements of Italian virtuosity and *ports de bras* to Russian schooling.

Pierina Legnani completed the Italian 'invasion' by creating the role of Odette/Odile in *Swan Lake* (1895). She imported the landmark feat of turning thirty-two *fouettés* – swiftly copied by the determined Russian *prima ballerina*, Mathilde Kschessinska!

Nicolai Legat and Anna Pavlova in La Fille mal Gardée (Petipa–Ivanov version 1885), pictured during a tour of Europe c.1909–12.

REVOLUTION AND CHANGE IN RUSSIA

The Russian Revolution of 1917 ended Imperial Tsarist rule, leading to the formation of Communist Russia and The Union of Soviet Socialist Republics (USSR). St. Petersburg was eventually renamed Leningrad, and the Imperial School changed its name accordingly. The Mariinsky Ballet became 'the Kirov', named after a ballet-loving general. Following the dissolution of the USSR in December 1991, the names of St. Petersburg and the Mariinsky were later restored.

Maris Liepa (1936–89), principal of the Bolshoi Ballet from 1960 to 1977, in his created role of Crassus in *Spartacus* (1968).

MOSCOW'S BOLSHOI BALLET

The separate, but interweaving, histories of the Mariinsky in St. Petersburg and the Bolshoi in Moscow have produced interesting stylistic differences. From 1738, ballet in St. Petersburg evolved a classically refined and polished style; by contrast, Moscow's Bolshoi (founded in 1776) developed a powerfully athletic, dramatic tradition. 'Bolshoi' means 'big' in Russian: monumental story-ballets, such as Leonid Lavrovksy's *Romeo and Juliet* (1946) and Yuri Grigorovich's *Spartacus* (1968), exemplify the Bolshoi's thrilling and distinctive repertoire. Its legendary dancers include Galina Ulanova, Maya Plisetskaya, Vladimir Vasiliev, Ekaterina Maximova and Irek Mukhamedov.

Agrippina Vaganova (1879–1951): Continuity of Style in Soviet Russia

Vaganova graduated from the Imperial School, St. Petersburg, in 1897. Her main teachers were Ivanov, Legat and, later, Olga Preobrajenska. Called 'the queen of variations' at the Mariinsky, Vaganova was promoted to the rank of principal late in her career (1915). At the outbreak of revolution in 1917, she started teaching at Akim Volynsky's Russian School of Ballet and, from 1920, at the former Imperial School, where she set out to analyse and codify Russia's system of ballet training.

Between 1931 and 1937, Vaganova was artistic director of the Kirov (formerly Mariinsky); she also published her teaching manual, *Basic Principles of Classical Ballet* (1934). Reprinted many times, it made a huge impact on ballet training worldwide. Vaganova taught until the year of her death in 1951 and, in 1957, the former Imperial/Leningrad School was renamed The Vaganova Ballet Academy. Her methods still lie at the heart of present-day training in Russia, and continue to resonate around the globe.

Rudolf Nureyev (1938–1993) was among the Vaganova Academy's most celebrated graduates. His dramatic defection to the West in 1961, and charismatic performances in both classical and modern ballets, renewed interest in male virtuosity. His onstage partnership with The Royal Ballet's Margot Fonteyn became legendary around the world.

CHARACTERISTICS OF THE RUSSIAN (ST. PETERSBURG) SCHOOL

As we have seen, the Russian School encompassed the teachings of the French School, together with elements of Italian virtuosity, mime and *ports de bras*; it was enriched by the creative versatility, and gender parity, of the Bournonville tradition. These factors combined with distinctive Russian traits to produce a special balletic style:

- Flowing *cantilena* (or 'singing') quality of movement.
- Luxurious extensions of line in the torso, neck and limbs.
- Expressive articulation of the wrists and hands.
- A sense of poetic spirituality (in both men and women).
- Contrasting dynamics: sustained *legato* and fiery 'attack'.
- Lavish use of space: around the body and travelling across the stage.

In both Moscow and St. Petersburg, this style was further expanded through:

- Combining folk dance with classical ballet steps in 'character dances'.
- Combining mime and gesture with ballet in *demi-caractère* dances.
- Development of athleticism and expressivity in *pas de deux*.

THE ENGLISH SCHOOL: HISTORY AND STYLISTIC FEATURES

English Classical Ballet: Parallels with the English Language

In many ways, England is a 'magpie' nation, adopting language, food and customs from abroad. Linguistically, English is a versatile mix of Celtic, Latin, Saxon, Norse and Norman-French; words like *pyjamas* and *bungalow* (Hindi) have also added to its vitality. English ballet similarly encompasses an eclectic range of influences from France, Italy, Denmark, Russia and elsewhere – as well as its own cultural traditions.

England has some of the earliest surviving folk dances in Europe, such as the *Abbots Bromley Horn Dance* in Staffordshire, the *Helston Furry Dance* in Cornwall and widely practised Morris dancing. Significantly, the traditional dances of England, Scotland and Ireland all emphasize a deft articulation of the lower legs and feet.

'The Dancing English'

During the sixteenth century, the Spanish *pavane* may have come to the Tudor Court with Katherine of Aragon, first wife of Henry VIII, while the French *galliard* arrived with her successor, Anne Boleyn.[34] Under Elizabeth I, dancing became such favoured 'sport' that Europeans referred to 'the dancing English'.

WILLIAM SHAKESPEARE ON THE POPULARITY OF DANCING IN ENGLAND:

They bid us to their English dancing-schools,
And teach lavoltas *high and swift* corantos;
Saying our grace is only in our heels,
And that we are most lofty runaways.
[Henry V, 3.5]

Four centuries later, English dancing continued to demonstrate such 'swift' and 'lofty' footwork – in the ballets of Ninette de Valois, Frederick Ashton and David Bintley.

Drama and Spectacle in English Theatre

Enactments of religious stories in medieval 'miracle and mystery' plays instilled a strong dramatic tradition in England. A vigorous theatrical culture included court masques featuring drama, music and dance. During the early seventeenth century, a celebrated partnership between Inigo Jones (architect-designer) and Ben Jonson (poet-playwright) created elaborate masques for the Stuart monarchy.

John Weaver (1673–1760)

Born in Shrewsbury, Weaver became a dancer and teacher in London under Queen Anne (r.1702–14). His most significant production was *The Loves of Mars and Venus* (1717); subtitled 'A Dramatick Entertainment of Dancing', this expressive ballet-pantomime enjoyed huge success at the Drury Lane Theatre. In 1721, Weaver gave a ground-breaking series of lectures aligning dance technique with anatomical science.[35]

MIME ON THE ENGLISH STAGE

David Garrick (1717–79) was the leading Shakespearean actor of his time; influenced by Noverre's *ballet d'action* reforms, he was famed for his 'naturalistic' gestures. Garrick also admired John Lun (1692–1761), England's celebrated Harlequin mime, observing:

When Lun appeared with matchless art and whim
He gave the power of speech to every limb...[36]

Arguably, this native British tradition resurfaced strongly during the twentieth century, with the dramatic ballets of Antony Tudor (1908–87) and Kenneth MacMillan (1929–92), and the dance-dramas of Robert Helpmann (1909–86) and Matthew Bourne (b.1960).

Auguste ('Goose-Toe!') Vestris at London's King's Theatre (1781); parliament was suspended so members could attend his performances.

The Royal Ballet's Valentino Zucchetti as Auguste Vestris in Ninette de Valois' *Every Goose Can* (1981).

Pre-Romantic Ballet in London

London's first principal opera and ballet house, the King's Theatre, Haymarket, was built in 1704–05. No ballet school was attached, since the British monarchy was not inclined to support one.[37] Consequently, ballet in Britain relied upon foreign guest artists, a model that persisted for another 200 years.

Romantic Ballet in England: Heyday and Decline

Many famous dancers from the Paris Opera appeared in London during the 1830s and 1840s. Young Queen Victoria was a notable 'fan', but as her long reign progressed (r.1837–1901), ballet in England gravitated from the respectable theatre toward music hall.

The Empire Theatre of Varieties in Leicester Square was a 'music hall' renowned for spectacular ballet productions. An Austrian dancer, Katti Lanner (1829–1908), choreographed over thirty ballets there between 1887 and 1897. At the time, male roles were often performed by women known as 'travesty' dancers. Ballet was seen as morally dubious entertainment, and only regained artistic credibility

Assembly ball waltz (English print, 1817); this charming parody of balletic style shows the close connection between social and theatrical dancing.

Danish-trained Adeline Genée (1878–1970), *prima ballerina* **of London's Empire Theatre 1897–1907; seen here as Swanhilda in** *Coppélia* **with Dorothy Craske as Frantz (1906).**

with the arrival of Diaghilev and his Ballets Russes (Russian Ballet) Company.

England Adopts the Russian Ballet

Lydia Kyasht succeeded Adeline Genée at London's Empire Theatre in 1908, the first of many Russian-trained ballet dancers to enjoy great success in England – most famously, Anna Pavlova, who arrived in 1909 and soon settled in London.

Diaghilev's Ballets Russes (1909–29), which had sprung from Russia's conservative Imperial Theatres, led the way in European modernism, and demonstrated how radical creative dance innovation could flourish when rooted in classical ballet traditions. Former Diaghilev dancers, Marie Rambert

and Ninette de Valois, followed this model when founding their own companies in England.

Marie Rambert (1888–1982): Creative Mentor

Rambert was a Polish-born dancer and teacher. A member of Diaghilev's Ballets Russes (1912–13), and student of Cecchetti, she opened her school in London (1920). Rambert's graduates formed the Marie Rambert Dancers in 1926; this became Ballet Club in 1931, Ballet Rambert in 1935, Rambert Dance Company in 1987, then 'Rambert' from 2013.

Rambert's acute theatrical and literary sensibilities encouraged creativity in her students, most significantly Frederick Ashton and Antony Tudor. Their different choreographic voices shared a musically

Vaslav Nijinsky's *The Rite of Spring* (1913); Diaghilev hired Marie Rambert (seen on left) to help the Ballets Russes navigate Igor Stravinsky's revolutionary score.

Ninette de Valois in the Ballets Russes production of Bronislava Nijinska's *Les Biches* (1924); Nijinska's artistry profoundly influenced both de Valois and Frederick Ashton.

precise, evocative use of balletic language that characterized an emergent English style. Surviving early works include Ashton's *Façade* (1931), *Les Rendezvous* (1933) and *Les Patineurs* (1937); and Tudor's *Lilac Garden* (1936) and *Dark Elegies* (1937).

Ninette de Valois (1898–2001)
Founder of The Royal Ballet

Born in Ireland and christened Edris Stannus, she moved to England as a child. Aged thirteen, she first appeared as Ninette de Valois with Lila Field's 'Wonder Children', becoming a soloist in major London pantomimes during the 1914–18 War. From 1923 to 1925, de Valois danced with the Ballets Russes, a formative experience that convinced her that England needed its own national ballet. Accordingly, she left Diaghilev's Company to open her Academy of Choreographic Art (March 1926). Later that year, de Valois approached Lilian Baylis (1874–1937), manager of the Old Vic and Sadler's Wells, to ask if her graduates might form a ballet company attached to Baylis' repertory theatres. A plan was agreed and implemented: by 1931, de

Valois' school had re-located to 'the Wells', and the Vic-Wells Ballet was established.

The Company was re-named Sadler's Wells Ballet in 1941, and gained national status through extensive touring during the 1939–45 War. In 1946, it became resident at Covent Garden's Royal Opera House, while a smaller 'touring' Company remained at Sadler's Wells. In 1956, this 'threefold institution' was granted a Royal Charter by Queen Elizabeth II, becoming The Royal Ballet School, Royal Ballet Company and Sadler's Wells Royal Ballet (Birmingham Royal Ballet since 1990). De Valois not only founded and directed The Royal Ballet until 1963, she had also been its first principal dancer, teacher and choreographer. Her own neat and accurate style strongly informed the qualities of an emerging English School.

BRITISH BALLET: INTERNATIONAL TEACHING ORGANIZATIONS

Several ballet examination bodies were established in Britain during the early 1900s, each developing its own training syllabus based upon the world's great schools of ballet. Over time, their reach extended globally, especially in Commonwealth countries such as Australia, New Zealand, Canada and South Africa.

In 1904, the Imperial Society of Teachers of Dancing (ISTD) was founded in London to improve the teaching of ballet and ballroom dancing; by 1924, it had incorporated the Cecchetti ballet syllabus. The renowned teacher Édouard Espinosa (1871–1950) was also committed to raising ballet standards in England. In 1920, he initiated the establishment of the Association of Operatic Dancing, known today as the Royal Academy of Dance (RAD). Espinosa later set up the British Ballet Organization (BBO) with his wife, Eve Louise Kelland, in 1930. The qualifications offered by the ISTD, RAD and BBO continue to expand and attract international recognition.

The English School: Fundamentals of Training and Choreography

From 1915 to *c.*1935, Ninette de Valois studied in succession with three masters of the world's great ballet schools then teaching in London: Édouard Espinosa (French School), Enrico Cecchetti (Italian School) and Nicolai Legat (Russian School). Their combined knowledge formed the basis of her own teaching, which she adapted for native dancers to develop an English training style.

British choreography reflected de Valois' belief that 'the teachings of the classic school are the sure and only foundation – limitless in its adaptability [and] power to meet the varied requirements of the theatre'.[38] De Valois' own ballets emphasized theatrical design and characterization, while Frederick Ashton was the great classicist of English ballet, who kept 'the *danse d'école* alive at the heart of his

Ninette de Valois' *Checkmate* (1937) with Harold Turner as the Red Knight and Pamela May as the Red Queen.

works'.[39] The composer and conductor Constant Lambert (1905–51), was The Royal Ballet's founding music director; for almost thirty years he instilled a deep musical sensitivity within its dancers and choreographers.

Frederick Ashton (1904–88) and the English Style

Ashton's versatile ballets contain both poetic classicism and rich theatricality; they are synonymous with the English choreographic style, and reflect multiple influences. The dancing of Anna Pavlova and Isadora Duncan informed Ashton's profound musicality and fluidity of movement. Having studied Cecchetti's method (with Massine and Rambert), Ashton believed the Cecchetti *ports de bras* instilled 'a wonderful feeling for line and correct positioning and

the use of head movement and *épaulement*', which was central to his work.[40] Like de Valois before him, Ashton had worked with Bronislava Nijinska (from 1928 to 1929), and absorbed her 'vivid way of making the upper body move as intensely as the lower'.[41] He also shared de Valois' instinct for intricate footwork derived from national and social dance forms, and her love of popular English theatre traditions.

Celebrated as The Royal Ballet's founding choreographer, Ashton joined de Valois' Company in 1935. For over fifty years his choreographic genius definitively shaped English ballet, as he 'poured into his ballets the flood of romanticism that he had hinted at in earlier pieces for Rambert' and 'exploited brilliantly the lyrical vein that he had uncovered in Fonteyn and, importantly, the rest of the Company'.[42]

Symphonic Variations (1946), Frederick Ashton's neo-classical masterpiece, was created for (left to right) Henry Danton, Moira Shearer, Michael Somes, Margot Fonteyn, Brian Shaw and Pamela May.

Vera Volkova teaching Margot Fonteyn (1919–91); Fonteyn became Frederick Ashton's muse and epitomized the English lyric style.

NICHOLAS SERGEYEV (1876–1951): STAGING THE CLASSICAL REPERTOIRE IN ENGLAND

Petipa and Tchaikovsky's *The Sleeping Beauty* was first produced in London by Diaghilev (re-titled *The Sleeping Princess*, 1921). Nicholas Sergeyev had reconstructed the entire work using his Stepanov Notation scores, salvaged from the turmoil of revolutionary Russia. He subsequently mounted several ballet 'classics', including *Giselle*, *The Nutcracker* and *Swan Lake*, for the Vic-Wells Ballet (all in 1934). Thus: 'The skeleton, if not the flesh and blood, of the Mariinsky style had been transferred from Imperial Russia to [Sadler's Wells] a modest theatre in Islington'.[43] The Company's seminal production of *The Sleeping Beauty* (1946) found its ideal Aurora in Margot Fonteyn – her clean, lyrical classicism became the hallmark of an English *ballerina*.

Postcard of Margot Fonteyn as Princess Aurora and Robert Helpmann as Prince Florimund in Petipa's *The Sleeping Beauty* **designed by Oliver Messel (1946).**

CHARACTERISTICS OF THE ENGLISH (ASHTON/DE VALOIS) SCHOOL

English schooling is rooted in Ninette de Valois' teaching, based upon the French, Italian, Russian and Danish Schools. A synthesis of Petipa's classicism, Diaghilev's modernism, and native British theatre traditions, created an English choreographic and performing style – primarily through the ballets of Frederick Ashton, but also those of de Valois herself.

Distinctive features include:

- Neat, quick footwork; *terre à terre* (low) jumps.
- Accurate alignment ('square' hip placement).
- Clean, uncluttered *ports de bras*.
- Control contrasted with fluidity.
- Strong use of *épaulement* and deep upper body bends.
- Musicality: rhythmically precise, lyrical and sensual.
- Narrative: strong characterization and dramatic 'truth'.
- Pantomime: travesty and comedy/pathos roles.
- Defined body directions and floor patterns.

THE AMERICAN SCHOOL: HISTORY AND STYLISTIC FEATURES

Early Ballet in America

Many American settlers held Puritan beliefs and thus disapproved of dancing. Even so, the British colony of South Carolina presented America's earliest known ballet in 1735, when an English dancer named Henry Holt appeared in *The Adventures of Harlequin and Scaramouch* – staged in Charleston's Courthouse, because the town had no theatre!

Following the American War of Independence (1775–83), a French ballet troupe led by Alexandre Placide performed in Boston, Philadelphia, New York and Charleston. 'Madame Placide' (actually Suzanne Vaillande) eventually became *prima ballerina* in New Orleans, and a pioneering choreographer. John Durang, the first American-born ballet dancer, also toured with Placide's company.[44]

Romantic Ballet Crosses the Atlantic

Soon after the Paris premieres of *La Sylphide* (1832) and *Giselle* (1841), both ballets came to America: Paul and Amelie Taglioni performed *La Sylphide* in New York (1839), while two 'home-grown' stars, Mary Ann Lee and George Washington Smith, danced *Giselle* in Boston (1846). Several European ballet celebrities successfully toured the United States, notably Fanny Elssler (1840–42), and Léon Espinosa (1850–56). The Cecchetti family (including seven-year-old Enrico), visited for eleven months in 1857. Ballet was slow to take root in America but a century later, Cecchetti's student and successor, Margaret Craske, would teach his training method at New York's Metropolitan Opera Ballet School (1950–68).

The Metropolitan Opera House opened in 1883; its ballet company was subordinate to the opera, and dependent on foreign guest artists. In 1909, 'the Met' established a school under the direction of Malvina Cavallazzi (dates vary: 1852/62–1924), a former *prima ballerina* of Milan, London and New York. By 1914, she had trained a truly American

The Black Crook (1866) premiered in New York and ran for over a year; various revivals toured the States until 1903, introducing many Americans to ballet. Illustration from the London version (1872).

corps de ballet, and produced the Metropolitan Opera Ballet's first American star, Eva Swain.[45]

Ballet 'Legends' in North and South America

Adeline Genée and Anna Pavlova independently toured the US in 1910, igniting new interest in classical ballet amongst press and public alike. Pavlova eventually spent almost a quarter of her entire career in the Americas, where she inspired many future dance-makers.[46]

As World War I took hold in Europe, the sensational Diaghilev Ballets Russes performed across the American continent (1916–17). Vaslav Nijinsky's appearances with the Company showed that ballet was no longer simply the preserve of the *ballerina*.

Diaghilev's Legacy in America

The five great choreographers of Diaghilev's Ballets Russes were Mikhail (or Michel) Fokine, Vaslav Nijinsky, Léonide Massine, Bronislava Nijinska and George Balanchine. Apart from Nijinsky, whose mental illness had ended his career, they all went on to spend many years, or to settle, in the United States, where their works dominated the repertoire, formed its dancers and made ballet a nationally recognized art form.

Following the death of Diaghilev in 1929, several rival 'Ballets Russes' companies had emerged. Colonel de Basil's Les Ballets Russes de Monte Carlo (1932–52) made a successful American debut in 1933, with Balanchine as ballet master. A breakaway group, formed by René Blum in 1935, became the Ballet Russe de Monte Carlo (1938–62), led by Massine. As war returned to Europe (1939–45), this Company established headquarters in New York and made America its home.[47]

AMERICAN SOCIAL DANCING AND BALLETIC STYLE

From the early seventeenth century onwards, waves of immigration – both forced and voluntary – brought a wealth of music and dance to America: English country dances became American square dances, while African–American traditions gave rise to new forms, such as tap, jazz, jive and many more. Irish reels, jigs and clog dances entered the mix, along with other popular dances from Europe. In America, these 'spread out and became quicker, longer and harder' to reflect the young nation's greater 'room and energy'.[48] In the twentieth century, Balanchine's choreography harnessed American speed, variety, dynamism and bold expansiveness.

(Left to right) Tamara Toumanova, Irina Baronova, Tatiana Riabouchinska and Alexandra Danilova (on floor), c.1936. Recruited by Balanchine for the de Basil Ballets Russes in their early teens, they became famous throughout Europe and America as the 'baby ballerinas'.

School of American Ballet (SAB) and New York City Ballet (NYCB)

The School of American Ballet was founded in January 1934 by Russian-born teacher and choreographer, George Balanchine, with American writer and dance-patron, Lincoln Kirstein (1907–96). From the outset, the School's training was designed to serve Balanchine's choreographic style, and SAB graduates were recruited for successive companies he and Kirstein co-directed: American Ballet (Metropolitan Opera House, 1935–38) and Ballet Caravan (touring 1936–41). In 1946, they started Ballet Society, which took up residence at the New York City Center of Music and Drama in 1948 to become New York City Ballet.

Milestone works from Balanchine's early years in America include Tchaikovsky's *Serenade* (1934), *Concerto Barocco* and *Ballet Imperial* (scores by Bach and Tchaikovsky, respectively, 1941) and *The Four Temperaments* (music by Hindemith, 1946). His iconic production of *The Nutcracker* (1954) established Tchaikovsky's ballet as an enduring Christmas tradition nationwide. Balanchine's creative partnership with the composer Igor Stravinsky (1882–1971) was central to the development of NYCB and its repertoire: astonishingly, Balanchine choreographed nearly 40 per cent of Stravinsky's published works during their life-long collaboration.[49]

Balanchine's dancers were his greatest inspiration; several generations of extraordinary artists gave life to his ballets, including such famous names as Maria Tallchief, Melissa Hayden, Violette Verdy, Jacques d'Amboise, Edward Villella, Allegra Kent, Suzanne Farrell, Peter Martins, Merrill Ashley and Gelsey Kirkland.

GEORGE BALANCHINE (1904–83)

Born in St. Petersburg (originally christened Georgi Balanchivadze), he graduated from the former Imperial School into the Company in 1921. Joining Diaghilev's Ballets Russes in 1924, he soon became Company choreographer, creating the iconic 'neo-classical' ballet *Apollo* in his first collaboration with Stravinsky (1928). (See the photograph of the original *Apollon Musagètes* (1928) in Chapter 5.) Following Diaghilev's death, Balanchine formed 'Les Ballets 1933' in Paris, before accepting Lincoln Kirstein's invitation to the United States, which led to their co-founding of New York City Ballet.

Over six decades, Balanchine's prolific, inventive and eclectic choreography was distinguished by his deep understanding of music – he was a trained musician – and the Mariinsky ballet tradition in which he was raised. His usually plotless, one-act works re-positioned the boundaries of classical ballet and shaped the American balletic style.

George Balanchine on a visit to London *c*. 1955.

Ballet Theater (Renamed American Ballet Theater in 1957)

Established in 1940 by the American actor-dancer, Lucia Chase (1897–1986) and theatre agent, Richard Pleasant. Chase's personal drive and fortune sustained the Company for over forty years. Two of Ballet Theater's founding choreographers were the native New Yorker, Agnes de Mille (1905–93), and London-born Antony Tudor (1909–87); both had absorbed the Diaghilev tradition during their early careers with Rambert in England.

From the start, Ballet Theater's broad repertoire included favourite twentieth-century ballets and traditional nineteenth-century 'classics', as well as new American choreography. The Company's inaugural season in New York (1940) presented Fokine's *Les Sylphides*, Tudor's *Lilac Garden* and Anton Dolin's production of *Giselle*. Its first decade saw important new commissions, notably Tudor's *Pillar of Fire* (1942), Massine's *Mam'zelle Angot* (1943), Jerome Robbins' *Fancy Free* (1944), Balanchine's

Theme and Variations (1947) and de Mille's *Fall River Legend* (1948).[50]

American Ballet Theater (ABT) toured extensively, having no permanent base until 1977, when New York's Metropolitan Opera House officially became its home. In 2006, an Act of Congress made ABT the National Ballet Company of the USA. True to the purpose of its founders, and in contrast to Balanchine's New York City Ballet – or the modern dance companies of Martha Graham, Merce Cunningham, Alwin Nikolais and others – ABT was never 'subordinate to a single artistic vision'.[51]

ABT widened the scope of the national balletic style, commissioning work from America's modern choreographers, including Paul Taylor, Cunningham, Twyla Tharp and Mark Morris. The Company nurtured many great dancers, such as Alicia Alonso, Cynthia Gregory, Fernando Bujones and Cynthia Harvey; also attracting an international roster of stars, notably Natalia Makarova, Mikhail Baryshnikov, Alessandra Ferri and Anthony Dowell.

BALLET AND BROADWAY

The creative interaction between ballet and modern dance with American musical theatre and film really began when Balanchine made his *Slaughter on Tenth Avenue* ballet for *On Your Toes* (1936). Agnes de Mille famously choreographed many original musicals, including *Oklahoma!* (1943) and *Carousel* (1945), in which ballet scenes provided motivational insight and moved the action along. American dancers were often fluent in classical ballet and musical theatre, affecting the style of both genres.

Jerome Robbins (1918–98) danced on Broadway and as a soloist with Ballet Theater (1941–44). He began his choreographic career with *Fancy Free* (1944), a ballet about three happy-go-lucky sailors on leave in New York. Set to a score by Leonard Bernstein, it was developed as a popular musical, *On the Town* (1944), and later filmed with Gene Kelly. Robbins and Bernstein went on to create the ground-breaking musical, *West Side Story* (1957). From 1949 to 1959, Robbins was associate director of New York City Ballet, returning as ballet master from 1969 until his retirement in 1990. He created many works for NYCB, including the gently comic *The Concert* (1956) and the lyrical *Dances at a Gathering* (1969), both to Chopin's music. His ballets encompassed the full range of American dance styles, from 'showbiz' to rigorous classicism.

Gelsey Kirkland in *La Sylphide c.*1975; trained at the School of American Ballet, she joined New York City Ballet (1968–74) and American Ballet Theater (1974–84).

The School of American Ballet Theater

There have been several training programmes associated with ABT: the first, directed by Antony Tudor, was attached to the Metropolitan Opera Ballet School in 1950; a second 'official' Ballet Theatre School was opened on West 56th Street in 1951, directed by Bronislava Nijinska, then Lucia Chase. The Jacqueline Kennedy Onassis (JKO) School is now the associate school of ABT (established 2005). It is interesting to note that the stated aim of ABT's national training curriculum is to combine 'elements of classical French, Italian, and Russian schools of ballet' (www.abt. training/).

CHARACTERISTICS OF THE AMERICAN (BALANCHINE) SCHOOL

- Vertical axis: hyper-extended body and limbs.
- Musical precision prioritised over placement.
- Fleet footwork (focus on pointework).
- Flexible alignment: 'open' hips and shoulders.
- Free articulation of joints (hips, wrists, etc.).
- Head and torso: lifted, open and arched.
- Physicality: bold, energetic, fast, elastic, expansive.
- Vocabulary: steps from tap, jazz and musical theatre.
- Phrasing syncopated: linking steps abbreviated.
- Highly developed floor and group patterns.
- *Corps de ballet* dance 'soloist'-level choreography.

In spite of their individual foundation stories and balletic styles, this chapter has shown how all schools of classical ballet share the same deep roots: notice, for instance, how many of history's great teachers and choreographers were taught by Auguste Vestris! Yet increasing levels of travel and media inter-connectedness might, in future, lead to the loss of distinguishing national stylistic features and expressive qualities – resulting in ballet across the globe becoming more standardized and less rich in variety. It is also possible that the opposite may happen, and that some exciting new styles will emerge as classical ballet becomes a truly worldwide performance art. What do you think can contribute to shaping the future? Will you be a part of it?

Nicola Katrak leading a movement sequence in the ballet class.

CHAPTER 3

TECHNIQUE AND BALLET CLASS FUNDAMENTALS
Nicola Katrak

ART AND SCIENCE

What happens in a ballet class? Ideally, it is the place where your body, mind and emotions combine to explore an important truth. You discover that the 'science' of technique serves to support and extend the flourishing and freedom of the art of dancing.

As we know, a class usually consists of 60–90 minutes of memorizing and executing syllabus or teacher-led movement sequences. Set at an appropriate level of challenge, such 'exercises' to music build gradually in physicality, speed and use of space. But how often do we remind ourselves that these sessions are so much more than a repetitive training programme in the balletic style?

From the earliest level as recreational students we explore the concepts of musicality and expression within classical boundaries. And, as we gain strength, knowledge and experience, class becomes the place where we focus each day on the physical and mental re-tuning of our instrument of performance.

Thoughts on Entering the Studio
When you place your hand on the barre afresh each time, remember that even a simple classroom sequence is like a conversation between still shapes and flowing movement, closely linked to your breath and sense of rhythm. The classical vocabulary is a living thing, not a set of old-style rules. Each time you adjust your eye focus, muscle engagement or musical phrasing, you subtly change the colour, flavour or meaning of a step. You may even discover that musicality can extend beyond dancing alongside or with the music, and experience yourself 'becoming' the music.

Participating in a ballet class is, of course, a deep personal study but also a group activity. It is worth reflecting that being able to switch focus from yourself to the team and back again is also an important skill needed in performance.

At the same time, are you are sharpening your own appetite for the basic fundamentals of ballet technique? Are you convinced that these are essential for every dancer and not just the beginner? While exploring the art of ballet in class, do you truly know, in your very bones, that the physical mechanics of balance and body position – placing and posture – need to be understood from a scientific point of view? Continuously demonstrating these correct underpinnings of technique will let you enjoy the physical freedom to move without tension, so you can indeed learn to dance to your full potential.

THE FOUNDATIONS OF TECHNIQUE

Ballet's technical demands are greater than ever before. Dancers now work toward having the strength and physique of athletes, extreme flexibility in extensions and ever-increasing virtuoso skill in high jumps, multiple turns, pointework and partnering. Yet they still need to know how to move with the simple classical grace that gives the illusion that their movements are effortless. In addition, they must be fully able to maintain those distinctively turned-out legs, plus the elegant lengthened spine that allows beautifully positioned arms to flow from the centre with ease.

So how can you aim to push your body to achieve always more, without the risk of injury? One way to sustain a long and healthy dancing life is to take time to understand and establish correct physical foundations. Consistently putting into practice the building blocks of a safe and secure technique is like an insurance policy for your future.

1. Placement of the Whole Body on Balance

The security of good balance starts with knowing you have stacked up your skeleton in a truly vertical line:

- With feet slightly apart and parallel, and thinking of the sideways view of your body, line up precisely these *five* points: ear, shoulder, hip, knee and ankle bone.

- It should be possible to trace a completely straight and perpendicular line between these five points (*see also* Chapter 6).

Imagine a builder using a 'plumb' line (aplomb) to ensure that their bricks are stacked exactly vertically, so that the forces of gravity help to maintain the stability of the wall.

2. Consolidating Correct Posture

To support your perfectly upright body, regularly check that you employ the essential elements of accurate posture, including:

- Lifting the bones of your pelvis into a 'neutral'* placement – neither arching your lower back nor 'tucking in' your bottom.
- Maintaining and supporting this correct pelvic placement by consistently lifting the abdominal muscles (stomach) upwards toward your sternum.
- Lengthening your whole spine upwards, imagining the vertebrae separating from each other.

Remember to lengthen the spine without straining the shoulders as you lift the abdominal muscles toward the sternum. Oona, in front, shows calm ribs.

*A neutral pelvic placement is when the hip bones and pubic bone are on the same plane.

In simple classwork, the back of your neck should feel particularly elongated, so your chin is level with the floor – for good balance – and your neck free from strain. Indeed, it is all too easy for dancers to be over-eager to 'pull-up' their spines by raising and thrusting out the chest and chin, which affects the balance and causes unnecessary tension.

To counteract this, draw your lowest two ribs calmly toward each other without shrinking your spine. Then open your shoulders sideways, simultaneously imagining your shoulder blades sliding downwards and outwards toward your armpits, rather than pinching toward each other. As you practise breathing deeply, sustaining this good posture, visualize your back widening to let the air in, rather than the stomach ballooning and the ribs over-extending.

3. Habitually Lining Up Knees and Toes

Our knees are particularly vulnerable to injury when twisted, so it is ideal to revise correct lower leg alignment while standing in this same parallel position:

- Feel your big toe joints well-planted on the floor, with all the toes in a forward direction, while you place your feet without the ankles 'rolling' either inwards or outwards. Problems often start with over-correcting here, so just gently lift the small navicular ankle bone, checking that your toes remain relaxed, not clawing the floor.
- The middle of your kneecap should be in line with the gap between your second and third toe. Notice how you will need to engage the tops of the backs of your legs a little in order to rotate your knees into this correct alignment.

SPECIAL TIP!

If you have hyper-extended knees, slightly release the backs of the knees and pull the fronts upwards toward your thigh, rather than sink into the swaybacks.

4. Correct Leg Rotation

Opening outwards, or *en dehors*, is a key element of the aesthetics of ballet. The turnout of the legs is also a critical aspect technically, so be sure to retain in your mind and muscles the image of that straight line reaching from the centre of your knee down to the spot between your second and third toes.

- When your heels are placed together in First Position those muscles at the tops of the backs of your legs should be fully activated, without 'tucking' the pelvis.
- To these rotators will be added your glutes – so maybe think 'glutators' – to help you support and maximize the turnout of the whole leg from the hip. This is further secured by using the muscles of your inner thighs to continue to 'spiral' your legs *en dehors.*
- Firmly resist the strong temptation to over-turn out your feet, roll your ankles and screw your toes sideways, particularly while you execute a *demi-plié*. This is a common trap and to work safely it is vital to maintain the correct alignment between knees and toes.
- Retaining the correct placement and posture you have already established (*see* The Foundations of Technique 1, 2 and 3) is the key to finding all the personal rotation you naturally have. When we turn out, it is all too easy to misalign those *five* points. So often we place our hips behind our ankles, counterbalanced by our shoulders and ears leaning forwards, especially in a *demi-plié*.
- Avoid 'sitting' in your heels, as if you are sticking your shoes to the floor to keep your turnout (all too easy on a lino floor!). Imagine the heels just lightly 'kissing' the ground as your perfectly poised body prepares for movement.
- If you then rise on to the balls of your feet – or *demi-pointe* – focus yet again on maintaining placement and posture to lift your body upwards all in one piece. If you are well-placed, you should not need to grip the floor with your toes. Imagine that the spot between your second and third toes is the centre point of your balance, to keep the ankles well-aligned and less susceptible to injury.

Placing and turnout in First, with and without *demi-plié*. On the left, Laura and Oona deliberately demonstrate what happens when the *five* points are not stacked up, so their hips are incorrectly placed behind their ankles and ears. Anita has centred her weight placement correctly with hip bones aligned vertically over ankle bones. Regan, on the right, has lined up his ear, shoulder, hip, knee and ankle, but demonstrates a very slightly tucked pelvis.

WAKING UP THE MUSCLES

It is important for your muscles to be warm before you work with your legs turned out, and as you gain more experience, you will develop a warm-up specific to your own body. Including 3–5 minutes of simple low-impact movements, like various walks, marches, knee bends, small jogs, with vigorously coordinated arms to raise your heartbeat and get the blood flowing, is an easy way to ensure that you have safely prepared your body. Your mind will benefit too, as this will stimulate the secretion of endorphins, hormones that enhance your mood.

(*See* Chapter 6 for more details.)

HOW DO I LEARN?
1. PRACTICE MAKES BETTER

These foundations of good technique can seem a lot to remember. However, dancers have always understood the value of repetition – hence daily classes – and in the past were often told 'practice makes perfect'. The truth is that intelligent, focused, personal practice absolutely makes things better, but perfection in a living art form that relies on the human body isn't really a useful goal.

As you develop your own way of practising, always check that you have really considered and understood any appropriate information and personal feedback that you receive. Apply it carefully to your unique body, knowing that each physique has different capabilities.

Remember that slow, thoughtful and, above all, accurate repetitions of small, crucial details will send increasingly helpful messages between your brain and your muscles. These will build enduring neural pathways that will enable you to achieve things with less conscious effort.

HOW DO I LEARN? 2. OBSERVATION AND PROPRIOCEPTION

Get someone to take a photo of you sideways to see if you are accurately lining up those five points of ear, shoulder, hip, knee and ankle bone. Use a mirror to really study your posture and lower leg alignment. Once you have used your eyes to observe and correct your work, stop looking and instead try feeling or sensing when you are right. A strong awareness of your body in space – proprioception – really helps you learn.

SPECIAL TIP!

You don't need a warm-up or a ballet studio to practise holding accurate posture, placing and lower leg alignment with those properly planted *parallel* feet. Imagine what you could achieve in the lunch queue, waiting for a bus, making a phone call…

THE FIVE POSITIONS

As we know, the classical vocabulary starts with the five basic positions of arms and feet. Although the names and exact poses differ between schools worldwide, such slight variations are not considered critical, as it is the job of a dancer to adapt to new stylistic details wherever they go. However, it is important for your mind and body to establish a clear version as you train in class. The shapes discussed here derive from what I learned as a child with the Royal Academy of Dancing and what I now teach at The Royal Ballet School.

So, what is the value of examining these fundamental ballet shapes, codified long ago? After purposefully revising some basic physical foundations, studying these default classical positions anew reminds us of that deep relationship between the science of technique and the dancer's artistry.

Ports de Bras

It is all too easy for us to become fixated on what happens from the waist downwards, but at least 50 per cent of our dancing involves the upper body. Frederick Ashton, after watching an 'Introduction to Ballet' lecture demonstration, remarked that it all seemed very focused on the legs and feet. 'There is no dancing without the ports de bras!'[52] he rightly exclaimed, and every moment of his choreography expresses this truth. Never forget that the movements and shapes of your arms frame the essence of your personality, your face, your heart and soul.

First Position

To the balletic display of the legs *en dehors* is added the classical element of curved arms. Drawing the legs upwards together, rotating and spiralling them outwards to reveal the heels, we employ all the science of posture (*see* Foundations of Technique 2) to suspend gracefully the arms before us in an artistically rounded shape, the hands apart by about the width of our cheekbones. Inclining the head graciously to gaze at our fingers brings an air of peaceful containment.

First Position. The height of the arms can vary. Here Oona shows artistic connection between her eyes and hands, and Laura's uplifted spine supports a well-rounded 'gateway'.

But there is also hidden power in the roundedness of the arms in First Position, accurately called the 'gateway' between positions. Used wisely, this shape sustains the uplift of the back and good weight placement. With the right force and opening of shoulders it facilitates multiple pirouettes. Crucially, it can help to coordinate the whole body moving at speed, such as when the arms swish musically through First in preparation for a big jump. Indeed, this shape of the arms could be visualized as the physical manifestation of the feeling that movement originates from the centre of the body.

Second Position

Transferring your weight so that your body is centralized between outstretched legs with arms extended sideways is a confident statement of the body *en dehors*. Physically it can be easy to 'sit' in the legs and heels. Have you retained the lift of the kneecap and the rotation of the inside thighs, feeling how the mass or weight of the body is energized? Then you will be ready for that jump or *relevé*, which will rely on an accurately aligned bend of the knees in a *demi-plié* in Second.

Aesthetically, it is crucial to retain that classical curve of the arms, now part of an arc of a much larger circumference and placed just below the shoulders.

HOW MUCH TO TURN OUT?

Every physique is different and, while you work safely toward maximizing your degree of leg rotation (*see* The Foundations of Technique 4), it is worth remembering that, when standing in First, anything beyond a 179-degree angle is likely to be incorrectly placed. Check all your science!

SPECIAL TIP!

Beware of revealing any weakness of posture by either drooped or hyper-stretched elbows. Position them fractionally in front of the shoulder and imagine a rotation *en dehors* of the shoulder and wrist with a simultaneous inward, *en dedans*, rotation of the elbow.

Second Position. The palms of the hands face the audience. Regan demonstrates that when the hips are incorrectly placed behind the feet, this is often counterbalanced by over-extending the ribs.

Third Position

Crossing one foot halfway in front of the other is commonly used before the student is proficient enough for Fifth Position. It is useful too in rehabilitation after injury when it reminds us that *both feet need always to bear equal weight and both legs use equal turnout.*

And in Third Position, with one arm in First and the other in Second, the dancer's torso begins to imply the play of opposing forces and develops the *épaulement* (which some call 'shouldering'). You can consciously develop the artistry of this opposition feeling by exploring your use of *épaulement*.

Anatomically, keep the hips squarely aligned with your feet as you subtly lift and twist your upper spine. Aesthetically, you are adding another dimension with your shoulders and a new flavour to the pose.

Third Position. Different 'flavours' of Third, with extra *épaulement* from Regan in the centre.

THE HEAD

The invitation to explore the artistry of *épaulement* can include discovering an extended range of head movements. Absolutely crucial for expression, your head angle and eye focus breathe life into each position, whether your upper body is in *épaulement* or square with your hips.

Physically lengthen your spine, especially the back of your neck, and rehearse the basic mechanics of head movement – nose up and down; right and left; ears tilting right and left. Then make the transformation from classroom to stage by subtly combining elements of these to produce a head position that, while harmonizing with the pose your whole body is making, adds a sense of character or mood. Remember to really 'see' with your eyes.

SPECIAL TIP!

If you keep your shoulders open, and remember to use your abdominal muscles, you can often twist the upper spine more easily to add *épaulement*. Remember, the knees and hips must not swivel round.

Fourth Position

With one leg planted in front and one behind the central axis of your body, there is a feeling here of movement, of advancing or retreating. Keeping both hips squarely facing your front (*en face*) and your knees aligned over toes (*see* Foundations of Technique 3 and 4) is a tough physical assignment. Tempting as it is to favour one leg, the weight on your feet should be precisely equal. On *pointe* and *demi-pointe*, toes should be well-crossed in line with each other but on flat feet, sometimes placing the front heel opposite Third rather than Fifth assists with accurate hips and safer knees. The width of your position is an aesthetic judgement based on the length of your legs, but too wide is unlikely to be helpfully placed.

With one arm curved above the head and the other in Second or First, the artistry of Fourth

Fourth Position. Many variations of the Fourth Position. Zoe on the right at the front fully rotates her upper spine while keeping her hips 'square'.

Fifth Position. From left to right: Denilson demonstrates over-crossed feet and over-stretched elbows. Anita sustains as much turnout with the back leg as the front, whereas Regan demonstrates the common faults of turning-in the back leg and not rotating the elbows _en dehors_. Zoe's pure position shows open shoulders and a clear eye line.

Position with its various head angles runs to many possibilities. Enjoy experimenting with their extensive expressive potential!

Fifth Position

> _What a dramatic and dynamic move this is, to pass the front leg across the line of the vertical._[53]

With the front foot crossed enough to conceal the bunion of the back foot and the hips resolutely square _en face_, Fifth is the ultimate technical expression of secure turn out and potential for movement in all directions.

Work determinedly toward keeping equal rotation of both legs and equal weight on both feet. Don't be tempted to 'sit' sideways on the back heel and hook the front toes around to over-turn out that front foot. This is critical: such an almost one-legged and unequal Fifth will never constitute a well-balanced foundation for the preparation or ending of a sequence. Instead, focus on strongly engaging those 'glutators' and feel the inside thigh of the front leg assist you in stretching the front knee. It will, of course, be safely aligned with that spot between the second and third toes (_see_ Foundations of Technique 3 and 4).

Meanwhile, the beautiful, stylish framing of your face with the harmonious oval of your arms requires a consistent curvature of the elbows, wrists and each finger joint. When this oval is repositioned downwards in the _bras bas_ or preparatory position, work toward avoiding the extreme tension of over-flexed wrists or angular elbows that often compensate for weak posture.

SPECIAL TIP!

Your hands should aim to be elegantly and economically shaped, soft but not lifeless, with thumbs gently folded toward the palms.

Oona angles her head harmoniously to match her arms in Fifth. Laura's hands are much wider apart than the width of her cheekbones, and demonstrates that the oval shape in her *bras bas* or preparatory arms is lost.

FOCUS ON FEET

As you explored poses with the arms in Third and Fourth, you may have used a *battement tendu* to move between them, suddenly becoming aware of how you are presenting your foot as an extension of your stretched leg.

Undoubtedly, the beautifully arched, pointed foot is an iconic element of ballet. Lengthening and completing the line of the leg, it can even add an extra dimension to a dancer's artistry. And perhaps the rather intense relationship we sometimes have with our feet is due to the desire to produce this best possible aesthetic line in still shapes or photos.

This aim is commendable but at least equal focus should, of course, be given to the way the foot is used in movement. Most of the classical vocabulary involves the foot transitioning to and from a stretched position. In jumps, maximum articulation of the toe-joints – or metatarsals – with split-second timing, will produce higher, stronger elevation. The return through a speedy *demi-pointe* will cushion the landing for greater control and safety.

The Characteristics of a Dancer's Foot

As with every aspect of our physique, we are all very individual, but ideal feet are considered those that have naturally high insteps, as well as mobile ankles that allow full extension. Well-articulated metatarsals are also needed for quick action and good *demi-pointe*, plus pointed toes that are strong and straight, never curled or floppy.

A well-aligned, pointed foot will continue that straight line from the middle of the kneecap toward the second/third toes, avoiding the more natural 'sickle', inversion or 'banana' shape. The opposite – an everted

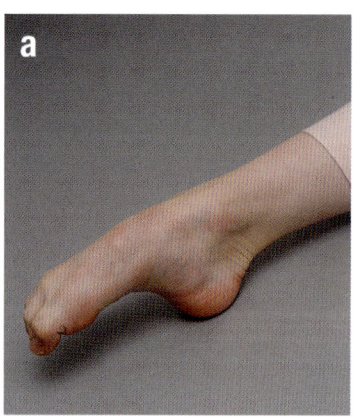
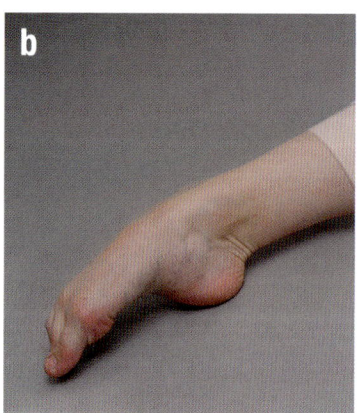
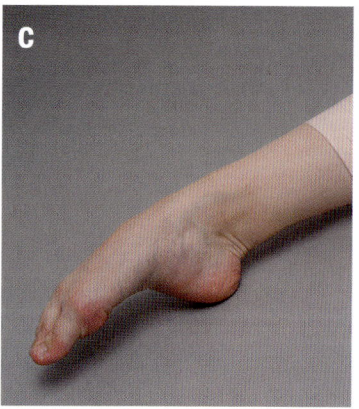

(a) The toes are never curled. (b) Beware of over-pointing your foot, crushing your Achilles' tendon and shortening your line. (c) Well-stretched toes and elongated ankle.

or 'fished' foot – is often thought of as a desirable line, particularly in arabesque, but it can easily result in the ankle being flexed and the toes disengaged. It should be used very sparingly in ballet class to avoid building weak habits.

Maximizing Your Feet

Each physique being different, part of the skill of learning effectively is knowing how to make the most of the body you have been given. It is important to know the difference between those aspects of your technique that you can develop and strengthen, and the areas that you have little control over, such as the shape of the bones. This particularly applies to our feet.

It is not possible to enlarge the size of our insteps, for example, but by hard work in class and gentle, wise stretching we can slightly increase the mobility of the ankles. Small adjustments to a sickled foot can be diligently practised over time and a restricted great toe that hampers the *demi-pointe* can be eased a little. But the greatest control we have over feet is increasing the strength and articulation of the metatarsal joints and toes. Developing long, steel-strong toes will allow a foot with less of an instep to look more arched and a highly arched one to gain more control, especially on *pointe*.

Metatarsal Exercise

Learning the habit of never curling or clawing the toes helps to avoid injury and is easier to establish when you are young.

Practise first with your hand and fingers, so that you know what you can expect from your toes. With the palm of the hand facing downwards on the floor and the fingers flat, raise the knuckles of your hand without curving any joint in the fingers. Then mirror this movement with your toes. Mental focus and regular repetitions will be crucial. When it is easier, try making the same shape without resting the toes on the floor, or with added resistance from a TheraBand. Know that every single time you point your foot in class, the toes should never be curled.

SHOES

The shoes worn in ballet classes are often very light, with the canvas hugging like a sock and the soles split to accentuate the arch of the foot. Although this can enhance the line for now, it does not help to build future strength. The resistance offered by more old-fashioned, full-soled leather or soft-block, ballet shoes adds extra value to all the footwork training within a ballet class.

Pointework

The ultimate expression of an exquisitely arched foot is the skill of dancing on *pointe*, assisted by the technology of customized shoes. In order to be safe, it is now even more essential to employ the correct foundations of technique. Check that you are fully spiralling your legs *en dehors* as you lift your perfectly placed body and strongly stretched toes upwards and out of your shoes.

Preparing your metatarsals and toes will help you to check if you are standing on the tips of your toes in your *pointe* shoes, rather than sitting in your knuckles or flopping on to the soft pads of your toes. It is a good idea to cushion your toes inside the *pointe* shoe with a little lambswool to begin with. This allows you to feel what your toes are doing more than the rather substantial toe pads that dancers tend to wear when shoes are worn for long periods of time.

On *pointe* the aim is to look as if the shoe is an elegant extension of your leg, not a hefty extra encumbrance. You should wear in your shoes before first working in them, so that you can use almost as much *demi-pointe* on the ball of your foot as in your soft shoes.

Choosing the ideal shoe is always a balancing act between how it feels and how it looks. Rarely will it be perfect, especially while your feet are growing, but consulting a highly-skilled shoe-fitter can be like a personal coaching session on how well you are training your feet, and whether a certain fit of shoe, or strength of sole, could help enhance the aesthetic line that you are constantly tweaking to improve.

MAKING THE MOST OF EACH BALLET CLASS

Arriving in good time for class allows you the space to recall the basic scientific foundations of your technique and to warm up your muscles. Many dancers like to stretch before working but it's worth considering the risk of injury in stretching cold muscles.

Maybe the previous evening you will have reflected on your current goals and planned how you will continue the process of patiently building them into accurate habits. This prepares your mind to consolidate your plans confidently and to be in a receptive zone for the next day's work.

Once class begins though, be alert to listening to more than your own thoughts. Allow yourself to be governed by the music and really hear your teacher's voice. Process instructions and advice as quickly as possible before each sequence so that, rather than worrying about what movement comes next, you can target and enjoy your progress.

Aim to start well, using all your concentration and effort. The first few sections of barre work are crucial to the rest of class. Achieving these to the best of your ability puts you on track to learn well.

Remember to apply the science quickly! You want to dance with freedom, not tension.

HOW DO I LEARN? 3. REFLECTION AFTER CLASS

Sometimes all the information received in class can seem overwhelming, so how do we remember everything we learn? As well as taking time to reflect, think and plan, writing notes afterwards can be a great way to make things clearer in your mind. Working with a friend when memorizing steps is often easier than doing it alone.

Don't forget how important it is to remember what went well in class and the words of praise you received! Those dancers who tend to obsess about their challenges all too often forget such compliments and ignore their strengths.

HOW DO I LEARN? 4. MENTAL REHEARSAL

If you are worrying about achieving something you currently find difficult, find time to lie down calmly with your eyes shut and mentally rehearse it. Imagine yourself in the studio, using all your senses to feel what you are wearing, what you are hearing and seeing. Then very slowly and deliberately visualize yourself performing that challenging step extremely well, several times. You will be enhancing the neural pathways between your brain and your muscles without physical exhaustion and stress.

At the Barre

Standing a comfortable distance from the barre, placing your hand gently upon it with a relaxed wrist and elbow to allow for an open shoulder, know that this is the moment when all your mental and physical preparation bears fruit. As you breathe and still yourself for the first sequence, reflect that you are in control of your learning, that your body is ready to create artistic beauty.

Pliés

This smooth-flowing exercise will include timely reminders of all the fundamentals of technique. Your body will revise the verticality of the spine, plus accurate posture and rotation of the leg with each bend and stretch of the knees. You can recall correct ankle and lower leg alignment with each rising and lowering from *demi-pointe*, and good use of the foot with each transition between the Five Positions.

Your arms rehearse their classical poses, sometimes holding still in a perfect curve, sometimes coordinating with the head, eyes and whole body to trace a circular pathway to the next shape, at a speed and dynamic in relation to the music.

Perhaps this sequence also develops your understanding of the fact that a *demi-plié* can be both a still shape and a dynamic action that links to, or prepares for, the succeeding movement. The mood and tempo of the music could encourage you to explore the speed and quality of the way you might stretch and bend your legs. Enjoy sensing the opposing forces of movement, by feeling the floating up as you go down and the pressing down as you come up.

SPECIAL TIP!

When you are on balance you can dance with much more confidence. Remember that the function of barre work is to find your centre of gravity and your 'plumb' line (aplomb), and to work the muscles to build up these good placing habits. Use the barre to develop this but beware of gripping it too tightly. Allow your hand to slip about as you transfer your weight.

Battements Tendu, Glissé and Jeté

When the dynamic sharpens to focus more on footwork, revise the sensation of the whole body extending upwards, before you begin each action with the thigh extending from the body to drive your leg and foot to stretch and return. Beware thinking of only a pretty pose of pointed toes forward, sideways or backwards. Enjoy activating your inside thigh to achieve the turnout of your heel as you slide your foot to the stretch ankle, metatarsal and long toes, gradually lessening the floor pressure to transfer your weight from two legs to one. Every *battement tendu* extension will be as weightless as a *battement glissé* or *jeté*: toes do not need to prod the floor!

KEEPING 'SQUARE'

Although your arms and head are moving freely at the barre, it is important for your ribs and hip bones to remain facing toward your front, to help you centre your balance and keep your classical shapes clear.

Develop your knowledge and feeling of where the centre of your body is facing (see How Do I Learn? 2 Observation and Proprioception). Stopping your hips from twisting around when you *tendu*, front or side, will help you to activate the turnout of both working (or gesture) leg and supporting (or standing) leg *equally*. It is all too easy to cheat by turning in the standing leg to try to achieve a better aesthetic line. Train yourself at the barre to maintain an honest habit of staying square and you will build true strength – and so avoid tension the audience can see.

When the leg is in the *derrière* position, there might be a very slight opening of the working hip to facilitate turning out, but certainly no lifting it up as if hiding your waistband.

Rond de Jambe

These circular leg movements *en dehors* and *en dedans* will remind you of the mechanics of elongating your spine and turning both legs out equally, as you keep hips and ribs square and your supporting side still. You may be adding full body bends in these sequences, combining the art of making the musical phrases satisfyingly visible in your *ports de bras* with accurate technique in the *cambrés*.

Check when you bend your whole body forwards, with well-stretched inside thighs, that hips remain vertically positioned over your feet. Likewise, a *cambré* sideways should not include transferring your weight on to one foot. To achieve a satisfying arch backwards, turn your head sideways and begin the movement by elongating and then bending your neck before shoulders and upper spine follow.

Battement tendu. Equal turnout of both legs.

A serene shoulder line and well-held abdominal muscles complete the picture.

Battements Fondu and Frappé

Here is a moment to reflect on the French names of these steps to increase your dynamic range. Repeating well-oiled 'melting' movements of the knees and a sharp 'striking' of the floor with the ball of the foot prepares you for the technique of jumping, as well as landing. Will that be on balance, with accurate safe turnout?

Battement Developpé

The slow unfolding of your leg to full height can demonstrate artistic serenity if those technical foundations are secure. Use all your placing and postural knowledge as you draw a line with your toes up your shin bone to make a *retiré* with square and level hip bones. Elongating the spine, without 'tucking' the pelvis, as you lift your knee to start the unfolding movement gives you space to aim for a beautiful, elongated, rotated line, on balance, with harmonious *ports de bras*.

See the photograph of Margot Fonteyn with Volkova in Chapter 2 for an ideal example of serene artistry. Margot Fonteyn demonstrates a flowing classical arabesque line, her well-rotated legs perfectly complemented by her elegantly curved *port de bras* and expressive eye focus. Notice how her teacher, Vera Volkova, is ensuring her fingers, wrist and arm create an unbroken line.

THE ARABESQUE

You will be practicing this signature shape of ballet both at the barre and in the centre. There are many variations of an arabesque, but it is helpful to study this one in detail before proceeding to explore different styles and a more exaggerated line.

In a First Arabesque, standing on the left leg, the left arm is extended in front of your left shoulder about eyebrow height and the right is lower, placed just behind a sideways position. Both elongated palms face the floor. Engage all the posture muscles of your ribs and abdominals (*see* Foundations of Technique 2) extra strongly as you *tendu* the right leg *derrière*, to avoid arching the lower back and to help protect it. Remember, you may slightly open the right hip, but make sure you have not shortened your line by hitching it upwards (*see* Box: Keeping Square)

For this pure arabesque you are aiming for your shoulders and ribs to face the forwards direction of your gaze and if you keep the back of your neck elongated, so that your ears are not forced behind you, your balance will be a lot easier. Feel your standing leg planted vertically on the floor and aim for a clear 90-degree height of the working leg. Sense your toes reaching far behind as your eyes project forwards toward infinity.

Arabesque – finding a strong use of the abdominals.

Arabesque – the dancers deliberately demonstrate how poor placement can spoil the purity of line: Laura (left) twists her whole body to the audience and leans backwards with a shortened back of neck, while Oona (centre) doesn't quite have both her shoulders and her ribs facing the direction of her eyes. Anita (right) focuses carefully on her upper body but the weight is placed backwards on the heel, so that the supporting leg is not perpendicular to the floor.

Grand Battement

The floor is your friend here, as you swish your heel with pressure and force to throw your leg fast and feel it fly to full height. Powerful foot use, secure connection to the floor through the stretched supporting leg, confident upper body and assured musicality give you a thrilling foretaste of *grand allegro*.

In The Centre of The Studio

Ports de Bras

Quietly bring your dedicated revision of all technical fundamentals with you as you leave the barre, so that as you intensify the focus on the upper body, your dancing flourishes without tension in what is often the expressive heart of a class. Here again, the French words throw extra light on our dancing intentions. Now, as you demonstrate 'carriage of the arms', consider that – 'implicit in the idea of carriage is deportment – how we carry ourselves as human beings'.[54]

Remember, beautifully executed *ports de bras* depend on the inner confidence of assured placing and posture. As you harmoniously link the classical positions you have studied, your breath, your use of eyes and, above all, your musical flow let your personal artistry take flight.

Feel that each extension of curved arms – or *allongé* movement – originates from the centre of your uplifted back to reach your enlivened fingertips. When you add the extra dimension of *épaulement* (*see* The Five Positions: Third), keep the correct square placement of your hips (*see* Box: Keeping 'Square'), so that you can add more of your own creative flavour with the whole of the upper body.

Centre Practice

Use this section of class truly to test the strength of your technical foundations as you perform elements of the barre vocabulary on your own balance in the centre of the studio. When travelling through space and changing direction at speed, increase your confidence by holding fast to accurate turnout and weight placement. Focus wisely, too, on the pathway of your arms and how they coordinate with the use of your eyes and the timing of each step. Then your balance will feel more secure, and less energy will be wasted on upper-body tension and fighting to catch up with the music.

DIRECTIONS

Significant parts of these sequences will face 45 degrees away from the audience in the *croisé*, *éffacé* or *écarté* directions. Keeping hips 'square' to your own changing front is particularly important here. Remember, as you turn your whole body 45 degrees away from *your* front, you will not necessarily be looking at the actual corner of the room.

(*See* Chapters 1 and 4 for more about directions.)

Adage

Balancing on one leg for extended musical phrases can seem daunting. However, before you commence, sense how the Fifth Position you make to prepare contains all those building blocks that you need to succeed.

Swiftly check that both legs are equally engaged and rotated, the weight evenly placed on both properly planted feet. Has the whole spine lengthened to secure the neutrally placed pelvis, calm ribs, serene shoulders and wide back? As you lift your abdominals, the upper body is poised to take the lead in anticipating each change of position. In your mind you have no doubts about what the sequence is and how it relates to the music. Then, from the start, you can focus on presenting the meaning of each phrase with the seamless flow of your *ports de bras*, securely underpinned by your technique.

Turning the whole body 45 degrees from the front to show grand pose in Fourth *croisé.* Always aim for equal weight placement on both feet and allow the arms to curve without upper body tension.

SPECIAL TIP!

Practise getting the initial *cou de pied* of a *developpé* confidently on balance. Anticipate getting there by letting your arms lead the way, and remember to simply bend your knee without leaning the torso or lifting the hip and distorting the rest of your placing.

Turning Steps

Beware of the conviction that the best turners are the best dancers! Multiple *pirouettes* do not make an artist. However, beautifully positioned spins that rotate several times exactly in relation to the music can be exhilarating to watch and to execute.

Revising the technique that achieves a confident double *pirouette* is a continuation of all that you have been studying. During the barre and centre practice, keep checking that you secure a vertical balance in every *retiré* position (for the turn) and that every *demi-plié* is upright, with the pelvis held in a neutral placement underpinned by strong abdominals (for the preparation) (*see* Foundations of Technique 2, 3 and 4).

The arms in First Position will need the strong habit of accuracy so that they do not waver mid-turn; this too depends on the consistency of your posture. Remember to level your chin for balance; this will also help you to turn your head more fully as you 'spot', with your eyes well-open and not looking down your nose.

When turning *en dehors* to the right, a well-opened right shoulder is your accelerator. Watch out that you never close it up before take-off by twisting your upper body round to the left in your efforts to find more force. Instead, imagine your left arm chasing your right and use the sensation of your metatarsals pushing off the floor as you *relevé* to find a swiftly turned-out *retiré* for extra impetus.

SPECIAL TIP!

Be economical with your energy in all ballet turns by using a well-turned-out leg to spin on. Test the difference it makes in your *chaînée* or *posé* turns *en diagonale* when your heels are well forward. So, in a *pirouette en dehors* from Fourth Position, do not slip your heel to a parallel alignment just before you set off.

Allegro
Wherever it is placed in the running order of class, you will always dance a simple two-legged warm-up jump exercise. Use this time wisely to rehearse the crucial foundations of that upright *demi-plié* and the full articulation of the metatarsals and toes, which will lead to successful *sautés* and safe, quiet landings.

Once this technique becomes an established habit, jumping to and from one foot as you progress through the rich variety of the classical vocabulary, holds no fears. Land on balance, with the whole body perpendicular, finding the centre of gravity with well-sustained turnout of the whole leg, and you remain in control. Then you can relish experimenting with your musicality and finding your own personal artistry within the given choreography.

Let the music lead you in your exploration of artistry during centre practice and *allegro*.

SPECIAL TIP!

How can you tell if your landings are off balance? Try checking if your toes need to grip the floor after a *glissade*. Do your feet shuffle in *demi-plié* in Fifth after a *sissonne fermé*? Land from a *sissonne simple* to *cou de pied* and see how long you can stay in the *fondu* position!

Well-crossed feet in a high
***soubresaut* in Fifth.**

HOW FAR TO *DEMI-PLIÉ*?

The length of the Achilles' tendon at the back of the ankle varies, so the actual depth of each dancer's *demi-plié* (with the heels on the ground) will be different. A naturally big *demi-plié* is not necessarily needed for a high jump. The bouncy *sauté* that spends little time on the floor – called *ballon* – does not depend on a deep knee-bend. Indeed, trying to make your *demi-plié* as low as possible, by pushing your heels into the ground and leaning the body forwards, is particularly counterproductive.

The best preparation for a jump is your own scientifically accurate *demi-plié*, with those five points stacked up correctly, so there is no lower leg tension and wasted energy. Back this up with well-worked feet as you spring upwards, and a confident musicality. Remember, the speed with which you stretch and bend your knees is your choice, so slow this down with muscular control if you have a shallow *demi-plié*.

Grand Allegro

As the music broadens and your movements expand, remember to 'use' the floor to the utmost to maximize your jump. For example, in a *grand jeté en avant*, enjoy feeling your heel swish dynamically through First Position and along the floor before you throw your leg and leap. Match your arm shapes to your legs, making good use of that gateway First Position of the arms to gather your coordination together and to keep your weight placement forward. Instinctively, you may have realized that the speed of your *ports de bras* can really add to the effect of your *grand allegro*. Arms arriving at a highlight just before the musical beat and lingering a split second afterwards can make your elevation seem higher. Enjoy developing the use of your head, and eye focus too, to create even more of an artistic illusion.

Imagine that your big jumps are like *adage* in the air. As you fly, once again you hold beautiful classical shapes, though now with split-second stillness. Then, as you land, you gather all those scientific fundamentals of technique to *plié* or *fondu* quietly and safely, while you transition with infinite grace to the next artistic highlight.

Révérence

And so, as you thank teacher and pianist with the time-honoured mime of a gracious bow at the end of class, know that you have made more wise progress toward dancing with that illusion of effortless power.

Perhaps you found more control in placing your body on balance, or strength in the posture of your positions? Maybe today you showed more consistency in rotating your whole leg and lengthening your spine to lift your torso. Did you develop the accuracy of your classical positions or perhaps increase the stretch and speed of your footwork?

Patiently proceeding with these building blocks of technique helps you to construct the palace of your dancing potential. But be vigilant about the accuracy of your science. Cheating your Fifth, placing your weight too far back, clawed feet, twisted hips or misaligned knees could all lead to injuries, and time away from the studio can be dispiriting for the soul. For your ballet class is the core of your dancing life. It is here that slowly, but surely, you will develop the strength and control you need, as you encourage your body toward its physical potential. Of course, there are times when this is exhausting. But on those days when the legs feel sore and unresponsive, always remind yourself to remain wholehearted about the artistic presentation of your upper body, never sinking into unfocused *ports de bras* and dropped eyeline.

Frederick Ashton with White Lodge students, including Nicola Katrak (left), in the studio named after him to mark his retirement as director of The Royal Ballet (1970).

Above all, breathe, so that always you are calming your mind, refreshing the blood flow to the muscles of your body and drawing emotionally closer to the phrases of the music.

Exiting the Studio

At the end of each class remember and celebrate those 'lightbulb' moments, when your mind and body understood something with a sudden clarity that helped you to find the technical key to greater freedom.

Before you leave, perhaps check the detail of something the teacher said or take time for slow, accurate practice. You might nurture your physique by stretching out warm muscles. Or maybe you stay to dance a step again simply because you loved it.

Cherish the exhilaration you feel in this joy of movement. Share it generously with the audience and let it inspire you to explore your artistry over a long dancing life.

Daisy Bishop and Regan Wilson, third-year
ballet students at London Studio Centre.

CHAPTER 4

ADVANCED TECHNIQUES – TRAINING FOR EXCELLENCE
Mark Annear

What can you expect in advanced training as a vocational dancer? Studying at this level focuses on excellence – on growing as an artist, developing deep knowledge and personal experience of the art form, being ready to take on the mental, physical and emotional challenges, and fulfilling your dance potential.

Achieving excellence may feel daunting, but thinking about your training as a process, which moves through three stages, consolidation, progression and refinement, is a good strategy. The intensive study in many vocational courses for students over sixteen years of age is structured over three years in just this way. You build on previous learning, embark on the study of more complex ballet vocabulary, learn to work productively with others, dance challenging extracts from the ballet repertoire, as well as new choreographies, and these experiences and opportunities will steadily refine your technical and artistic skills.

The concept of consolidation, progression and refinement is a great model and can be evident in the way you approach and embody each move and stage of development. Why not make it as applicable to performing a *demi-plié* or to approaching a solo, as it is to training over three years?

Throughout this chapter you will see photographs of two dancers who have achieved excellence: Zoe Arshamian, who trained at The Royal Ballet School and Central School of Ballet and is now a professional dancer, and Denilson Almedia, who also trained at The Royal Ballet School and, having recently completed his advanced training, is starting his professional career.

WHAT IS EXCELLENCE?

Excellence is arriving at a point where you have mastery over your technique and expression. You have the knowledge and ability that allow you to be in control of your body in movement, giving you freedom to perform to your best and let the dancing happen. It's something to constantly strive for.

AT AUDITION...

Expect to audition for vocational training! Typically auditions include a ballet class, a prepared solo, physical examination by a medical team and often an interview. It's an exciting opportunity to share your 'own dance'; it may be a new experience and you can expect to be nervous. However, focus on what is important and remember that the panel of teachers is looking for positives, as well as your potential to thrive and develop on a course of study. So trust the process, be sensitive and responsive, ask questions if you don't understand and enjoy the chance to meet others and get a taste of what might be in your future. Be yourself and you'll find the right course for you.

CONSOLIDATION

The first stage of advanced training looks very similar to your early training. Deep understanding of the technical foundations and classical principles underpins your artistic growth and your whole dance career. You will consolidate your fundamental skills and knowledge of your own body, so that they are an *integral* part of your dancing.

As you refresh your understanding and ability, you may find yourself 'unlearning' – rethinking some habitual moves – in the effort to integrate the foundations more clearly. You need an 'automatic' physical recall of how to dance according to the underpinning science and artistic principles. Be encouraged. It's in the actual doing that your knowledge of ballet as a performing art and your expertise as an artist grows. Whether for recreation or as a career, this is a lifelong process and richly rewarding. Re-thinking the familiar helps you to be more adept, overcoming inefficient habits and developing more efficient ones. Don't worry about this, it is part of the learning process and all dancers constantly address this as they develop a deeper understanding of technique.

APPLYING THE FOUNDATIONS OF CLASSICAL BALLET TECHNIQUE

Five areas of technique are evident in *all* classical ballet vocabulary and support your performance of both simple and complex vocabularies. These are the foundations that are explored in Chapter 3 – ensure that they are secure.

- *Posture* is the stacking up of the shoulders and neutral pelvis over the feet.
- *Turnout* is the rotation of both legs.
- *Weight distribution* is the balancing on one or two feet.
- *Placement* is the aligning of legs and arms with the torso.
- *Lengthening and counter-pull* give breadth to movement.

Consolidating the fundamentals of technique requires a deep investigation of the basic positions and movements studied in early training. Ensuring that the five foundations of technique are evident in all aspects of dancing will form a strong basis for advancing your training.

An advanced movement or position on the *demi-pointe* requires the foundations of technique to be executed accurately. Here the dancers pay attention to posture, weight distribution and placement to ensure stability in *retiré*. The equal use of turnout on both legs, and lengthening and counter-pull through the whole body, refine the pose and give it the 'classical aesthetic'.

Understanding the Mechanics of Technique

The mechanics of technique refers to the way the bones and muscles activate to execute the ballet vocabulary. Understanding *how* ballet movements work helps you to apply your knowledge to perform them correctly every time.

What is this understanding of ballet movement? What do we mean by correct? It is knowing *how* to use your own body efficiently – safely and with sufficient effort – and that *each* movement has a technical *and* a musical and expressive function.

For example, in a *pirouette en dehors* from Fourth Position, focus on connecting the basic elements together. Apply the basic foundations to the *demi-plié* in Fourth Position, along with well-placed arms. Transfer your weight during the *relevé* by pressing down into the floor, so that you have the resistance through your standing leg to lengthen the hamstrings and make your leg straight and secure. Maintain leg rotation constantly on both the standing leg and the gesture leg that is in *retiré*. Ensure that the placement of the arms helps you to achieve balance and stability during the turn. Developing strength to maintain your alignment and placement gives you freedom to spot the head during the turn, as well as an overall sense of freedom in the movement.

Artistic Exploration

Artistic and musical expression are an integral part of your study, so your teachers will encourage these aspects in your everyday practice. Artistry grows alongside your deepening technical understanding and knowledge of ballet as a performing art. This is particularly important in training for the stage. Communicating with an audience requires you to express meaning by exploring musical and dynamic relationships and character in the dance material. Explore your understanding of the expressive potential of the vocabulary itself. Be aware of how you respond to music, what inspires you and fires your imagination. The thoughts behind the movement will communicate to an audience.

PROGRESSION

How Do You Bring What You Have Learnt to the Next Level?

You progress all aspects of your dancing with the study of advanced vocabulary and more complex *enchaînements*, building the capacity to pay attention to every detail of technique, musicality and expression. Advanced ballet vocabulary often takes a simple step and increases its difficulty and complexity. For example, you can add more turns to a *pirouette* sequence or finish in positions like *arabesque*, add a jump to steps like *rond de jambe en l'air* or add beats to jumps such as *cabriole*.

You consistently apply the foundations, performing linking steps with accuracy and coordinating the arms and legs through each movement and position with precision.

Pointework for female dancers will also increase in complexity. The time you spend studying pointework also increases with *pointe*-specific classes, repertoire, *pas de deux* and, possibly, part of your ballet class taken *en pointe*.

Why Tackle Difficult Vocabulary and Develop New Levels of Attention to Detail?

Increased complexity enables you to build strength, speed, accuracy and precision in all movement phrases, so that your body becomes more finely tuned. By accurately and consistently aligning your

The *allegro* section of any lesson often contains challenging vocabulary. Accurate placement of arms and legs requires control over the limbs, and considerable power is needed to achieve elevation, particularly on one leg.

bones and muscles, they function smoothly and the ballet 'aesthetic' can become integral to your practice of the *enchaînements*, poses and movements. You build freedom in your ability to make choices in your musical and expressive exploration, thereby adding nuance and individuality to your dancing. Liberate your inner artist!

Musicality and Expression

Look out for different opportunities to explore a wide range of artistic and musical expression. Notice the inherent dynamics that your teacher indicates through their demonstration and voice. These will indicate how to approach the musical dynamics of a movement. These dynamics are the different movement qualities (slow, quick, soft, strong, fluid, staccato) that give variety to your dancing. You could make your focus in a lesson the exploration of dynamics, by seeing how one *enchaînement* differs from another in its dynamic approach or you may even experiment in dancing an *enchaînement* with a different dynamic when you perform it again.

As training develops, dancing now includes more musical complexity with varied rhythms, challenging your ability to phrase movement in relation to the music. Artistic expression covers a wide range of moods and styles and different *enchaînements* require different expressive qualities. Develop nuance, light and shade, so that you can perform with sophistication. Pay attention to how various types of music influence the way your body moves.

Musical and Rhythmic Qualities

Music that accompanies an *enchaînement* is a key to identifying its quality. An *adagio* flows and has soaring, sustained passages, while *allegro* has bounce and shorter, staccato movement phrases. A polonaise or mazurka has a distinct rhythm to emulate and clear accents to highlight. Think about how you can use your breathing to highlight accents in the music. Punctuate transitions with a 'comma' or show the end of a phrase with a 'full stop'.

The use of eye focus can change the feeling and expression of a pose. Zoe projects confidence by focusing toward the audience.

In the same pose with the eye focus lowered, Zoe displays an introspective quality.

Develop expression by differing your physical approach to reflect the mood of each dance: use eye focus to project different moods; 'colour' movement with different dynamics and intention. Notice how the use of the head can change the expression of a movement: holding the head upright and projecting the eyes strongly toward the audience can express confidence or power, while inclining the head softly toward the shoulder can give an introspective expression. The same pose or movement can take on many different expressive qualities with just a subtle change of focus.

DEVELOPING AN INDIVIDUAL APPROACH

Consider the following:

- How might different tempi affect the same step, and what does that do to your body?
- How does the movement impulse and conclusion help to develop phrasing or a feeling for punctuation?
- How does the ebb and flow of energy affect movement?
- Does changing the emphasis and accent of a phrase produce different nuances?
- How does the eye focus change the look of a pose or movement?
- How does imagery, imagination and feeling affect the way you perform a movement phrase?

While all dancers have a style of movement that is natural to them and feels comfortable, expressing movements in different ways gives you versatility and is explored further in the next chapter. If you are comfortable performing strong, dynamic characters, try to develop your ability to express lyrical movements and styles. If you prefer to direct your dance inwards toward yourself, try projecting more to the audience.

Knowledge and Skill

As you train, each time you learn new skills you move through four stages or learning:

- **Unconscious incompetence** – you are not aware of what you cannot do, this is when you first begin training.
- **Conscious incompetence** – as you begin to learn you know what you are supposed to do but are not always able to do it.
- **Conscious competence** – this stage would be at the beginning of your advanced training. You know what to do and you are aware of how you go about doing it.
- **Unconscious competence** – during your advanced training you develop the embodied knowledge and skill to dance with expertise. It can feel like it just happens!

An example of working at the unconscious competence level would be executing a controlled sequence of movements during an *adage*. At this level you understand how to sustain long, controlled sequences and the technical foundations during the *adage* without having to consciously think about them. This means you can perform effectively without getting tired. It also means that you can focus on integrating artistry and musicality into your practice.

As you take on new vocabulary or choreography you will be going through each of the four stages in order but, perhaps, more quickly as your knowledge and skill grow. This helps you to develop expertise in the new movements or roles you learn. The process is not just a 'one off' situation. It takes daily practice to keep up a high level of skills and prepares you to take on professional practice.

Developing your knowledge also relies on processing your teacher's feedback. Be willing to

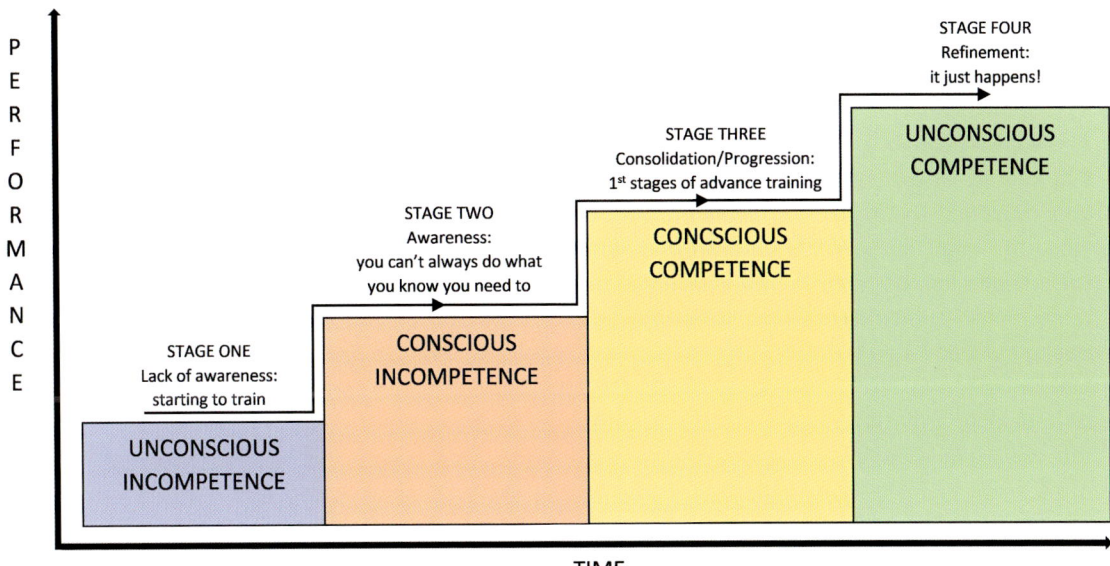

Dancers progress through four stages of learning over the course of their training, as well as when learning a new step or role. Developing the knowledge and skills to successfully execute movements without conscious thought about what is required is one of the aims of advanced training.

listen to the information you receive from both your teacher and your body. This will be valuable information to apply to every part of your dancing.

Supplementing your dance training with a fitness programme and somatic techniques, such as Pilates, helps to develop strength and the neural pathways that create efficient movement patterns.

Step by Step Guide – Tackling a *Fouetté Sauté*

Even straightforward steps such as *fouetté sauté* require attention to seemingly small details. Note how the foundations of technique are present in each part of the sequence.

1. Begin by standing in Fifth Position *croisé* on the *demi-pointe*, lengthening the torso and projecting toward the audience.
2. On the preparatory jump (e.g. *failli*), face squarely toward *de côté* with clear direction. Activate the torso for stability. Rotate, lengthen and place both legs. Keep the arms in front of the body, ready to coordinate with the next movement. Clarity in direction and position makes this part of advanced technique.
3. The *failli* passes through First Position into a lunge, demonstrating an advanced use of transfer of weight on to the front leg.
4. *Grand battement devant* with rotated and articulated legs. Maintain your direction. The strong dynamic of this movement assists your elevation. A full *ports de bras* to Fifth Position assists the jump, with attention to the curve and placement of the arms in *bras bas* and First Position. Accuracy in each part of the movement, particularly with the arms, brings this to an advanced level.
5. Arms remain in Fifth and the torso actively shifts *en face* and the leg moves from *devant* to *à la seconde* to maintain placement. The leg

that extends toward the floor should rotate. Both legs stretch with well-pointed feet. Maintain accurate placement to achieve advanced execution.

6. Arrive in *arabesque*, arms Fifth, facing the opposite side to where you started. Keep engaging your rotation. The raised leg remains placed, while the other leg lengthens toward the floor underneath the body ready for landing. Your arms remain curved throughout, without anticipating the *arabesque* position.

7. On landing, the leg in *arabesque* maintains its position and the weight is placed over the *demi-plié*. This eliminates any hops. The arms arrive in *arabesque* at the same time as the landing. The smooth, stable landing and considerable energy required through your body for clarity in each part of the jump makes this an advanced step.

Step 1. Denilson starts in Fifth Position *croisé*.

Step 2. Preparatory jump facing toward *de côté*.

Step 3. Pass through First Position into a lunge.

Step 4. *Grand battement devant* with articulated legs.

Step 5. Turn in the air from *devant* to *à la seconde.*

Step 6. Still in the air, arrive in a well-placed *arabesque.*

Step 7. On landing, maintain the *arabesque* position.

Learning Repertoire – Contextual Understanding

Learning about the historical context of classical ballet and its development as an art form will inform your dancing, particularly your artistry. For example, look at the contrasting styles and their characteristics in Chapter 2, and where you would locate the ballets and choreographers you are studying within the tradition.

You may study dance history in an academic context alongside developing practical knowledge of the art form through learning excerpts from the classical ballet repertoire, such as a solo from nineteenth-century ballets like *The Sleeping Beauty*, *Swan Lake* and *Giselle*. Solos from the twentieth and twenty-first centuries then give you an embodied and practical understanding of how ballet technique and performance have developed.

Studying a solo may follow the consolidation, progression and refinement model. You begin by learning the movements, consolidating the technique and breaking up the solo into sections. You progress by joining phrases together and increasing stamina. Refinement is incorporating a contextual understanding into the solo.

This study involves much more than the sequence of movements, so develop your curiosity about the choreographers, composers and designers who created the ballets. Knowing the synopsis of the ballet will enable you to place the solo in the context of the storyline and to understand the relationship that your character has to the rest of the ballet. Imbuing each solo that you study with its context will enable you to develop an artistic approach to your performance, ensuring that you do not focus solely on the steps you have learned.

REFINEMENT

This stage is the culmination of your training, where you bring together all the areas that you have studied – technique, artistry and knowledge – to make sure that you are a dancer who moves, performs and thinks at a high level. Dancers who achieve this, perform with precision, purpose and understanding, while their research, understanding and characterization of the ballets they are dancing will be grounded in artistic expression. Such dancers value the place of current ballet choreography in the context of ballet history. Which dancers do you think achieve this? Next time you view a performance or video think about those dancers who demonstrate these qualities.

Aim to apply the attention to detail that you have developed throughout the progression stage to all aspects of your dancing. Your knowledge of classical ballet technique informs the way you move, eventually developing the skill to reproduce movements accurately each time you perform them, while your knowledge of classical ballet history informs the way you express yourself. Imagination and intention are integrated into your dancing, so that your performance can become an artistic endeavour and not just the reproduction of steps without meaning.

Katharina Nikelski, 2018 Royal Ballet School graduate, as the fairy of the golden vine in *Aurora's Wedding* staged by Anthony Dowell from Marius Petipa's *The Sleeping Beauty*.

Overall, this last stage of training culminates in your ability to integrate everything that you have learnt into being a dancer of confidence and with a high level of ability.

GROUP PRACTICE

One of the interesting differences between early and advanced training is the move from focusing on the solo body to working within a group. Whilst you continue the development of a personal technique, dancing with others, whether as a pair in *pas de deux* or as a member of a larger group, is a natural extension of early training.

Pas de Deux

Pas de deux, the art of two dancers working together, presents specific challenges. In the traditional format of classical ballet, female and male students are paired together.

Royal Ballet Principal, Francesca Hayward epitomizes a dancer who is able to integrate technique, artistry and contextual knowledge, constantly refining her dancing through daily practice and rehearsal.

Working as a couple requires synchronicity and rapport to achieve harmony between the two dancers.

A big challenge is for both partners to work in synchronicity. Because you have spent many years focusing on your own body and technique, working in contact with another dancer feels very different, particularly at first. You have another person to be thoughtful about and you need patience and respect to be able to work effectively with your partner.

Before you begin to study *pas de deux*, your teachers will make sure that you are the appropriate age and at the appropriate stage of physical and technical development. This is particularly important for male students, so that movements such as lifts, which can be a cause of serious injury, are not attempted too young. Female students need to have achieved the appropriate level of technique and the movements studied in *pas de deux* will have been first mastered in their own classes.

Zoe and Denilson demonstrate the correct hand grip and weight distribution to create a well-balanced position. You will see a similar position in the *Rose Adage* from Act 1 of *The Sleeping Beauty*. The man walks in a perfect circle around his partner allowing her to promenade perfectly on her axis, displaying every angle of the position.

In the same pose, Zoe uses more *épaulement*, which creates a feeling of greater rapport between her and Denilson.

Female Students

For female students, classical ballet *pas de deux* is an extension of the technique studied as a solo dancer. The challenge is to sustain the structure and form of the ballet poses and to become used to having the male dancer support you through-out movement. For example, in supported *adage* movements, where your partner holds your waist or hands, you rely on him to maintain your balance *en pointe*. While your partner is developing stabil-ity and the sensitivity in his arms and hands to know where your point of balance is, you need to resist fighting to adjust your body. This can be a challenge as it feels uncomfortable and possibly frustrating – however, trying to get yourself back on balance, won't help your partner to feel how to centre you on your point of balance. What is pref-erable is to let him know if you are too far forward, backward or to either side of your balance. This helps your partner to understand where to place you on balance.

Another difference for female dancers is in travelling lifts. As a solo dancer you are used to moving through space in travelling jumps; however, when executing travelling lifts it is your partner who provides the impetus for travel. As an example, when you perform a *grand jeté en avant* by yourself, you use the impetus of the preparation and jump to propel yourself forward, as well as into the air. When lifted in this step, you use the same impetus, but only toward the elevation of the jump in coordination with your partner. It is your partner who provides the travel through walking or running.

Zoe and Denilson demonstrate the trust and cooperation required between partners when studying advanced *pas de deux*. Notice how Denilson has his weight behind his centre of balance to counterbalance Zoe who is forward from her centre of balance.

Male Students

Pas de deux technique for male students involves a whole new technique to learn that is different from what was studied in daily ballet class. The main aspects are:

- Supporting your partner on balance during movements such as *pirouettes* and *promenades*.
- Lifting your partner through a range of small and big lifts.

Supporting your partner on balance requires you to be 'grounded'; that is, secure on your legs, with your weight more into the floor with less counter-pull away from the floor than you aim to achieve in your ballet technique. Depending on your partner's position, sometimes the weight is placed evenly on both legs or it may be more on one leg. Matching your partner's position is an important part of the synchronicity required in *pas de deux* and you should focus on blending with your partner at all times.

Successful lifts are achieved through working in coordination with your partner, as much as developing strength. Working together with shared attention to musical phrasing gives a lot of impetus, particularly for overhead lifts. You also need coordination within your own body as both the legs and the arms play a vital role. Using your *demi-plié* in the rhythm of your partner's preparation is the initial impetus for a lift; this is followed through with your arms, which come in close to your body, so that you can use the leverage of your elbows to push your partner into the air, as your legs stretch out of the *demi-plié*. In fact, you should really think of these movements as pushing into the air, rather than lifting, as the impetus is coming from low down into the floor, rather than from above.

Developing upper body and leg strength is beneficial for your partnering technique but core strength is just as important. Core strength stabilizes your body, helping you to be 'grounded' when supporting your partner's balance and to prevent back injuries. It helps to give you the physical security and stability you need and that your partner appreciates, feeling comfortable and secure in the knowledge that she is 'in good hands'.

GROUP REPERTOIRE

Dance training is rarely an activity you perform by yourself. Unless you are undertaking private coaching, dance classes are taught in a group. During advanced training, this extends to learning group (or *corps de ballet*) repertoire. Like the solos that you study, group repertoire is taken from the nineteenth-century classics, as well as from twentieth- and twenty-first-century ballets. When you work in mixed gender groups, some of these dances are an extension of the *pas de deux* work you have studied. Other dances are for single genders. Some of the dances you study, particularly from the nineteenth century, may be the character dances from such classical ballets as *Coppélia* or *Swan Lake*.

Beyond the benefits of enhancing your knowledge of ballet repertoire, there are other advantages from learning these group dances. Working with other students on the same choreography teaches you the ability to synchronize with other dancers, but it also teaches you how to work cooperatively. Learning to work with others is not only important for the success of the group dance, but it is a skill that you will take into other areas of your life.

To synchronize with other dancers in a group choreography, focus on musicality and space. Spend time listening carefully to the music and know on which 'count' the movements occur, to perform precisely on the beat and with rhythmic clarity. Develop a shared understanding of phrasing with fellow dancers and the ability to time movement in space precisely with music. (See Chapter 8 for discussion of beat and phrasing.)

Maintain spatial clarity, being precise in the direction of travel and orientation in space – where you face in relation to the 'dancer's square'. Develop your peripheral vision and awareness of the distance between you and other dancers, in

Year 10 and 11 students of The Royal Ballet School
in *Coppélia Suite* by Marius Petipa, Enrico Cecchetti
and Peter Wright.

Year 10 and 11 students of The Royal Ballet
School in *Pulcinella Suite* by Mark Annear.

order to maintain spatial relationships on stage and in group choreography. This spatial awareness can be learned in a ballet class and then progressed to group dances.

You may also have the opportunity to work with other dancers through studying choreography, either by creating a dance for your fellow students or dancing in another student's work. This increases your knowledge and ability of how to work cooperatively with others and provides you with greater insight into how group dances are constructed.

Ultimately, dancing is most often something you do with others. While you spend a lot of time thinking about your own body when dancing, you do this alongside fellow students. Take advantage of this experience, not only to learn from them but to create lifelong colleagues and friends.

CHARACTERISTICS AND VALUES

What are the characteristics and values that I have found are important for students in advanced study, particularly those who are thinking of dance as a professional career?

Having curiosity helps you to thrive as an advanced student and to value all aspects of the art form, including its beauty. Be quick to

William Bracewell centre front with Matthew Ball kneeling and artists of the Royal Ballet in rehearsal for *Corybantic Games* **(2018) by Christopher Wheeldon.**

comprehend what is required of you. Learn how to process instructions, choreographic and technical information efficiently, and to integrate artistic expression into your dancing. Understand the self-discipline required for dance training and how the more advanced you are, the more focused you need to be to produce and maintain a high standard. This self-discipline will stand you in good stead throughout your life, both in dance and anything else you pursue.

Professional Dancer Perspectives

These ideas are echoed by dancers who, having trained vocationally, now have thriving careers – successful professionals like the dancer in the photographs, Zoe, and Royal Ballet Principal and Soloist dancers, Francesca Hayward and William Bracewell.

When asked to reflect on the aspects of advanced study that they found especially useful, they offered the following insights.[55]

Foundations
For Zoe, 'the emphasis on your centre and your aplomb, is a useful foundation for everything' and she sees particular value in working on *pointe*: 'the control and a certain length that's found is quite a unique sensation – and that strength… can be used for all types of movement'. Francesca highlights 'the discipline. Always being focused and prepared. Picking up exercises and material quickly.' William also appreciates how the dancer's daily ritual develops the understanding that allows the 'freedom to forget it all when you work with a choreographer and concentrate on what they're searching for': *The repetition of extremely precise movements gives you an incredible sense of where your body is and how it's feeling – like a tool that's gradually being honed to become more effective, more precise, stronger and pliable.*

Creative Responses
Zoe finds that ballet training also prepared her to work creatively in response to instructions:

Your brain is always being challenged with each ballet class because everyone has their own way of composing exercises and you're constantly building that memory – which I think is a muscle – that gets better with time. William hugely enjoys exploring different intentions: 'for example, you can perform the same a movement with the intention of empathy and it will look completely different if it's performed with anxiety'. Francesca talks about the subtle responses required when working with a choreographer. 'You need to work out what they need from you as a dancer with their creative process. Do they need you to be creative, think outside the box, show them what your body is capable of doing or where their movement is capable of going in that space? Or are they someone who wants you to clearly show them what they're demonstrating to allow their brain to see the potential?'

What these dancers look for in other dancers has changed over the years. They all now value musicality and the ability to move the audience, over technical prowess. Zoe reminds her younger self 'to be freer and let the artist out rather than focus all the energy on being a perfectionist'. She adds, 'it doesn't have to happen all at once, there is time to evolve and be the artist you want to be'.

Above all else, advanced training requires you to work with integrity, both for yourself and for others. Although dance is a very personal activity, being reliable, working cooperatively with others and being humble about everything you achieve makes you valued by the dance community and allows you to achieve your best.

Francesca advises the aspiring professional dancer:

Always work your hardest and push yourself, but also listen to your body. Know the difference between good and bad pain, and don't be afraid to speak up if you need to stop or pace yourself. Think about your body in the long term. Be open to different opinions about your art, about technical steps and execution and your approach to your art form until you find what's right for you. Always be listening and learning from others. Watch your colleagues. Don't get into bad habits. Always be polite and respectful, but know when to speak up for yourself. Don't *be scared, or try not to look it if you are, on stage or in the studio. The most powerful thing is to see a dancer enjoying themselves, so dare to enjoy it for you. Your audience will feel that and love that more than a perfect* pirouette.

'In flight': Harris Beattie, dancer with Northern Ballet; his career has been shaped by diverse training in both ballet and contemporary.

CHAPTER 5

DEVELOPING VERSATILITY AND CREATIVE THINKING
Karen Berry

Being a dancer can be one of the most rewarding careers to follow, but it is not without major challenges. Only a small minority of dance students succeed in becoming professional dancers, and huge competition and a significant amount of psychological pressure face those who do. Getting a job is tough, and being able to sustain one, even tougher!

Leaders in the dance industry look for dancers with the versatility, skills and creativity to meet current demands and to help shape the future of the profession. Christopher Powney (2019), director of The Royal Ballet School, advises that 'dancers must not only have the highest technical capability, but be versatile, autonomous and creative all-round artists who are well informed about the dance industry as a whole. They need to be able to adapt and navigate through the ever-changing and increasing demands on our art form'. International teacher and director Matz Skoog agrees that in order to thrive, dancers require, 'resilience, mastery of many skills and the drive to carve out a place within this complex, competitive system'.[56] This chapter draws on such thoughts about how to build towards a future career. You will find the dates of my interviews with industry leaders, listed beside their names, as you read through the text.

AN EVOLVING ART FORM

The call for dancers to be versatile isn't new. Consider how the influence of Italian *ballerinas* and

Serge Lifar as Apollo and Alice Nikitina as Terpsichore in Balanchine/Stravinsky's *Apollon Musagètes* (1928) with Diaghilev Ballets Russes.

the integration of folk elements in nineteenth-century choreography by Marius Petipa demanded new and virtuosic performance skills. The mixed repertory model that we often see today, characterized by double or triple bills, originated in the early twentieth century. The emergence of neo-classical works by Balanchine and Massine required dancers to interpret music and explore their technique in different and challenging ways. Just as they do now, dancers at that time had to slip effortlessly between varying choreographic styles. Historian Anna Meadmore (2019) considers that the impact of modern dance on the classical form has also tested dancers' versatility. Isadora Duncan's free interpretative dance, the American movement led by Martha Graham and Merce Cunningham, and the influence from 1960s of choreographers such as Paul Taylor, Jiří Kylián and Twyla Tharp, have resulted in the blending of new techniques into ballet.

Cross-Over of Dance Styles

In this post-modern era, the blend of ballet with musical theatre is exemplified by commercial shows like Christopher Wheeldon's *An American in Paris* (2014), and most ballet companies programme a mixture of historical and modern repertoire, ranging from the traditional to the innovative. Works such as William Forsythe's *In the Middle Somewhat Elevated* (1987) and Wayne McGregor's *Woolf Works* (2015), require dancers to use their classically

SCENERY BY E. LOURIÉ FOR "CHOREARTIUM"

Illustration from a programme, showing the scenic design by E. Lourié for Léonide Massine's ballet *Choreartium* (1933).

trained physiques to the extreme, whilst being in full command of their weight and movement dynamics.

As the classical/contemporary divide lessens, so the demands on classical dancers increase. Director and choreographer Mathew Bourne points to the 'cross-fertilization' of dance styles in the repertoire of many companies. 'Things are getting blurred in a way and the dancers are having to be very versatile to take on those different movements'.[57] With this 'fusion' of dance styles and choreographic forms, audiences expect a variety of movement styles to be performed on the ballet stage. So, classical dancers in the twenty-first century need to be chameleons, quickly and aptly expanding their movement profile as the industry evolves. Versatility, therefore, is key: the essential factor in training that will help to ensure your future and sustained employability.

TRAINING FOR VERSATILITY

Make Sure Your Passion Isn't Blind!

If you are considering a performing career, take advice from trusted professionals. Discuss whether, when or where to start further training. If you decide to accept a place at a vocational school or Further Education establishment, do so with an open mindset that acknowledges you may not end up as a dancer. Start dreaming big, but if you find, for whatever reason, that performing is not for you, there are many opportunities available for those able and willing to look beyond the stage. The industry offers rich career possibilities, only one of which is performing, and whilst a performance career may be short, a career within the dance industry can be for a lifetime.

Broaden Your Perception of What Your Training Can Do for You

Consider technical training to be just a part of your broader education as an artist. Look for schools that will develop not only your performing versatility, but those that will also expand your transferable skills. Training in one particular school, or working with one particular choreographer or company, may be a luxury of the past. Shift your thinking, and new,

unexplored territory opens up. Whatever school you do attend, consider these essential tips whilst training to help you realize your full potential and enable you to work in diverse settings:

- Embrace a range of styles to develop your performance versatility.
- Take on new skills and consider which might be transferable to other areas of your learning, thinking creatively about the relationship between different processes.
- Take advantage of *any* opportunities to learn, inside and outside the school environment. What may not appear relevant now, can be invaluable at a later date. You may discover new interests that can lead to related or alternative employment opportunities.
- Be proactive: take responsibility for your learning and don't always wait for instruction.
- Be enterprising: look for and initiate opportunities to explore what excites and inspires you. Be aware of the world around you and how the art form influences, and is influenced by, the cultural landscape.

EARLY TRAINING CONSIDERATIONS

Your early training is the time to try out any technique that encourages you to move, think and express in a different way to ballet. Using what you learn in your classical ballet classes, aim to gain experience in a variety of other dance styles. Techniques such as jazz and modern, along with contemporary dance, can be particularly useful for settling in a movement profile that can then develop and expand throughout your vocational training. Choreographer Wayne McGregor warns against allegiance to one technique, adding that 'sometimes technique gets in the way of letting dancers be curious and open to try new things'.[58] Discovering the expressive language of any particular style – the intent, movement and musical dynamics, phrasing and geometry – can allow the mind and body to develop and respond more confidently to stylistic nuances and subtleties of choreography and repertoire.

ADVANTAGES IN DIVERSE TRAINING

Principal Dancer Steven McRae's (2019) experience of different styles shaped his career:

> I wouldn't be the same dancer today if I hadn't had a diverse training. My teacher's mentality was to experience everything and so I did: tap, jazz and ballet. I didn't really focus on ballet until around fifteen years of age and even then, I didn't stop learning other subjects. If I had experienced only ballet when I was younger, I would have felt restricted and would have left!

The Dangers of a Narrow Focus

If you study toward examinations, it is important that this does not become the sole focus of your training. Syllabus study, although rewarding, can inhibit broader and deeper learning, while excessive time spent on a specific activity, such as a show or competition preparation, can also restrict your growth. Too narrow a focus can result in you being unable to respond appropriately with vocabulary, combinations and concepts in an unfamiliar context – for example, in an audition. Diversity in your early training allows your body and mind to be wired for change and to relish the unexpected.

Studio practice: Royal Ballet Principal Steven McRae epitomizes the versatile twenty-first century classical dancer.

COMPLEMENTARY STYLES AND HOW THEY ENHANCE VERSATILITY

Versatility can be implicit within your training from the outset of your serious study for professional performance. Jazz and contemporary techniques, such as Horton and Limon,[59] are usefully explicit in the use of language for developing your dynamic and expressive movement potential. Being exposed to different ways of responding and moving can help awaken your understanding of how movement principles are applicable across different styles.

Traditionally, classical ballet has a codified vocabulary for positions, steps and movement. But it is easy to forget that its language for dynamic qualities and intention also derives from the movement actions; for example, *frapper* (to strike) and *jeter* (to throw). As a result, they tend not to be discussed or valued in the same way as mechanical aspects of technique in ballet class. But this does not mean that dynamic and expressive qualities are not just as much a part of your practice and creative thinking. Also consider the way that the form has developed over time. On the one hand, in studying the vocabulary, you need to understand and follow the rules and principles precisely, so that it is aesthetically legible and understood. On the other hand, it is a shared vocabulary that has evolved from human endeavour over many centuries; therefore, it is multi-layered in meaning and intention and, like any language, open to individual interpretation and the artistic imagination. If ballet is understood as 'a vocabulary of human expression',[60] each individual will be unique in the way they dance the gestures and movement.

UNIQUE MOVEMENT PROFILE

Consider that every dancer already has their own 'unique movement profile'. This refers to a personal style or way of moving, as well as to the complex ways in which you develop your own body and potential for movement. It is influenced by factors such as gender, personality, age, body type and cultural background, and the range of dance and choreographic styles that you encounter. Teachers have an impact on your movement profile as you absorb and replicate technical and stylistic nuances through observation and repetition. The impact of observational learning on your practice is significant, especially as we are now beginning to understand the neurology of movement and the impact of 'mirror neurons' on our performance.[61] How you practice – the choices that you make, what you focus on, the questions you ask, the depth of your passion and curiosity – become embodied as your 'unique movement profile' that continues to develop throughout your dancing life.

Begin to think creatively about exploring and blending relevant principles into your ballet technique. For example, compare and contrast qualitative movement concepts, such as release with tension, fluidity with resistance and expanse with contraction. Learn how to use space dynamically, to shift your weight and expand the use of your body in your practice of the codified classical vocabulary. Take time to reflect on the feeling of moving differently and make connections for yourself between the contrasting experiences, so that your learning is embodied more quickly and deeply.

Given the mix of techniques in current repertoire, the study of contemporary dance and improvisation is a must. Angela Towler (2018), former dancer and rehearsal director for Rambert explains:

Regardless of what contemporary technique you study, you will develop your freedom of expression and explore your creativity. Learn how to use your weight and body in a different way from ballet which will challenge your physicality and artistry, making you a more versatile performer.

Former Rambert dancer and rehearsal director Angela Towler in a perfomance driven by improvisation (2017).

EXPLORE AND DEVELOP YOUR MOVEMENT POTENTIAL: IMPROVISATION

Improvisation is an effective technique for freeing the body from habitual movement patterns. By responding spontaneously to music or stimuli, you learn to trust your impulses, to move and explore the use of space, varying geometry, lines and dynamics. Musically – different rhythms, styles and genres can allow you to experience emotional range, and discover intention and connections through your movement. Not only can the process be liberating, but applying your new-found artistic tools in your ballet practice can give you a framework on which to build stylistic versatility.

Repertoire and choreography are also vital components in your weekly training programme. Repertoire study educates your practical understanding of the stylistic range of ballets from the nineteenth century to the present. Choreography offers the opportunity to explore your own and others' movement potential and creativity.

Experiencing other performing opportunities, such as acting and singing, adds to the range of skills that you might call upon now and in the future. For example, Adam Cooper's exposure to different dance styles and theatre arts enhanced his performing and choreographic ability throughout his career. When Leanne Cope left The Royal Ballet to star in *An American in Paris*, her passion for both ballet and musical theatre flourished and underpinned her success. Her co-lead, Robert Fairchild, was at the height of his ballet career when he left New York City Ballet in 2018. His early training in different dance styles, as well as his call to

Leanne Cope and Robert Fairchild in Christopher Wheeldon's *American in Paris* (2014), Dominion Theatre, London, 2017.

Utilizing a blend of somatic techniques within your training will help you to develop holistically: reflecting on what you do, think and feel, and enhancing your movement awareness. Ask your teachers to support your engagement by encouraging you to explore imagery and strategies to make relevant connections between doing, thinking and feeling. Becoming your own agent for change will enable a swift response to technical or artistic issues that you may encounter. Technique classes have the potential to be infused with somatic strategies to develop a more sensitized approach to learning. These approaches are becoming a vital tool.

PERFORMANCE STRATEGY: A SENSITIZED APPROACH

It can take thousands of hours of practice to hone your technique and performance abilities. Progress is not always linear and can seem contrary to the hours you have invested. Frustration can set in. However, the right mental tools and attitude of mind can support your progress, directing your focus toward the sensation of movement and 'accessing' motor patterns at a deep, neuromuscular level through kinaesthetic awareness. Feeling the movement as a whole, rather than as a sequence of individual actions, can help with flow and transitions.

To help embed ideal performance, try this strategy immediately after you have performed a movement sequence particularly well:

Close your eyes and 'relive' the movement again, exactly as you did physically but now in your mind: reflect on the action, intention, rhythm and feeling. 'See and feel' what you have just done. When you want to perform that movement again, consciously access that particular sensation movement map in your mind, remembering what you had experienced before. The more you utilize this procedure, the more effective it can become.

'embrace your individuality',[62] served him well on stage and in his feature film debut as *Munkustrap* in Tom Hooper's film adaptation of Andrew Lloyd Webber's *Cats* (2019).

WHOLE-BODY LEARNING: A SOMATIC APPROACH

In recent years, somatic practices have been used as a tool to help facilitate movement awareness in dance training. According to Sally Fitt, somatics is 'a means to acquire bodily-based access to the whole system and its interactive patterns, or very simply knowing oneself from the inside out'.[63] Alexander technique, Franklin method, Pilates, Feldenkrais, yoga and ideokinesis are some of the more familiar somatic approaches that can be studied alongside, or principles used within, your technique classes. All these approaches affirm the first-person perspective on bodily experience: the physical sensation as you experience it.

Intrinsic 'Feedback'

Intrinsic feedback is internal sensory feedback from the body perceived during and after performing a movement, whereas extrinsic feedback comes from an external source – for example, an instruction from your teacher or a visual input from a mirror. For extrinsic feedback to be effective, it should connect to your own internal or felt experience: your attention to, and awareness of, the sensation of the desired position or movement. The sensations tell you when the feeling aligns with the aesthetic function, and this can result in harmonious shapes and effective movement patterns.

Somatic Awareness of Shape and Movement

Educating your body from within involves somatic attention to its unique profile and structure. This awareness of the 'feeling' of the forms (the shape and movement) can be a vital method of intrinsic feedback, which is an essential tool for reflective practice and can also support injury management. Try and distinguish between different kinds of tension in your body – for example, the positive feeling of stretch to elongate muscles, the dangerous feeling of stretching out of alignment, the 'good' tension required to sustain an elevated shape or elongated spine.

Daisy Bishop (2019 London Studio Centre Graduate) had opportunities to develop her movement profile and versatility in a variety of dance genres and somatic practice throughout her training.

LEARNING STRATEGY: INTRINSIC FEEDBACK

A 'teacher do, student copy' model can neglect the need for intrinsic feedback, for the dancer to cultivate awareness, self-reflection and individuality. When copying dance material, seek to know why and how. Think of the many ways that you receive feedback on your practice: teachers' comments, your peers, video, the mirror are all useful and necessary forms of extrinsic feedback. Rather than being totally reliant on extrinsic feedback, use somatic techniques to evaluate and analyse in order to become your own reflective practitioner. Accessing and developing your inner awareness will enable you to self-monitor and adapt your practice throughout your career. Take responsibility to shape your learning, make choices and be a thinking dancer.

For example:

- Think of a still shape, such as Fifth Position of the arms, as dynamic and, therefore, malleable. Be aware of the flow of energy around the circumference of the arms, as well as the inside.
- Identify opposing points in the imagined architecture of your body, and expand the inner space between those points – for example, the 'inner diagonal' in the torso between the tip of the hip bone and opposite shoulder.

- Build an inner 'sensation' picture of the balanced vertical stacking of the vertebrae within your skeleton around your aplomb.
- Sense the equal distribution of weight on both feet and imagine the spiralling musculature around the aplomb; in the First, imagine the energy flowing down the back of the legs and up the front.
- Feel the floor pressure in a jump and the associated counter-pull as the body lifts into the air.

The Athleticism of Today's Repertoire Is Demanding

Your training should include body-conditioning techniques to ensure your health is not compromised by increased physical demands and intensity. Professor Emma Redding, head of dance science at Trinity Laban Conservatoire of Music and Dance, explains that in order to develop factors such as strength, stamina and power, dancers need to supplement their daily class with a variety of cross-training.[64] Two aspects of general fitness that have been found to be particularly under-developed are muscular strength and cardiorespiratory fitness.

There are different schools of thought about aspects of training. For example, how the barre is used differs from one school to the next. Within class, teachers can adapt the structure and pace of the class to challenge your stamina and strength in *allegro,* whilst balancing recovery and endurance with *adage.* Barre and centre practice can be interspersed to allow for development of control, alignment and transfer of weight. Fitness specialists can offer guidance in how to apply these strategies to help bridge the gap between the constantly evolving choreographic demands and the skills developed within training. Many schools recognize and address the need for cross-training by programming supplementary classes and healthcare support within the curriculum. The Royal Ballet School's *Healthy Dancer Programme,* launched in 2015, is at the forefront of best practice in this area by consistently applying research relevant to the training of pre-professional dancers in order to maximize their potential, physically, emotionally and mentally.

Be mindful, however, that biomechanics, body conditioning and somatic development are not the focus of your training: they support the bigger goal of becoming an expressive agent. As a dance artist, you are in command of your technique and condition, in order to be able to portray the athleticism, intention and emotion of the choreography. Take care with all types of supplementary classes (somatic and conditioning), so that new learning is transferred effectively within the context of your ballet training.

LEARNING STRATEGY: USING A BLEND OF DIFFERENT SOMATIC TECHNIQUES

Imagery and tactile feedback together can enable transfer of learning to occur and stimulate the mind and sensory awareness. Not only can imagery and visualization be used to affect movement quality and artistry, but they can help to facilitate neuromuscular repatterning.[65] Touch can make the same impact by creating a 'sensation map', where the body understands the energy, relationship and coordination of body parts to each other, as well as the peripheral space.

continued

For example:

- To gain a feeling of extension and weightlessness in the upper body, imagine the head as a balloon floating away from the torso, along with a light finger brush from a peer or teacher from the base of the neck to the crown of the head.
- To feel the spiralling effect of turnout, use TheraBands to wrap and spiral around the top of the thigh to the ankle bone. With a partner, gently pull from either end in opposite directions. This is can awaken the postural muscles that control and strengthen turnout, initiating the correct neuro-muscular flow and patterning. Once felt, you can remove the TheraBand and use the image and sensation of spiralling in practice.

ARTISTIC DEVELOPMENT – CREATIVE THINKING IN PRACTICE

When much of ballet practice can appear to focus on conforming to an existing aesthetic line or technical demand, are there tools or strategies that develop your 'personal signature' as an artist? How do you deepen your knowledge of the art form itself and how does that knowledge nurture your individual artistry? What might help to develop authenticity and creativity, qualities that also mark out the dance artist today?

If you are reflecting on these kinds of questions and ideas, you are already thinking creatively and practising on many levels like an artist. We can quantify physical aspects of performance, such as the height of the jump or leg in extension, the number of *pirouettes*, or degree of turnout, strength and coordination. These are 'measurable' outcomes of technical training. They are important – and consistency, discipline and attention to detail will refine these aspects. But the quality of practice cannot be quantified; it is something that you feel and sense, rather than just see – and that the audience also perceives. It involves individuality, imagination and play.

In a form that has such a rich history and is already full of remarkable artists, finding a sense of place and personal confidence can be daunting. Fears, of course, are natural and human but they can be helpful tools for assessing risk. But to make art, you must have courage to step into the unknown. Adam Cooper (2018) credits his career breaks to his ability to take risks:

The swan (1995) – Adam Cooper in Matthew Bourne's *Swan Lake*.

It's easy to play safe but you need to experiment and not be frightened to lose control, or of not being perfect. With Swan Lake*, I fully bought into the idea of male swans and was highly excited, but I realized it was a huge risk. Many people laughed at the idea and didn't take me or Matthew [Bourne] seriously. We went into the first performance not knowing how the audience would react: however, it was an instant success!*

The risk paid off! How many dancers and audiences, who otherwise would not be interested, have been inspired by this iconic performance and subsequently immersed in dance?

STRATEGIES TO DEVELOP ARTISTIC QUALITIES

What is it that makes one performer touch you and another not? It may be how they relate to the music, or how they move or express the intention and connect with the audience. Artistry is open to interpretation and unique to the individual person. Ensuring that your artistic development is embodied within the physicality of your learning can, in turn, develop, challenge and refine your versatility and your knowledge and understanding of ballet as art. Finding strategies to explore artistic qualities feeds your technical execution and develops your personal practice or craft as an artist.

Laban Movement Framework

Rudolf Laban revolutionized our understanding of human movement in the workplace and, especially, in dance. Laban categorizes movement into four theoretical categories: body, effort, shape and space. Each category is concerned with a specific aspect of human movement. Laban's movement framework is an excellent tool to analyse and to understand qualitative movement factors and their effect on dance performance.

LEARNING STRATEGY: UNDERSTANDING QUALITATIVE MOVEMENT DYNAMICS

The following strategy uses Laban's effort category, which describes the *how* of human movement. Each of the four efforts has two contrasting qualities:

Time: sustained–quick
Weight: light–heavy
Space: indirect–direct
Flow: free–bound

To play with movement quality, think of the contrasting efforts as being plotted at opposite ends of a line – so that, for example, sustained is at one end and quick at the other. The movement qualities associated with any particular action or movement can then be plotted at some point along the line, depending on the extent that the quality is demonstrated or needs to be demonstrated.

Contrast and compare this example of two different performances of a *port de bras* from preparatory to Fifth. Dancers A and B perform the same action of the arms, starting and finishing in the same position:

Time: Dancer A demonstrates a relatively sustained (slow) timing throughout, whereas Dancer B starts with a quick lift of the arms, slowing down as they arrive at First and continuing very slowly thereafter to Fifth.

continued

Weight: Dancer A demonstrates a heavy (strong) effort to First position and then releases tension to continue to Fifth, whereas Dancer B demonstrates a lightness to First and onwards to Fifth.

Space: Dancer A demonstrates a more direct pathway than B, who performs with a slight indirect pathway (foreshortened arms with hands closer to the body as they pass from First to Fifth).

Flow: Dancer A demonstrates a continuous free flow throughout, whereas Dancer B starts and finishes with free flow, demonstrating a degree of bound flow as the arms pass through First.

The differences can be understood when analysing the movement qualities as weighted at either end of a scale, allowing the theory to become visible and tangible.

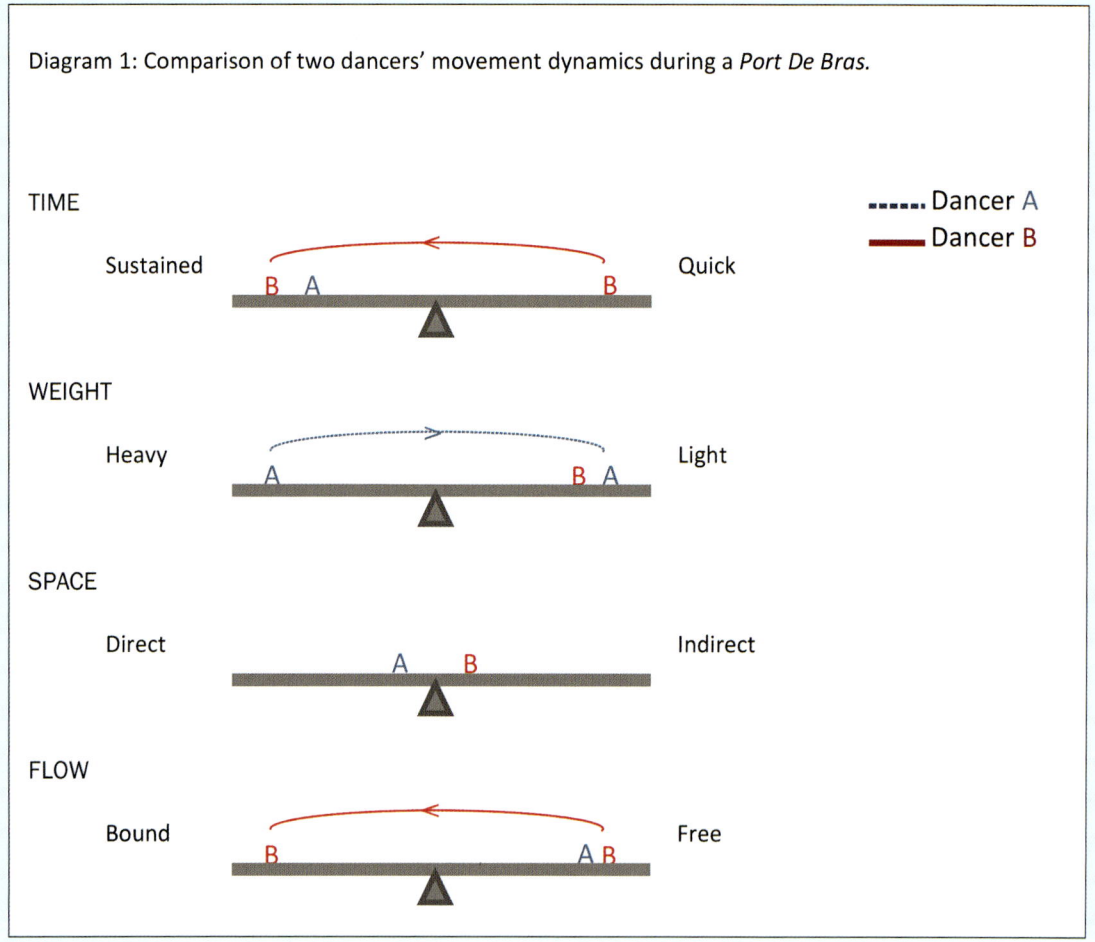

Diagram 1: Comparison of two dancers' movement dynamics during a *Port De Bras.*

Qualitative movement dynamics.

Individual interpretations of the same action in a photoshoot (left to right): Angela Wilson, Laura Bratek, Marta Cabot, Anita Feerick, third-year students, London Studio Centre.

Using any strategy or framework that allows you to analyse and explore movement dynamics within daily class deepens your embodied knowledge, enabling versatility and artistic quality to grow organically, as part of your technique. In the effort strategy provided, although the action or sequence performed is the same, the dancers differ in their qualitative movement interpretation, or *how* they move. The reason may be unique to that individual dancer in terms of how they express the music, the mood and their intention, or it may be driven by physical demands of the choreography – or both.

Working creatively with your movement profile is an effective tool to 'colour' your dancing, and for experiencing and embodying a richer expressive language. Understanding the qualitative aspects of movement helps develop precision, expression and versatility in your practice of classical ballet and other styles.

LEARNING STRATEGY: DEVELOP YOUR USE OF QUALITATIVE MOVEMENT DYNAMICS

Observe, reflect and adapt.

- Consider the extent to which time, weight, space and flow efforts are demonstrated when varying the musical style, tempo or rhythm for a specific *enchaînement* or movement sequence. For example, try performing an *adagio* sequence set to a habanera and then repeat the performance using

continued

a minuet. Observe others, as well as analysing yourself: use Laban's effort framework as a starting point to discuss the stylistic nuances between the two performances. When and why did variations to performance occur? Were there any changes to the breath or suspension? Were there similar or different areas of impulse, tension or release? How did the spatial aspects within the dancer's kinesphere and peripheral space differ? Were there any areas of juxtaposition or harmony you could use in performance and choreography to deepen expressive interest?

- Observe other dancers in class for their varied use of movement dynamics. Is there a common factor in how they move? Are they using a familiar movement profile for a range of movement sequences? Does it alter with their intention or music? To what extent do you or the other dancers imitate your teacher's movement profile? Discuss the differences and similarities. Use a peer's movement profile rather than your own to perform a certain *enchaînement* and discuss with your teacher and peers how this feels and also how it looks to others.

SEEING – WHAT MAKES A GREAT ARTIST?

As well as practising versatility, make sure you are seeing it! Expand your knowledge-base through observing a wide range of dancers and repertoire from different eras and choreographers, as well as those closer to home. The digital era gives us easy access to a range of high-quality dance. Compare and contrast choreography, dancers' intention, artistry and physicality, as well as sets, costumes, music and other production values. Invest time in working out why a particular show did, or did not, move you: was there something you didn't like and why? Was it because you couldn't relate to it or didn't understand it? Did it invite you to re-examine your values and open your mind to new possibilities?

When you watch – reflect on what you value. Consider what makes the artist. Are you seduced by virtuosic physicality or aesthetically refined technique and artistry? Beware the lure of the instant fix: Instagrat! Positions and tricks, such as those on Instagram, may have the 'wow' factor and give instant gratification, but do they generate a lasting emotional response?

Digital media platforms for dance differ from live dance performance on stage. Live performance gives us the action, framed in real space and time, whereas social media gives us a fragment of the action in mediatized time and space: that is, social media clips may be edited and often manipulated to create the illusion of mastery or excellence, and removed from live time and space; you can't edit a live performance. As a dancer, you need to be able to respond to varying performance conditions, as well as your own and other dancers' performances on that day – you can't stop the performance and 'cut' what you see as imperfect. On stage, learn how to adapt, to maintain focus and carry the audience with you.

Mikhail Baryshnikov sums it up well:

Sometimes there is an obsession with technique that can kill your best impulses. But communicating with an art form means being vulnerable. Being imperfect. And most of the time this is much more interesting.[66]

VERSATILITY AND ADAPTABILITY

Often 'versatile' and 'adaptable' are used synonymously, but in describing a dancer it is useful to differentiate. Versatility indicates that you embody the technical and imaginative abilities to respond appropriately to stylistic and artistic challenges.

Adaptability, however, is the ability to respond quickly and fluidly to the performance conditions outside of yourself; for example, being able to adapt to a smaller performance space, a raked stage, the different teaching styles of teachers or the approach of a choreographer.

Being able to adapt to new teachers, choreographers and directors is essential. Although having one regular teacher can provide clear focus, it can also inhibit your ability to cope with different methodologies, ideas and personalities. Valeri Hristov (2019), the ex-Royal Ballet soloist, describes how his adaptability and versatility were affected by his allegiance to his teacher: *I had an exceptional teacher, but it made me very one-directional: I judged other classes and teachers based on the one formula I knew. As a result, I couldn't learn from them and I was limited in my ability to perform modern work. Experiencing a variety of teachers, methods and styles is so important in training, so that you can learn to be dynamic from the beginning.*

Northern Ballet dancer Harris Beattie (2020), comments on how his early core training, in both ballet and contemporary, gave him the confidence to tackle richly diverse opportunities that shaped his career: *Throughout my vocational training I experienced a wide range of theatrical arts, dance styles and choreography from performing the title role in* Billy Elliot, *summers spent at Netherlands Dance Theatre to The Royal Ballet School, and by experiencing choreography from artists as diverse as Wayne McGregor, Michael Clark, Kenneth MacMillan and John Neumeier. All these experiences have had a significant influence on my movement profile and who I am as a dancer.*

Try to take classes or workshops with teachers from different schools and backgrounds. Reflect on what you have learned and how their approach varied from what you are used to. How did you respond? How did you apply your knowledge in the new situation? Always look for something that you can take away and something you can work on – even if it's learning to hide your unrest or insecurity!

Director of Northern Ballet, David Nixon (2019), believes that dancers are required to be flexible in the way they interact: *I look for more in dancers than having stylistic versatility. I look for an ability to listen to what people say, to be responsive to varying situations and to be able to work with people with varying personalities and ideas.*

LEARNING STRATEGY: ADAPTING TO CHANGES AND CHALLENGES – BE CURIOUS

- Adopt a 'can do' mindset. Having a dynamic approach to new situations and responding positively to different environments and social situations will make you more employable.

- Be a team player. Being able to contribute and operate as part of a team are essential skills for any career. Dance training involves hours of study with like-minded peers, but participation can be alongside, rather than amongst, your peers. When given the opportunity, contribute to group tasks and choreography: learn to listen to the opinions of others and to respond to challenges creatively, rather than defensively.

- Embrace the unfamiliar: take risks and be open to different teaching methodologies, teachers and choreography. Don't allow your own opinions and beliefs to stop you exploring the new.

Be excited by challenge rather than reticent, accept that learning takes time and that progress, not perfection, is the aim of your education as a dance artist.

Royal Ballet Principals Marcelino Sambé and Francesca Hayward in a choreographic workshop. Francesca says – 'we must dance in all styles of dance now, so being versatile is crucial. I believe you have to wrap your mind around a different style, before you can adjust your body'.

WORKING WITH CHOREOGRAPHERS

Having a curious and open mind will not only allow you to flourish as a dancer, but will make you attractive to choreographers. Versatile dancers can help feed a choreographer's creative vision and thus help push the development of the art form. Darcey Bussell highlights how 'the young choreographers are constantly delving to produce something that hasn't been done before'.[67] All ballet dancers today are expected to come to rehearsals already equipped with a diverse skill-set and to be physically and mentally, thus artistically, curious. Many choreographers expect dancers to contribute to making movement and a trace of your 'personal signature' becomes embodied in the choreographic text. Christopher Hampson (2019), director

of Scottish Ballet, also notes that in his company, a dancer's rank is no longer a barrier: 'There used to be more a hierarchal structure that determined who was used within a new creation; however, now there is a flatter landscape: … Being versatile allows dancers more opportunities to be used regardless of company rank'.

Importantly, be curious about life in general. Be aware of what is outside the studio and theatre: nature, art, literature, music, science and world affairs. Know what's important to you, your family and your community. Try different sports and pastimes, engage through human contact and not only through virtual reality. Wayne McGregor recognizes such qualities that make for an exceptional artist:

Intellectual curiosity for me is as important as physical curiosity because I think they are the same thing. So, if you look at Steven McRae, he's got so many interests outside dance, so actually it feeds his brilliance inside dance.[68]

IT TAKES TIME

Developing refined technique and artistry takes time – a minimum of seven years of serious study – and continues for as long as you keep dancing. Experience and sustained practice allow you to integrate the corresponding aesthetic gestures, actions and intentions, so that they are 'embodied'. The essential foundational 'movement maps' are established through slow, careful practice, thereby helping facilitate and develop the versatility and range you need in your career. Fast-tracking specific skills – for example, executing complicated steps at the expense of clean technique – can have serious long-term consequences: bad habits are engrained, making you prone to injury. Too much too soon, along with a narrow focus on specific skills, can result in you failing to reach your dynamic movement potential.

Be patient. Know that the effort to embody the fundamentals, to develop versatility with virtuosity and to make creative space for your inner artist to flower, is time well spent. With the right mindset and carefully considered training you can achieve great things.

Choreographer and dancer, Dame Gillian Lynne (1926–2018) epitomized an artist of great versatility with a 'can-do attitude'. 'Try whatever is asked of you – because even if you are bad, you will learn something and if you are good you will make a massive and happy discovery' (One Dance UK Conference, London, 2015).

Dancer: Anna Heery.

CHAPTER 6

TAKING CARE OF YOUR BODY AND MIND: APPLYING DANCE SCIENCE TO PRACTICE
Stephanie De'Ath and Laura Erwin

INTRODUCTION

As a dancer, you know that how the body and mind feels on any given day can have a big impact in the studio. Whether you feel technically 'on form' and focused, or 'off balance' and distracted, can hugely affect the ability to enjoy dancing and feel that you are making progress. This is why taking care of your body and mind should be an integral part of every dancer's daily routine.

The area of 'dance science' aims to help the dancer to:

- prevent injury
- optimize their performance

It includes such aspects as anatomy, strength and conditioning, lifestyle advice and psychological skills.

Use of dance science within dance training has grown rapidly over the last ten years with students, teachers and professionals recognizing its vital importance in supporting successful dance practice. As well as the International Association of Dance Medicine and Science (IADMS), UK-based organizations such as the National Institute of Dance Medicine and Science (NIDMS) and One Dance UK conduct research and disseminate this information to the dance community. They have also set up healthcare initiatives, such as the NHS dance injury clinics. Dance schools, secondary schools and community dance groups are increasingly incorporating fundamental aspects into their work. The Royal Ballet School, for example, has pioneered a new healthy dance programme, using the latest injury management technology and skilled professionals to empower, support and equip the dancer to take charge of all aspects of their wellbeing.

This chapter gives some key thoughts and top tips to help you consider and apply dance science knowledge to your training, helping you to get the most from your dancing. We recommend taking time to cross-reference this information with Chapters 3, 4 and 5, exploring the exercises in your own time with precision and awareness, to supplement your ballet class.

We begin 'In the studio' and look at each area of the body in turn – considering structure, purpose for the dancer, alignment and technique. For each, we will reflect on key goals and point out common pitfalls in order to help you to avoid them. We include essential exercises to support these goals that can either be done in isolation or combined to give you a whole-body training plan.

'Outside the studio' will then look at the vital elements of self-care that a dancer should aim to consider in their week. This includes such aspects as rest and recovery, supplemental training, nutrition and injury. Finally, 'Psychological skills' will discuss specific concerns that may affect you, such as perfectionism, body image and anxiety. It will also introduce key coping strategies that any dancer can use to assist with their training. At the end of the chapter we point you to further resources so that you can continue your research beyond this book.

We bring to the table our own theoretical knowledge and practical experience of working with, and supporting, dancers in training over many years. We encourage you to reflect on the different areas that affect your dance practice, many of which are interlinked. It is often small changes that make a big difference. Work through the chapter logically, spending more time on issues relevant to you but not missing anything out.

We have chosen to feature different dancers within the chapter to illustrate the ideas discussed – dancers who specialize in ballet (Angela Wilson, Anna Heery, Daisy Bishop, Laura Bratek and Regan Wilson) and those who are musical theatre and jazz specialists (Abbie Hollis and Mark Coates), yet also consider ballet an essential and highly beneficial part of their technique training.

Let's get started…

SECTION 1: IN THE STUDIO

INTRODUCTION

In general, a dancer training in ballet should be working toward the following:

- Balanced strength and flexibility to enable controlled movement, held positions and freedom of movement.
- Awareness of correct alignment enabling the dancer to achieve good posture and technique.

TERMINOLOGY

Neutral Posture and Placement

This refers to anatomical neutral. When standing, the positioning of each skeletal joint, including the curves of the spine, means the line of gravity passes vertically through the centre of the body. It provides the dancer with a lengthened and supported position, which is efficient with no unnecessary stress on the skeleton or muscles.

Neutral posture can be found by using an 'axis' or 'plumb line'.

We use the term 'posture' to refer to the whole body, and 'placement' when we are focusing on one part that makes up this whole-body neutral posture, such as 'neutral pelvic placement'.

Balanced Strength and Flexibility

To aid dance practice, one goal is to have equal strength and flexibility in all the muscles surrounding each joint. For example, around the hip joint, the dancer's hip flexors are equally as strong and flexible as the hip extensors (hamstrings and gluteal muscles). Where there is an imbalance in opposing muscle groups, this can affect the aesthetic, performance level and increase injury risk.

There is a reciprocal relationship between neutral posture and balanced strength and flexibility. Each is key to achieving the other.

Alignment

The above concepts support the dancer to sustain good alignment when moving. Good alignment means that the dancer carefully considers the position of their joints when moving, so that they do not place excessive stress on the skeleton or muscles, supporting efficient movement (where one muscle group is not being overused or underused).

YOUR SPINE, PELVIS AND CENTRE

Often dancers feel that the spine is 'at the back' of the body due to the 'back bones', which are visible from behind. In fact, as the image shows, these are just the very tips of the spine bones (spineous processes); the spine actually runs much deeper through the centre of the body.

The spine begins with the round skull at the top, which is supported by twenty-six mobile and neatly stacking vertebrae, then slotting into the wide and stable base of the pelvis. The twenty-six bones and discs that lie in between are built in an alternating structure of curves. In neutral posture, the weight of the head and upper body, as well as the impact from jumps, is absorbed through the centre of each bone and disc.

Explore: Neutral Posture

Neutral posture can be understood by lining up your body with its plumb line or central axis.

You can see that, when standing, the ear lobe, centre of the shoulder and middle of the pelvis are all sitting on the same vertical line, with the head over the centre of the body mass (*see* Chapter 3). It sounds simple, but we can see that the pelvis, ribcage and head, in particular, need to relate quite precisely to one another to find neutral posture. Then you have to be able to maintain the relationship while moving. Tricky!

When standing, jumping or performing *pirouettes*, the dancer needs to have the awareness and balanced strength to maintain neutral posture. This is crucial for injury prevention and great dancing! When performing spinal movements such *épaulement* and side-bends, flexibility and alignment continue to be integral for injury prevention.

To help you understand and find this detail for yourself, we have broken it down into four separate goals for you to then layer up.

Goal One: Finding and Maintaining Your Neutral Pelvic Placement

Aim for this to be your 'default' position of the pelvis during the majority of ballet technique and performance, such as *tendus, pliés*, jumps and *pirouettes*. This position, when combined with the second goal below, enables you to find your neutral posture, also creating the beautiful lengthened spine of ballet technique. It enables even shock absorption through the vertebrae, and the muscles around the core, back and hip joints to be balanced in strength and flexibility.

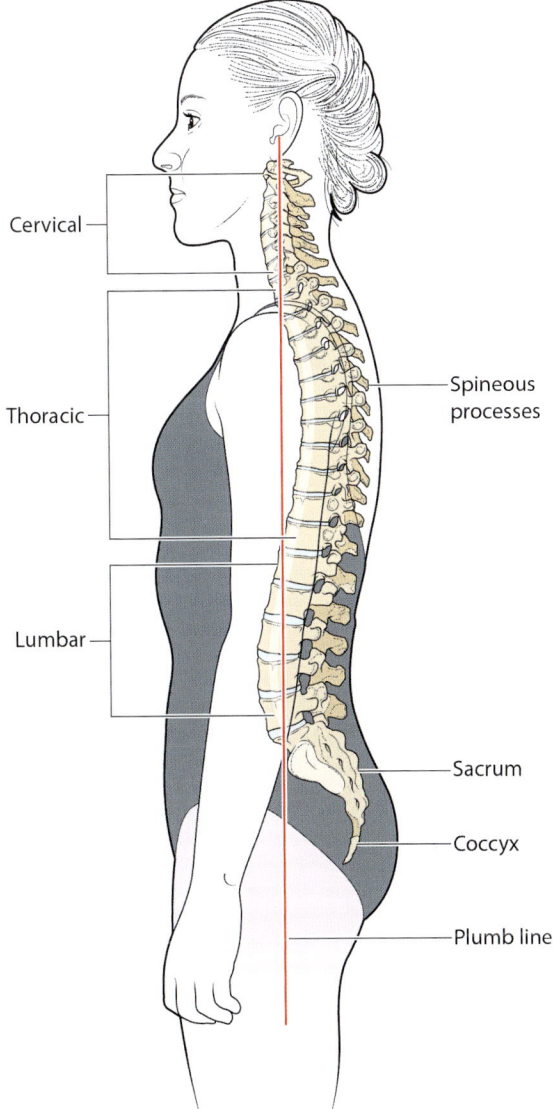

Cervical

Thoracic

Spineous processes

Lumbar

Sacrum

Coccyx

Plumb line

A side view of the spine and neutral posture using a plumb line.

Explore: Neutral Pelvic Placement

A neutral pelvic placement is found by keeping the 'hip bones' (ASIS – anterior superior iliac spine) and pubic bone in a vertical line when standing, and the two 'hip bones' level horizontally.

During some movements, your pelvis will move a small amount from neutral placement to facilitate shifts of weight and movement range. First, during work *derrière,* where one 'hip bone' will open slightly whilst still remaining level with the other. Second, during high leg work above 90 degrees (hip height), where the 'hip bone' of the gesture leg will lift slightly.

The most common pitfall is standing with the pelvis in either an 'arching' or 'tucking' position; this impacts on skeletal alignment and the five alternating curves, as well as on the lengthened spine.

When 'arching' with a forward (anterior) tilted pelvis:

- The lower (lumbar) spine over-arches (lordosis), placing more pressure on the back of the spinal vertebrae (instead of passing through the middle), increasing risk of injury to the discs and bones.
- The lower back muscles become tight and over-used and the core disengages, becoming weak and underused. Both increase the risk of back injuries.
- The hip flexor muscles become short and tight, while the gluteus maximus and hamstring muscles become weak and long. This makes them more susceptible to injuries, such as hamstring tears or hip joint injuries, and may also affect *arabesque* height.

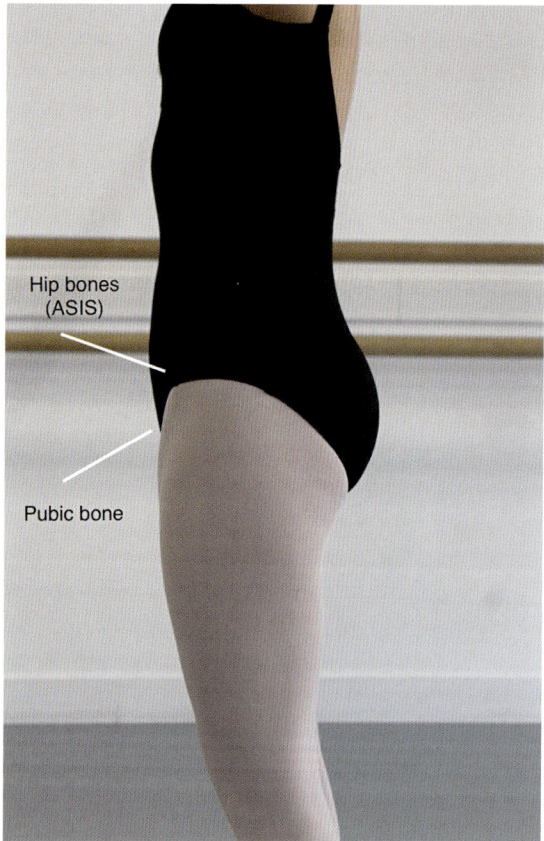

Neutral pelvic placement side view: the 'hip bones' and pubic bone are in a vertical line. Dancer: Angela Wilson.

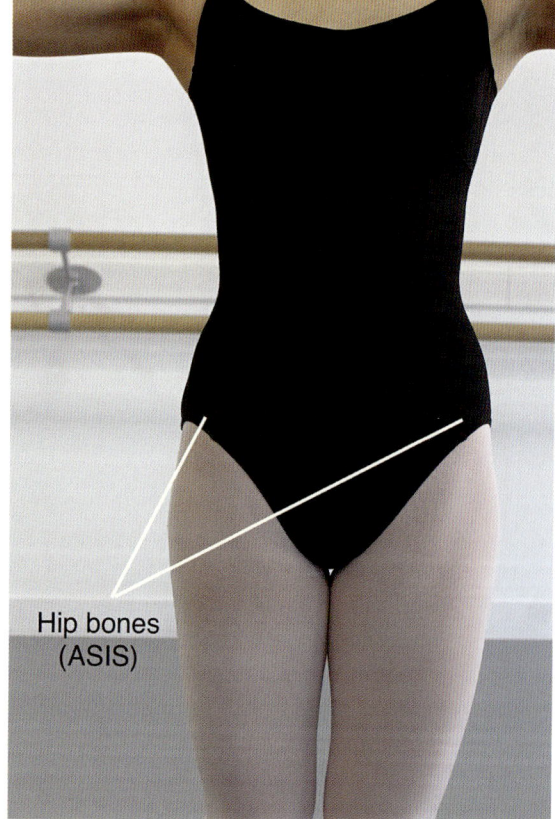

Neutral pelvic placement front view: the 'hip bones' are level horizontally. Dancer: Angela Wilson.

'Arching' with a forward (anterior) tilted pelvis, the 'hip bones' are in front of the pubic bone. Dancer: Abbie Hollis.

'Tucking' with a backwards (posterior) tilted pelvis, the 'hip bones' are behind the pubic bone. Dancer: Abbie Hollis.

When 'tucking' with a backwards (posterior) tilted pelvis:

- The lower (lumbar) spine flattens, placing more pressure on the front of the spinal vertebrae (instead of passing through the middle), increasing risk of injury to the discs and bones.
- The lower back muscles become long and weak and the core is over-engaged, limiting its ability to function efficiently and restricting breathing.
- The gluteus maximus and hamstring muscles are overused, becoming short and tight, susceptible to injuries and restricting turnout due to increased tension.

While these are the most notable impacts, often there are others as the rest of the body shifts around the new, incorrect posture – for example, the chest drops and the shoulder blades 'wing' (do not lie flat across the ribcage). Often dancers adopt these postures as a way of increasing turnout, because they appear to enable more external rotation at the hip. However, this may lead to negative impacts to knee and foot alignment, as well as restricting the muscles that control turnout from engaging correctly and efficiently. The dancer who has one of these incorrect postures will find that, as well as injuries, soreness and poor alignment, it is difficult to maintain balance in *pirouettes* and improve leg height.

Goal Two: Incorporating Your Ribcage and Head Placement

Once you have understood neutral pelvic placement, you can find ribcage and head placement balance on top to complete the axis or plumb line. This first promotes fluidity and freedom of movement for the vertebrae and, second, balanced muscle strength surrounding the spinal joints in both the abdominal and back muscles. This will enable you to engage the whole spine in a neutral posture, and then sustain this support and aesthetic during movements such as jumps, balances and *pirouettes*.

The most common pitfalls are that dancers tend to:

- 'Flare' or 'disengage the ribcage', shifting the front up away from the pelvis. This can often happen as the dancer tries to 'get taller' or 'pull up' from the chest, rather than finding length by growing up from their deep core. This also affects the pelvis, most often causing 'arching' and a forward tilt. The impact is that this leads to over-arching of the lower back curves and overwork of the lower back muscles. It also disengages the core muscles.

- 'Drop' or 'slump' the front of the ribcage down and shift the head forward. This can be a default posture for dancers in everyday life that then follows into the studio. It is often compounded by the overuse of technology such as mobile phones and computers. Dancers frequently hold their head forwards from their plumb line and, with the skull being so heavy (about 4.5kg), this over-loads the supporting muscles. This commonly

'Flaring' or 'disengaging the ribcage'. Dancer: Angela Wilson.

'Dropping' or 'slumping' the front of the ribcage down. Dancer: Angela Wilson.

also results in 'tucking' and a backward-tilted pelvis. The impact is that this can often make the dancer's neck and shoulders very tight, also impacting the ballet aesthetic. The dancer can then mistakenly stretch these muscles, which does not actually address the problem.

ESSENTIAL EXERCISE: FINDING YOUR NEUTRAL POSTURE

1. Begin by standing and find your neutral pelvic placement with the 'hip bones' and pubic bone in a vertical line. Also check that the 'hip bones' are level horizontally.
2. Next, find your neutral ribcage. First, try 'flaring' the ribcage out, then 'slumping' it down. Then find the mid-point where the ribs are softly 'tucked in' to your abdominals but not 'pinned down'.
3. Finally, consider neutral head placement – your earlobes balancing over the middle of your shoulders, with your chin parallel to the floor.

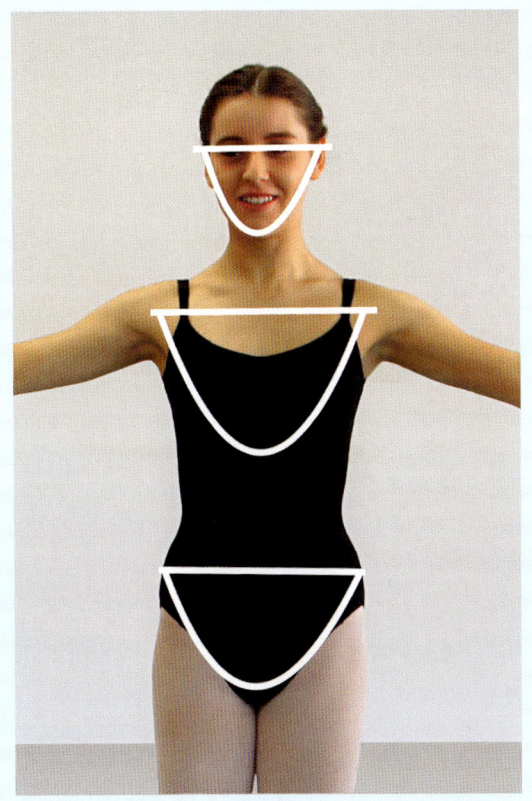 

Your pelvis, ribcage and head can be visualized as three bowls of water, with the aim being to keep each one level, as opposed to being tipped or spilled in any direction. Dancer: Angela Wilson.

The dancer can also think of the tailbone dropping or lengthening down, then the back of the skull floating up to create length and opposition. Dancer: Angela Wilson.

continued

Practise finding this as often as you can, both in everyday life and during class.

Technique Notes

- You might want to use a mirror, photos or another dancer to help you – what feels like neutral from your perception often is not from an outside view.
- Neutral may feel quite strange; for example, if you are used to standing with the pelvis tilted forward (more common in ballet dancers), it may feel like you are 'tucking under' when actually this your neutral posture.
- Try to find your breath moving freely in your ribcage throughout, as opposed to holding. Place your hands on the side of your ribcage and focus on moving them in and out, pressing into and softening away from your hands like an accordion or fish gills.

ESSENTIAL EXERCISE: MAINTAINING YOUR NEUTRAL PLACEMENT DURING LEG AND ARM MOVEMENTS

1. Take your time to find your neutral posture. You will need to watch/feel for any small movements away from neutral with the pelvis, ribcage or head throughout the exercise.
2. Move your arms through First, Fifth and Second Positions slowly. Repeat four times and reverse direction.
3. Take your time to transfer the weight to one side using *retiré*. Repeat four to eight times each side.
4. Slowly *tendu* in each direction. Repeat four to six times each side.

Technique Notes

- Look out for forward lifting or 'flaring' of the ribcage, particularly when then arms go to Fifth as this disconnects the abdominals and loses neutral ribcage placement.

- Focus on using both deep core support and the gluteus medius with your standing leg, to maintain your neutral pelvic placement and your 'hip bones' level horizontally throughout.
- Take care not to lift one of the 'hip bones' above the other when transferring weight. This stability will help you during balances and *pirouettes*.
- Be aware of the habit of forward tilting the pelvis during *tendu derrière*; focus on using your gluteal muscles to create the leg action.

Goal Three: Understanding Deep Core Support

The neutral posture and lengthened aesthetic of ballet are not possible without the correct core support. Your 'core' generally refers to all the muscles that provide stability for the centre of the body. This includes your abdominal muscles (rectus abdominus, transverse abdominus, internal and external obliques) and pelvic floor muscle. These core muscles perform different roles.

TERMINOLOGY: DEEP CORE SUPPORT

For the dancer, deep core support is of particular importance to be able to find and sustain.

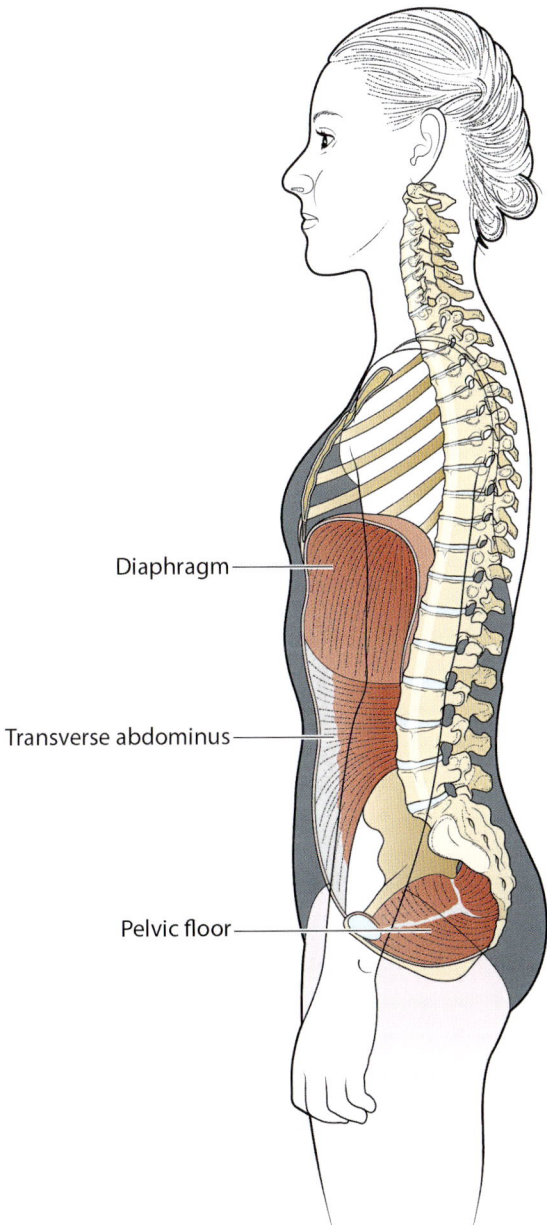

Diaphragm

Transverse abdominus

Pelvic floor

The muscles that can be considered to provide deep core support.

This includes the deepest layer of the abdominals, the transverse abdominus and the pelvic floor. The transverse abdominus muscle wraps from the spine at the back of the body round to the front, providing a 'corset' or 'cylinder' of support underneath the diaphragm. The pelvic floor sits like a parachute or sling underneath the pelvis from front to back and side to side.

Practise finding your deep core support using the essential exercise in the box to feel the engagement of the transverses abdominus and pelvic floor drawing gently 'up and in', then relaxing. This feeling can be connected at around 20 per cent of maximum contraction to provide support during dancing. Your breathing then takes place in the expansion of the ribcage to the back and side, so that the abdominals can stay gently engaged. This provides core stability and supports neutral posture, without creating tension and restricting breathing.

It is also important that the dancer maintains deep core support when performing all spine movements such as *épaulement,* full circular *port de bras* or *cambré*. This supports flexibility of movement, avoids overuse of the back muscles and helps to maintain the pelvis and spine in correct placement.

The most common pitfalls are that dancers tend to:

- Disengage the deep core (though other abdominal muscles, such as rectus abdominus, may be strong and they may be able to perform many other abdominal strength movements). The impact is an increase in lower back tension and injuries as these muscles work harder to compensate for weakness at the front.
- Overuse and constantly tense all the core muscles. The impact is increased overall tension, including in the shoulders and neck, which can affect performance aesthetic, and also shortness or restriction in breathing, as the ribcage cannot move freely.

ESSENTIAL EXERCISE: PRACTISE FINDING DEEP CORE SUPPORT

1. Place your hands just beneath your navel and cough or sniff to feel the engagement of the pelvic floor and transverse abdominus.
2. Now engage these muscles gently and constantly 'up and in' at around 20 per cent of maximum contraction.
3. Sustain this abdominal support while you allow the ribcage to move freely to the back and side, like an accordion or fish gills, for six to eight breaths.
4. Practise finding this in your warm-up and between class exercises. Gradually your understanding will improve to maintaining this support throughout class.

Technique Notes

- This feeling of core strength should be used in any abdominal exercise, such as toe taps, plank or sit-ups, drawing gently 'up and in' without 'doming' the abdominals. It is also the same feeling you should have throughout class.
- You can also think of 'wrapping around' like a corset from back to front.
- This skill of breathing freely above this deep core support takes practice, but do stick at it!

Goal Four: Upper Back Strength and Flexibility

Whilst your lower (lumbar) spine has the most flexibility, your upper (thoracic) spine also should be strong and flexible enough to participate in movements such as *cambré derrière* and *arabesque*, giving you the muscle support needed to avoid injury.

The most common pitfall, often due to the 'tucking' posture, is that dancers tend to lack this upper (thoracic) spine strength and flexibility, and so end up performing extension movements predominantly using their lower back. This can give the appearance of 'hinging' in one area of the spine, as opposed to using abdominal support to create a long curve throughout its whole length. The impact is that the dancer then disengages the abdominals, overuses the lower back muscles and puts pressure on the spinal joints – increasing risk of injury.

Often the gluteal and upper back muscle strength needed to create higher *arabesques* is lacking. The dancer will try to increase their *arabesque* height by working the lower back muscles. Instead, they need to develop balanced strength and flexibility in the upper back alongside deep core support. Once this has been understood, the dancer can explore greater leg height using the gluteal muscle to reach a fuller arabesque. (*See* the associated image and also The Arabesque in Chapter 3).

The dancer 'hinges' and disengages the abdominals. Dancer: Abbie Hollis.

The dancer achieves a lengthened spine in *arabesque*.

ESSENTIAL EXERCISE: YOUR TECHNIQUE FOR UPPER BACK MOVEMENT – EXTENSION, SIDE-BENDING AND ROTATION

1. Begin standing by finding neutral posture, 20 per cent deep core support and free ribcage breathing for five breaths.
2. As you exhale, use deep core support to keep your pelvis neutral and start lengthening your spine up to the sky. Think of opening your heart to the ceiling and melting the shoulders down the back to guide yourself into an upper back extension. Inhale to hold and exhale to return, re-checking your neutral posture before repeating four times.
3. Now repeat the same technique for rotations four times each side and side-bending four times each side. Think of reaching your heart up and away, as the back of your pelvis drops down.
4. As you get more confident with maintaining placement, you can try more complex versions:

    – Add arm movements to the above positions, e.g. holding Fifth throughout.
    – Combining different spine movements, e.g. *ports de bras*.

continued

Technique Notes

During upper back extension:

- Focus on getting maximum movement of the spine between the shoulder blades, as opposed to just 'hinging' from the lower back. Imagine shining a light from your heart up to the ceiling or use your hands to gently press your ribcage down to encourage more movement above.
- Be careful not to tilt the pelvis forward and over-arch the lower back, stay neutral and drop the tailbone throughout.
- A variation of this exercise called 'breast stroke' can also be performed lying face down.

During rotation and side-bending:

- Check that the 'hip bones' are level horizontally and take care that they don't rotate or lift.
- Try to lengthen the ribcage evenly away from the pelvis at the front, back and side to stop one area lifting more than the other. For example, it is very common when side-bending to lift more at the front and 'flare the ribs'.
- Keep the 'hip bones' and pubic bone in a vertical line. It is very common for ballet dancers to go into a forward tilt here.

Further Research

Exercises that may assist you:

- For dancers who are used to 'arching' – stretches for hip flexors and lower back, particularly the quadratus lumborum muscle.
- Pilates deep core and upper back strength exercises, such as toe taps and breast stroke.
- Strengthening exercises for gluteal and hamstring muscles.
- Stretches for front of the chest and pectoralis muscle.

YOUR SHOULDER COMPLEX

The shoulder joint has a large range of mobility. This is because the shoulder blades slide freely on the ribcage and the shoulder joint capsule is shallow, with only a third of the socket in contact with the ball. As a result, it is very easy for a dancer to lose correct shoulder placement. The muscles surrounding the joint are key to creating the support that the skeletal structure cannot. The 'fan' of the rotator cuff muscles, along with the serratus anterior muscle around the shoulder blade, are vital for correct scapula placement, including 'supporting the arms on the back' and preventing winging.

Goal One: To Find Your Shoulder Located Within the Socket

Within neutral placement, your shoulder joint should sit evenly within the shoulder socket, as opposed to dropping forward or back, down or up. This balances the fan of muscles at the front and back of the shoulders and around the shoulder blades, providing even strength and flexibility, so that movement is not restricted in any direction. Importantly, it also creates the ballet aesthetic of having 'wide and open collarbones or chest' and provides the foundations for successful partner work.

The most common pitfall is that dancers tend to drop their shoulders forwards and down out of the shoulder socket. This posture can often be caused by technology use, carrying heavy bags or bags on one shoulder, or postures such as 'arching'.

The impacts on the dancer are:

- Tight pectoralis muscles at the front of the shoulder, which will affect the ability to have

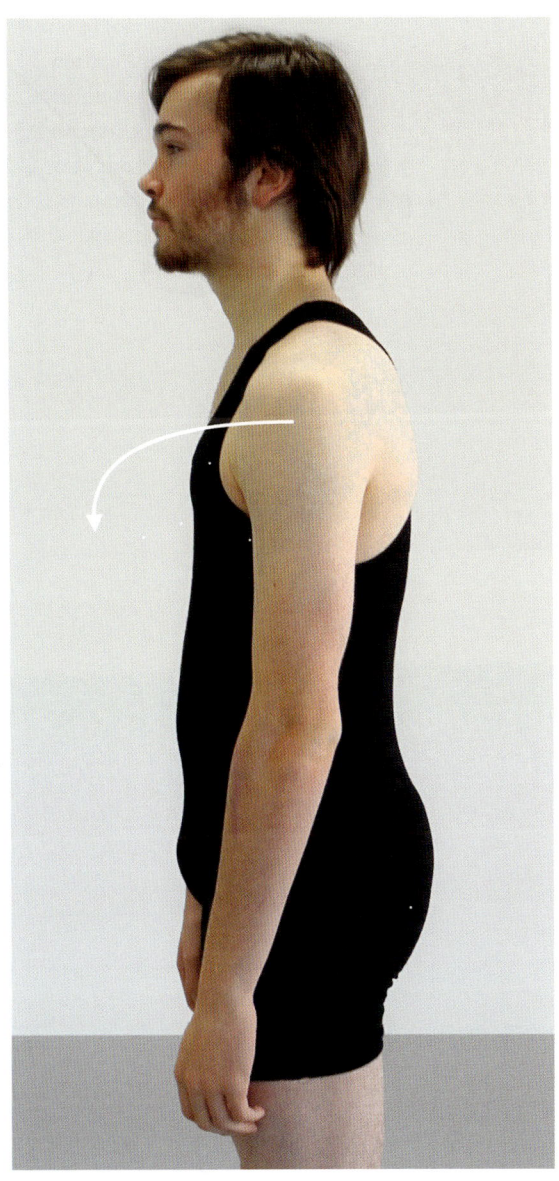

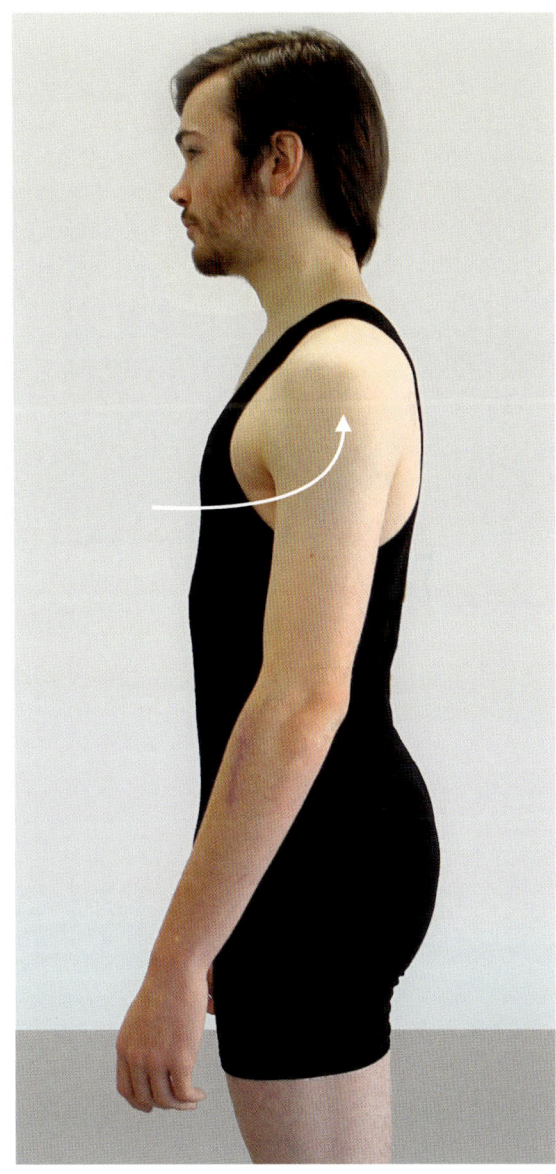

A dancer with shoulders moving down and forward out of the socket. Dancer: Mark Coates.

A dancer with neutral placement, the shoulders 'suctioning' into the socket. Dancer: Mark Coates.

the aesthetic openness desired with ballet. For example, when performing Third Position, the shoulders will round forward and the chest will have the appearance of being closed.

- Weak and long muscles at the back of the shoulder and around the shoulder blade. This

can affect the ability of the shoulder blade to be flat on the ribcage, resulting in winging and leading to tension in the upper shoulder and neck muscles.

- Injury risks, including shoulder dislocation, nerve impingement in the neck and muscle strains.

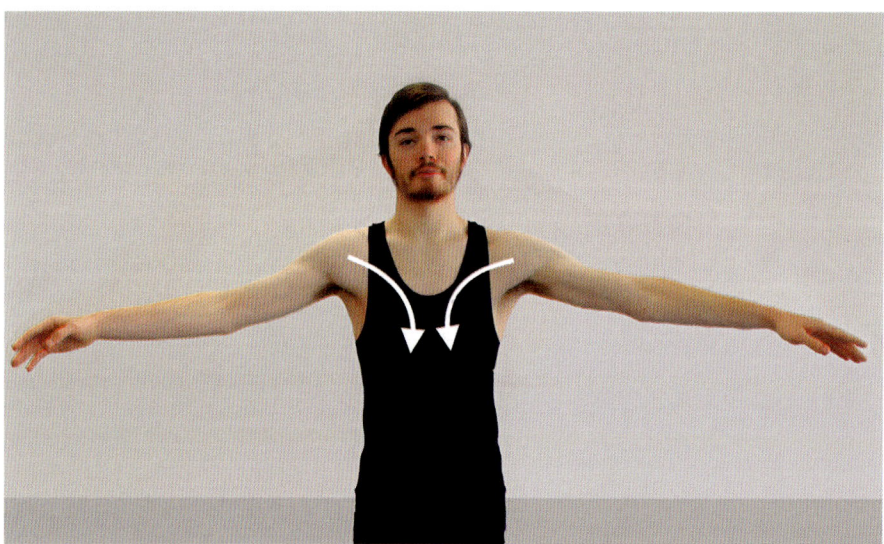

The dancer in Second Position with the shoulders moving down and forward out of neutral. Dancer: Mark Coates.

The dancer in Second Position with neutral shoulder placement. Dancer: Mark Coates.

ESSENTIAL EXERCISE: FINDING YOUR NEUTRAL SHOULDER PLACEMENT

1. Experiment yourself with the associated images. First, drop your shoulders down and forward out of the socket. Then draw the ball of the shoulder up and into its socket neutral placement. Note the difference in aesthetic, how it feels muscularly and the comparison with how you normally stand.
2. See if you can maintain your shoulder in your socket while you take four to six breaths, and make this placement your new habit.
3. Add combinations of arm positions, such as a *port de bras*.

See if you can do shoulder placement checks a few times each class and maintain them for a few breaths each time.

Technique Notes

- Apply this principle to any other conditioning exercises you do, such as sit-ups, plank and free weights.
- Enlist the help of a physiotherapist to help you to understand this further; it's a really difficult concept with a lot of fine-tuning needed.
- By 'supporting the arms from the back', try to release tension in the neck and shoulders.
- Stretching your pectoralis muscle may also help, as tightness here can make it difficult for a dancer to find neutral shoulder placement.

Goal Two: Feeling Your Shoulder Blades Connecting 'Back and Wide'

Aim for both shoulder blades (scapula) to lie flat and 'hug' around the sides of your ribcage. This feeling of gently drawing the shoulder blades 'back and wide' or creating a 'J'-shape should be maintained during your arm movements to enable them to be supported by the correct muscle use. Aesthetically, it also enables you to prevent winging and to maintain the flat appearance of the shoulder blades on the ribcage. When performing movements of the arms, this enables the shoulder blades to glide freely across the ribcage to allow full movement range.

The most common pitfall is that dancers' shoulder blades 'wing' (the edges stick out away from the ribcage). This impacts the dancer's alignment, muscle use, movement range and aesthetic.

Winging can indicate that the dancer is not in neutral posture; for example, they may be 'tucking' the pelvis, causing the

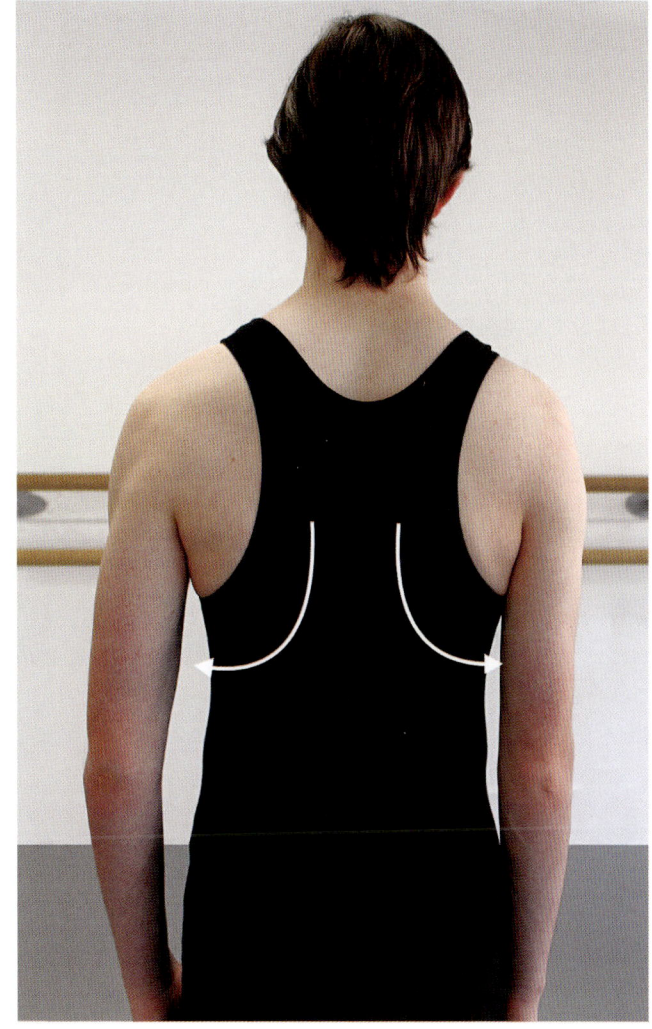

The shoulder blades reach 'back and wide'. Dancer: Mark Coates.

thoracic spine to round and affecting shoulder blade placement. The shoulder blades can also be either fixed, not moving freely enough to enable unrestricted arm movement, or move too freely, lacking muscular support and aesthetically appear to be 'boney' and 'sticking out'.

In order to correct this, dancers often, with the best intentions, 'pin the shoulder blades back'. This causes the ribcage to stick out, creates tension in other areas, such as the neck, and does not enable the dancer to learn the correct placement and strength, merely masking the actual issue.

'Pinning' the shoulders back causes the dancer to lose neutral spine and ribcage placement. Dancer: Abbie Hollis.

ESSENTIAL EXERCISE: REACHING YOUR SHOULDER BLADES 'BACK AND WIDE'

1. Begin standing and find the shoulders neutral in the socket. Now think of 'back and wide', creating a 'J'-shape on the back or 'tucking the shoulder blades into your jeans' pockets'.
2. Slide or reach your shoulder blades apart (this uses your serratus anterior muscle) and let this action float your arms up to second position. Hold and breathe.
3. Again, send your shoulder blades apart to float your arms to Fifth, feeling a sense of support and 'connection down the back'.
4. Now move through various arm positions for a couple of minutes, keeping the 'back and wide' sensation. Rest and repeat.

Technique Notes
- Remember that shoulder blade placement can also be affected by your posture, so do check this also.
- Hold light weights (or tin cans!) to help you to feel and strengthen these muscles.

ESSENTIAL EXERCISE: ACTIVELY STRENGTHEN YOUR ROTATOR CUFF MUSCLES

1. With the elbows tucked into the waist and bent 90 degrees, face the palms up in front of the body, like you are holding a tray. Find and maintain your neutral shoulder placement with the shoulder blades drawing 'back and wide' throughout the exercise.
2. Keeping your elbows tucked into your waist, outwardly rotate one arm so that the hand goes to the side, then return.

3. Repeat eight times, then swap sides. You can also do this holding a flex band to add resistance.

Technique Notes
- Maintaining neutral shoulder placement throughout is key.
- Watch out that you engage the deep core 20 per cent and breathe into the back and side of the ribcage throughout the exercise.
- Use your breath to stay soft and prevent tension creeping into other areas, such as the lower back and neck. If it does, this may mean you need to check your neutral spine placement and deep core support.
- Use this same placement with all shoulder-strengthening exercises, including wall push-ups (less weight means you can focus more on correct placement), side plank and flex band combinations.

YOUR HIP JOINT

The ball-and-socket-shape of the hip joint and the action of turning out (hip external rotation) allows the dancer a wide range of movement and expressive potential from *ronds de jambes* to *grands battements* and high leg extensions.

Explore: Range in Turnout and Parallel
To see the difference in movement range, lie on your back and raise one leg to the ceiling (hip flexion) without the pelvis moving, first in parallel and then in turnout. You will see that your range in turnout is much greater.

The dancer needs to understand and use correct muscle engagement, alongside optimum placement of the pelvis and hip joint itself, when moving. Both strength and flexibility also need to be balanced around the different muscle groups at the front, back and sides of the hip joint.

Terminology: Hip Joint Muscles
Note the different muscles we will be discussing most in this section:

- The deep gluteal muscles – the gluteus medius and minimus, which stabilize the dancer's standing leg.
- Gluteus maximus – the biggest gluteal muscle, which creates leg movement *derrière*.
- Deep six rotators – at the bottom of the back of the pelvis, underneath the gluteals, these create turnout.

Goal One: To Keep Your Pelvis Neutral and Stable During Leg Movement
Once neutral pelvic placement has been understood, seek to maintain this stability during low leg movements, such as *tendus, retirés* and transfers of weight. To do so, first feel your gentle 'up and in' deep core support. Second, use the deep gluteal muscles (gluteus minimus and medius) to stabilize the standing leg.

With higher leg movements, above 90 degrees, your pelvis will shift slightly from neutral placement, but this should always be kept to a minimum. Length in the lower back should always be maintained by 'dropping or reaching the tailbone' and engaging the same deep core and gluteal muscles.

The most common pitfalls are that dancers:

- To stabilize the pelvis on their standing leg and over-engage the hip flexors at the front (particularly the tensor fascia latae), instead of using their deep core and deep gluteals.
- When moving to the front or side, tilt the pelvis or lift one side of the pelvis, instead of keeping the 'hip bones' level horizontally.
- When moving the legs to the back, tend to shift the pelvis first, overusing the lower back muscles.

The impact of these is that the dancer loses correct pelvic placement and muscular support. Most commonly in ballet dancers, the pelvis tips excessively forward (anterior). This means the deep core and deep gluteal muscles are underused, which affects pelvic placement and stability on the standing leg. It results in overuse of the lower back muscles and hip flexors, which become tight and prone to injury. The gluteus maximus muscle also is underused, which means the dancer struggles to achieve good *arabesque* height, instead trying to achieve this by further overworking the lower back.

The dancer uses the lower back to *tendu derrière*, therefore loosing neutral pelvic placement, overusing the hip flexors on the standing leg and relaxing their deep core support. Dancer: Abbie Hollis.

The dancer uses the gluteus maximus to *tendu derrière* whilst maintaining neutral pelvic placement by engaging deep core support and deep gluteal engagement. Dancer: Abbie Hollis.

ESSENTIAL EXERCISE: FINDING YOUR NEUTRAL PELVIC PLACEMENT AND MUSCLE USE WITH TRANSFERS OF WEIGHT

1. Find neutral pelvic placement when standing with support on both legs in First Position, noting the engagement of the deep core and deep gluteal muscles.
2. Shift the weight on to one leg and note that deep core and standing leg deep gluteal engagement should increase to support a neutral pelvis. Repeat four times each side.
3. Experiment with several *tendus* and balances, keeping the above correct placement and muscle use. Rest and repeat the other side.

Technique Notes
- You can test if your deep gluteal muscles are engaged throughout by feeling for their contraction with your fingers in the side of the gluteal muscle
- Particularly watch out for a feeling of tightness or 'gripping' at the front of the hip, this probably means you are overusing your hip flexors
- Keep watching for dropping the tailbone and fairly level horizontal 'hip bones'
- This same feeling should apply to all work on one leg, including *tendus*, balances and *pirouettes*

STRENGTHENING YOUR GLUTEUS MAXIMUS FOR *ARABESQUE*

1. Standing in First Position or lying on your front, start by finding your neutral pelvis and deep core support.
2. Very slowly, reach one leg into a *tendu*, being careful not to tilt the pelvis forward too soon, but instead engage the gluteus maximus to create the movement. Repeat eight times, then swap sides.

Technique Notes
- Useful for dancers who overuse the hip flexors or tilt their pelvis forward during *tendu derriére*, as they will lack gluteal strength.
- Think quality not quantity; with correct technique, your movements may be small at first but don't worry, your strength will soon build.

Goal Two: Finding Your True Turnout and Using Your Deep Six Rotators

First, assess your turnout passively, with someone else moving you to see what range your bone structure allows. Do this by lying on your back and (with your knee bent at 90 degrees) having someone gently rotate each leg in turn outward, one at a time, taking note of your range on each side. After this, assess your active turnout. Standing in parallel, engage your muscles to create turnout yourself. Ideally do this with rotation disks (or by standing on socks!) to ensure you do not cheat and use the floor. Most dancers experience that their passive range is greater than their active range. This means they have the bone structure and muscle flexibility to achieve greater turnout but lack the strength to do so.

To create turnout, the deep six rotators pull the back of the thigh (femur) toward the back of the pelvis. This fan-shaped group of muscles is at the back of the body underneath the gluteus maximus and close to the bottom of the pelvis. Their action is supported by the inner thigh muscles (adductors), which wrap the thigh (femur) from back to front.

Building strength in the deep six rotator muscles will enable you to get your active turnout range closer to your passive one, whilst still maintaining a neutral pelvis. This is typically 120 degrees in normal healthy hips (60 degrees each side).

When it comes to finding higher leg movements, the deep six rotator muscles first act to create turn-out. Second, the deep hip flexor (iliopsoas) guides the femur bone down into the socket, dropping one end of the femur bone, so that the other lifts. These two anatomical details enable minimal shifting of

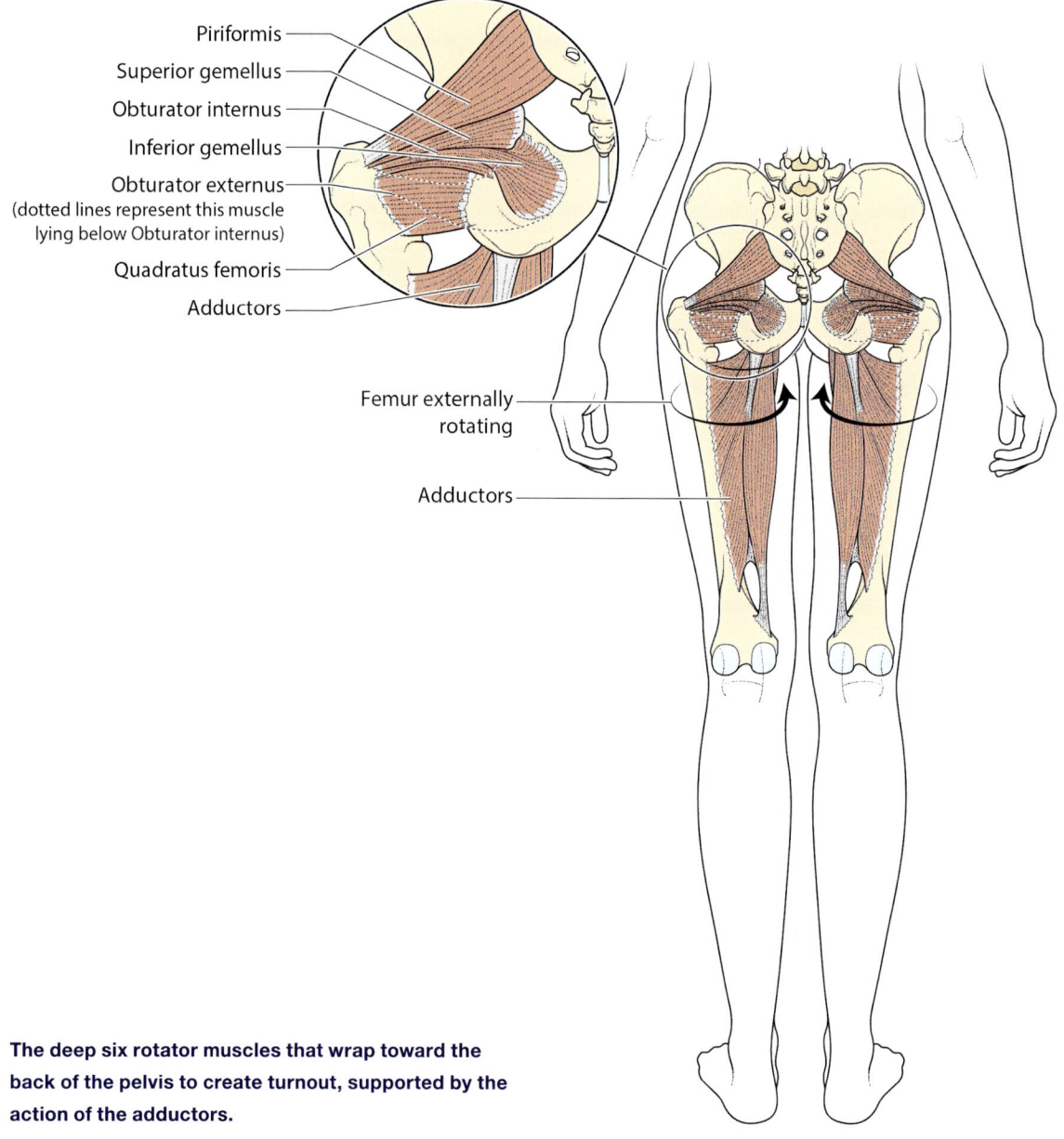

Piriformis
Superior gemellus
Obturator internus
Inferior gemellus
Obturator externus
(dotted lines represent this muscle
lying below Obturator internus)
Quadratus femoris
Adductors

Femur externally
rotating

Adductors

The deep six rotator muscles that wrap toward the back of the pelvis to create turnout, supported by the action of the adductors.

the pelvis and create freedom in the hip socket to enable higher leg movement. They also prevent restriction in the hip joint and the resulting 'hip clicking' and superficial hip flexor (rectus femoris) overuse that can often occur.

The most common pitfall is that dancers try to achieve turnout by other means – for example, one or a combination of:

- 'Arching' and tipping the pelvis forward (anterior tilt).
- Overusing the hip flexors at the front (most commonly the tensor fascia latae).
- Overusing the bigger gluteus maximus muscle, this actually inhibits the deep six rotators from firing.

ESSENTIAL EXERCISE: STRENGTHENING YOUR DEEP SIX ROTATORS

1. Begin lying on your side with your legs on the floor, knees bent at a 90-degree angle, feet underneath your pelvis. Try to find neutral posture and pelvic placement with the waist lifted away from the floor.
2. Pressing the heels gently together, open the top knee toward the ceiling, turning out the top leg, then close.
3. Repeat for eight to twelve sets. You can also hold open for five breaths. Repeat on the other side.

Technique Notes
- Keep the pelvis stable as you perform the exercise, noting your deep core support.
- Check that you are breathing in and out through the side and back of the ribcage.
- Other strengthening exercises include parallel and turnout *retirés* and work with sliding disks.
- You can add resistance to these exercises by using a flex band around the thighs and also investigate other variations.

- Hyperextending and misaligning the knees.
- Rolling in at the feet and ankles.

The impact is that these incorrect techniques lead to a dancer losing their neutral posture, resulting in tightness and overuse of the lower back and hip flexor muscles. This increases risk of muscle tension, strains, damage to vertebrae and hip impingement. It also means that the dancer cannot reach and support maximum turnout range, as they are not engaging the correct muscles, thereby limiting their technique and progression.

YOUR FOOT, ANKLE AND KNEE

The foot and ankle are made of twenty-six bones, which form a flexible yet strong arch structure. The knee joint forms where the upper (femur) and lower (tibia) leg bones meet. Unlike more enclosed ball-and-socket joints, such as the hip, the meeting of flatter bone surfaces leads to more open joint structures, requiring support from ligaments and muscles to retain joint position. This means that a dancer needs very precise alignment and to focus on muscle stability around these joints in order to have the strength to repeatedly support balances, jumps, *pirouettes* and pointework without injury.

Goal One: Finding Stability within Your Foot Arches and Ankle

When optimally aligned, your foot bones' unique arch structure provides enough strength to support your body weight, including landing from jumps (where up to ten times your body weight goes through your foot!).

When standing, your weight should be distributed evenly between three points of the foot:

- base of big toe
- base of little toe
- the heel

The arches between these three points are gently and continually lifted off the floor, using the numerous ligaments and muscles looped underneath the foot. Aim to find and maintain arch engagement at all times, as in shifting weight to the ball to go *en relevé* or *en pointe*. The three-point weight distribution should then be re-found each time your heels return to the floor.

The most common pitfall is that dancers 'roll in' or 'roll out'. This means that the arch is dropped and more weight goes to one part of the foot, as opposed to being evenly distributed. The impact is weakness in the ligament and muscle structures that support the arch. This can also affect further up the body; for example, causing the knee to roll in over the big toe.

Dancers are particularly prone to losing this arch and foot stability during preparation and landing for balances, jumps and *pirouettes*. As well as impacting on jump height and balance time, ankle injuries such as sprains are more likely due to 'going over' on the ankle.

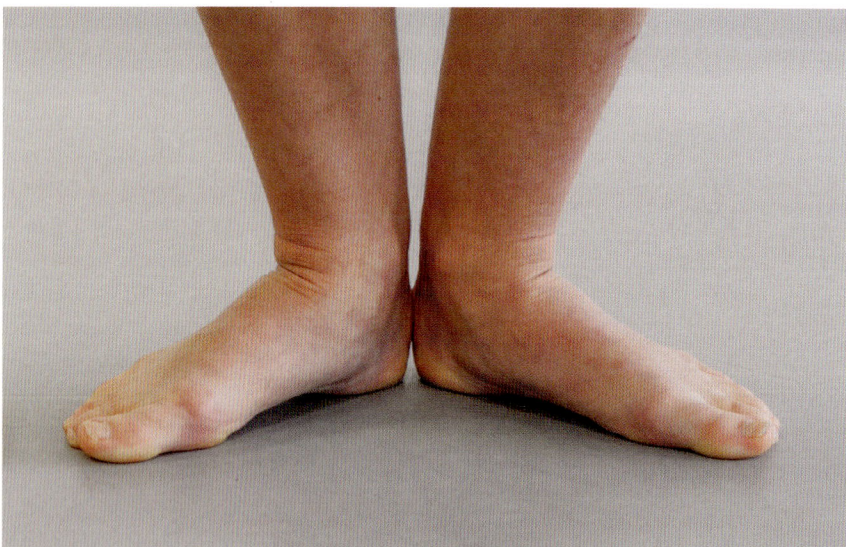

A dancer who is 'rolling in'. Dancer: Angela Wilson.

A dancer with even weight distribution and lifted arches. Dancer: Angela Wilson.

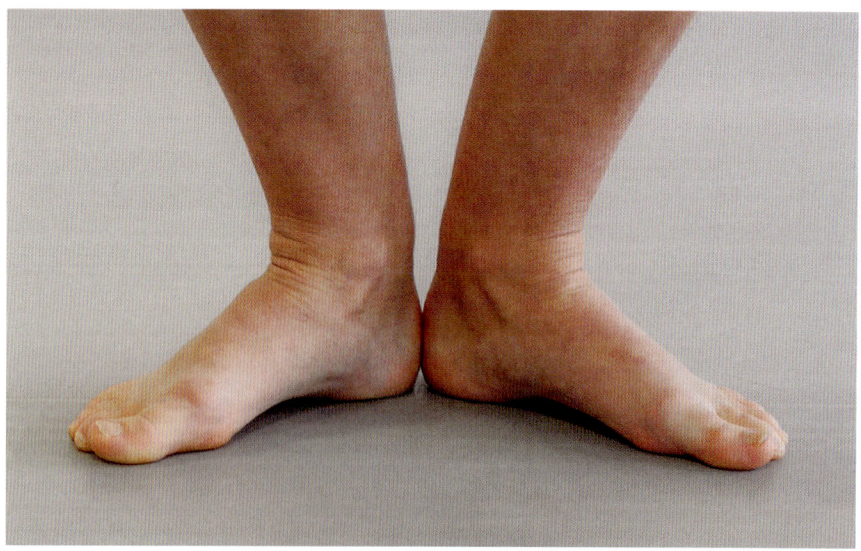

ESSENTIAL EXERCISE: CHECK YOUR WEIGHT DISTRIBUTION AND ARCH SUPPORT

1. Begin standing with your feet in parallel and a neutral posture.
2. Lift your toes to engage your arch and shift the weight until you feel it distributed evenly between the base of your big toe, base of your little toe and heel.
3. Now release your toes and note how the arch can also drop and disengage. Now repeat step 2, this time lowering your toes gently and keeping your arch engaged.

Technique Notes

- Take care not to hyper-extend the knee; keep a soft bend.
- Note what your habit is – do you usually 'roll in' or 'roll out'? While you teach yourself a new habit, it may feel strange to distribute the weight evenly, but it will pay off in the long run!
- Once you have mastered this you can repeat in First Position. You can also increase the difficulty by balancing on one leg, then even closing your eyes!

Goal Two: Tracking Alignment Correctly Through Standing, *Pliés* and *Relevés*

You can find and observe correct placement by very precisely lining up three key points on the lower leg and foot:

- The bony prominence on the shin, below the middle of the knee (tibial tuberosity).
- The muscle at the middle of the front of the ankle – found by lifting the toes (flexor hallucis longus).
- The gap between the second and third toes.

Aim to keep these vertically aligned during all movement, from standing in turnout to *pliés, relevés,* jumps and pointework. This enables the bones of the lower leg to align in a position that optimally supports weight-bearing and high-impact work. (*See* Foundations of Technique in Chapter 3).

The most common pitfall is that dancers misalign one or more of these three areas. This can happen due to a lack of awareness of the sensation of the correct placement, insufficient muscle strength or by forcing turnout at the feet or pelvis.

The impact if a dancer adopts this incorrect placement with jumps or balances is that they become prone to injuries such as ankle sprains, shin splints, knee dislocations and ligament damage. It will also affect the dancer's ability to hold balances, have strong pointework and achieve good jump height.

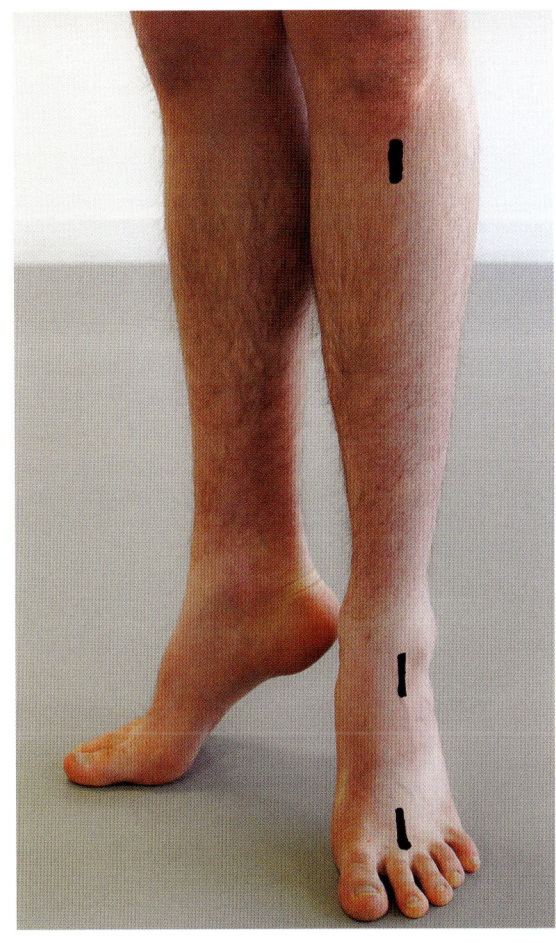

The dancer has aligned the lower leg and foot *en relevé.* **Dancer: Mark Coates.**

ESSENTIAL EXERCISE: SINGLE LEG *PLIÉS* AND *RELEVÉS*

1. Standing in parallel on one leg in front of a mirror, begin by checking your neutral posture. Second, your arch engagement and weight distribution.
2. Using the mirror, line up your three points:

   - boney shin prominence
   - middle of ankle
   - gap between the second and third toe

3. Now keep watching as you take controlled single leg *pliés*, only moving as far as you can maintain the alignment.
4. Now repeat the same for single leg rises.
5. Rest and repeat on the other side. Note the number and movement range of single leg *pliés* and rises you can do while maintaining perfect alignment. Then you can build the number of repetitions and range from there over time.

Technique Notes

- If you don't have a mirror you can use a friend or film yourself to help you check alignment.
- Drawing vertical lines on the three points can help you to line them up at the start and keep checking very closely all the way through.
- Beware of concentrating so much on the three points that you forget about your arch, weight distribution or neutral posture!

ESSENTIAL EXERCISE: STRENGTHENING YOUR ANKLES

1. Seated with a flex band around the ball of the foot, pull back on the band to create resistance. Flex and point the foot, pushing against the band. Do this for ten to twenty repetitions.
2. Next you can try pulling the band diagonally across your body to the opposite shoulder to your foot. Now press the foot to the outside against the resistance, strengthening the outside ankle muscles for ten to twenty repetitions.
3. Pull the band to the other diagonal, away from your body, and press the foot to the inside against the resistance for ten to twenty repetitions.

Technique Notes

- This is a great position for you to see if all three points (bony shin prominence, middle of ankle and second and third toe gaps) are lined up throughout.
- Watch for any small deviations in alignment and try to correct them; for example, you might see that halfway between pointing and flexing, your foot draws a slight arch inwards or outwards. Any habits you see here will be magnified during jumps, *pirouettes* and balances.
- When working diagonally with the band, be sure to stabilize the knee so that only the ankle moves.
- The tighter you pull the band, the harder the muscles have to work against the resistance.

SECTION 2: OUTSIDE THE STUDIO

INTRODUCTION

Whether you are training to be a professional dancer or studying dance as a hobby, the training is demanding and, therefore, your lifestyle needs to support the workload. This section aims to simplify lifestyle recommendations and provide you with some easy and manageable tips to:

- Identify important areas and key information for consideration in your day-to-day routine.
- Be equipped with information on where to seek further guidance or support.

SLEEP, REST AND RECOVERY

Many dancers are so passionate about their vocation that they are keen to take every opportunity to train, rehearse or perform. This can sometimes be difficult when juggling other commitments, such as family, work or school and a social life. Some dancers think that resting or taking a few days off can lead to poor performance, but research says quite the opposite! Rest is a necessary tool for optimal performance, so you shouldn't be waiting until you feel tired to take a break. It is fundamentally important that you schedule rest periods throughout the week and consider how much training you are doing in the lead up to important events, such as performances or exams. If a dancer does not allow for rest and recovery, this often leads to injury and burnout, which can leave you feeling fatigued, demotivated, irritable and with an irregular appetite. Let's take a look at how you could improve your rest and recovery…

Sleep

The quantity and quality of good sleep is vital for a dancer. Individuals aged fourteen to seventeen are advised to have 8–10 hours of sleep per night and those over the age of eighteen are recommended 7–9 hours. This may require going to bed slightly earlier or having everything prepared the night before so that you can wake up later. A lack of sleep can lead you to feeling fatigued during the day, being forgetful or finding it hard to remember sequences in class or choreography, learnt the previous day. You may also become irritable and see a change in your appetite.

In terms of quality, you should ideally find it easy to go to sleep once you get into bed and be sleeping throughout the night. A sign of a good night's sleep is to wake up feeling refreshed. Sleeping well is a skill, so it is important to develop a good routine and keep refining it over time.

TOP TIPS FOR GETTING GOOD-QUALITY SLEEP

- Reduce the amount of noise and light, perhaps having a pair of earplugs ready if you live in shared accommodation or on a busy road.
- Avoid technology use at least one hour before bed and utilize the 'night mode' feature that is on most devices to reduce the blue-light exposure. Alternatively, consider activities like reading, journal writing or doing breathing exercises during this time.
- Get comfortable. Where possible, have a comfortable mattress or topper, supportive pillows and a duvet that is the appropriate thickness.
- Avoid caffeine after midday.

If you experience issues with sleep, such as difficulty falling asleep or waking up lots during the night, that continue for a prolonged period of time, speak to your GP for advice.

Rest and Recovery

It is important to see rest as a vital component of your training and to value it just as much as flexibility or technique. Rest and recovery should be considered on a short-term (daily or weekly) basis and also on a long-term (monthly or yearly) basis, to allow you to achieve optimal physical and psychological potential. This type of planning is often referred to as periodization and it is starting to be used more frequently by the (vocational and professional) dance community. You may find it useful to plan out the weeks leading up to an important event and consider:

- Having at least one, but ideally two, days a week of complete rest or light active rest.
- Spreading your physical activity throughout the week.
- Leaving 48 hours between strength training on a particular body part.
- Including something called 'tapering', where you gradually decrease the amount of physical activity you are doing during the two weeks prior to the event you are working toward. For example:

    - Fewer classes or training sessions.
    - Shorter or less intense training sessions.

For further advice on this, seek the support of an accredited strength and conditioning coach.

SUPPLEMENTARY TRAINING

Surprisingly, numerous researchers have identified that technique classes and rehearsals are not enough to prepare you for the physical demands of performance. This means that you will need to carefully plan your time throughout the week to do additional fitness training, scheduling these sessions around your rest days. There are many fitness components that are important for a dancer, but two that are vital to work on outside of classes are cardiovascular fitness and strength.

Cardiovascular Fitness

Improving cardiovascular fitness allows you to perform choreography with more ease and so focus on the artistry. It can enable you to have more stamina for longer pieces or exert more power during quick, short sequences and to have better recovery

between classes or performances. The two cardiovascular systems that you will need to train are:

- The aerobic system, which will support you over a longer period for moderate or low intensity activities, e.g. *adage.*
- The anaerobic system, which will support you over a short period for big bursts of energy, e.g. *grand allegro.*

Including cardiovascular training in your weekly routine does not have to be time-consuming. You have a variety of options, including swimming, running, cycling, high-intensity interval training (HIIT) or the cross-trainer.

TOP TIPS FOR INCLUDING CARDIOVASCULAR TRAINING IN YOUR ROUTINE

- Aim for two to three sessions a week. Start with shorter sessions and increase over time.
- Ideally one aerobic (20–40 minutes) and one anaerobic (10–30 minutes) plus one more, depending on the demands of your repertoire, e.g. if your choreography is a long piece of moderate intensity, you would add in an extra aerobic session.
- Spread the sessions throughout the week.

Strength

Strength training is important not only for supporting good posture, but also for maintaining and increasing bone mineral density, and improving elevation in partnering. Female dancers, for example, are now often required to lift other dancers and to do floorwork. Strength training can take many forms and a session might include body weight exercises, resistance bands, weight machines or free weights. If you are new to strength training, you should ideally work with a Pilates' instructor. If you wish to incorporate free weight and machine-based exercises, in addition to body weight exercises, you should seek the support of an accredited strength and conditioning coach before training independently. This will enable you to focus on exercises that are appropriate for your goals and physique, alongside developing good technique.

TOP TIPS FOR INTEGRATING STRENGTH TRAINING INTO YOUR ROUTINE

- Aim for two to four sessions (30–45 minutes each), spread out across the week.
- Aim to maintain whole-body strength but focus attention on improving strength in certain areas that will encounter higher demand from any upcoming choreography

PSYCHOLOGICAL SKILLS

Working on the physical aspects of your training is only addressing half of the puzzle. Mental health should be valued just as highly as physical health to achieve positive wellbeing and optimal performance. Developing your mental health strategies should be a continuous effort, rather than only addressing it if issues arise. In this section, we will explore some of the more common psychological concerns that dancers experience and some coping strategies to integrate into your routine to strengthen your mental health.

Common Psychological Concerns

It is common to have days when you don't feel yourself, when you feel sad, anxious or irritated. It

Dancer: Laura Bratek.

is normal because our emotions fluctuate, depending on the circumstances we are facing. However, it is important to be able to regulate emotions and to process them, rather than allowing an emotion to linger. If you are finding it difficult to manage your emotions or you feel you are constantly in a low mood or the thoughts you are having concern you, a GP or a counsellor can support you.

A number of things can take their toll and allow psychological concerns to accumulate; for example, the pressures to achieve elite performance, the limited opportunities for taking a substantial break during the year and the expectation to embody an aesthetic that pleases a teacher or a choreographer. Some commonly occurring concerns are:

- Perfectionism: sometimes the pressure to achieve excellence can result in you raising your standards too high and only expecting perfection. You may experience this if you often compare yourself to others or when receiving a lot of constructive or critical feedback with a lack of praise. This can result in feeling dissatisfied with your achievements, leading to overtraining and possible burnout.
- Negative body image: the frequent exposure to mirrors, accompanied by the close-fitted clothing and continuous feedback about the way your body is moving could promote critical thinking about your body. This may result in a negative and often distorted opinion of your own body shape or capabilities, and encourage you to try to change areas of your body when it is not necessary.
- Anxiety: dancers are expected to be versatile, so your timetable will be populated with numerous exciting classes that leave little time for rest or reflection. In addition, you may have many other commitments to juggle, whether academic studies, a job, family or social life. A busy timetable with multiple commitments coupled with high expectations could enhance feelings of anxiety or, in more acute circumstances, a panic attack.
- Negative self-talk: this often presents as numerous and reoccurring thoughts that can be critical, belittling or demotivating about oneself. You may

experience this if you have a lack of praise or a negative training environment. It may also occur if you have negative perfectionistic tendencies, as your high standards may lead to you feeling like you are failing or not reaching your goals.

MEETING A MENTAL HEALTH PROFESSIONAL

If you feel concerned about your mental health, it is important to seek advice from your GP or a counsellor. Before meeting with them you could prepare for the appointment by:

- Talking to a friend or family member first to practice sharing it with someone more familiar.
- Write down your main concerns and how they are affecting you.
- Ask a friend or family member to come with you.

On the other hand, sometimes people may want to share their problems with you. In these situations, it is important to be a good listener, whilst also setting up healthy boundaries to protect yourself. Ensure you do not take on too much when helping someone else.

SUPPORT FOR MENTAL HEALTH

If you are concerned about yourself, someone else or feel overwhelmed supporting them, you may wish to disclose and seek support from:

- your school or college safeguarding lead
- someone impartial and supportive whom you trust
- NHS 111 (UK)
- Samaritans 116 123 (UK)

If your life or someone you care about is in danger, call 999 immediately.

Coping Strategies

Coping strategies are a set of psychological skills that you can practice regularly and utilize to improve your mental health. You can also use them during challenging situations to help you regulate your emotions. These skills should feature as frequently in your routine as stretching and fitness; your mental health is something you should always be evaluating and positively addressing. Similar to the body, the brain also needs to take time to warm up prior to activities, to be strengthened and conditioned, and to cool down after stressful or demanding days.

PRACTICAL COPING STRATEGIES

Try to integrate these strategies into your routine one at a time. This will allow you to form a habit and stick with it.

- Practice positive self-talk: phrases such as 'I can't do this', could become 'I'm going to give this a try' or 'I'm working toward this'. This means that when you have a challenging situation, your internal monologue can be rationale and supportive, rather than negative and destructive.
- Try goal-setting: often people will refer to 'SMART' goal-setting, which means creating a goal that is Specific, Measurable, Achievable, Realistic and Timely. This strategy helps you to set goals that boost your motivation and sense of achievement.
- Write in a journal: this can be a good outlet for any thoughts you have had that day, positive or negative, and can be written daily or sporadically as you see fit. As a private activity you can be honest, which may sometimes be easier than if it were a conversation.
- Mindfulness: take time to have moments of calm where you focus and reflect on what has happened that day. There are lots of apps that can help you with this, such as *Headspace*.
- Breathing work: practicing different breathing activities, such as those found in yoga or mindfulness apps, can help to reduce the feeling or accumulation of stress and anxiety.

To get more specific guidance on coping strategies, arrange an appointment with a counsellor or a psychologist.

Dancer: Daisy Bishop.

WARMING UP AND COOLING DOWN

A good warm-up focusses the mind for the upcoming activity, increases blood flow to the muscles, restores range of movement and primes the nervous system. A cool-down is an opportunity to increase flexibility, promote an efficient recovery and reflect on the activity to set goals for the next day. However, many dancers tend to rush a warm-up and forget about a cool-down altogether because they have a busy schedule and need to dash off to their next class.

WARM-UP AND COOL-DOWN – ESSENTIAL GUIDELINES

- The full warm-up or cool-down should be done at the beginning or end of the day, or if you have a long break between classes or performances.
- If you have a small gap between classes (45 minutes or less) focus on dynamic stretching of the muscles that were used heavily during that class and add more layers of clothing to maintain your body temperature. When arriving at your next class, do a shorter version of stage 1 and 2 outlined below (5 minutes each), before focusing on stage 3.
- Dynamic stretching is a moving stretch in which you do not hold a position, e.g. leg swings.
- Ballistic stretching should be small, slow, controlled bouncing (barely visible movement), e.g. a bouncing lunge.
- Static stretching is holding a position, typically for 30 seconds and never for more than 90 seconds, e.g. side-bend.
- PNF (Proprioceptive Neuromuscular Facilitation) stretching is often done whilst resisting a partner but should be done carefully and correct posture should be maintained, e.g. hamstring stretch.
- Avoid static stretching in a warm-up, as some research suggests it may decrease muscular power.

Warm-Up

A warm-up should last about 20–30 minutes and include:

- Stage 1: 10–15 minutes of pulse-raising activity, e.g. jogging, star jumps, burpees.
- Stage 2: 5–10 minutes of moving stretches, e.g. dynamic or ballistic stretching.
- Stage 3: 5–10 minutes of preparation that is specific to your class or performance. This typically involves some strength and balance exercises, along with some basic technical preparation, e.g. before a ballet class you may do some core and turnout muscle activation, with some single leg balancing and pirouette preparation exercises.

Quite often dancers find themselves short of time due to a busy schedule; although it's not an ideal training structure, it is often the reality. On occasions where you are not able to follow the guidelines above, you could save some time and instead use your commute to the studio as your pulse-raiser (perhaps by jogging, cycling or a quick-paced walk).

Cool-Down

A cool-down should last about 20 minutes and include:

- Stage 1: 10 minutes of activity to gradually decrease the heart rate, e.g. jogging into walking into roll downs.
- Stage 2: 10 minutes of static or PNF stretching.

If you need any support or guidance with your warm-up or cool-down routine, ask your dance teacher.

NUTRITION

Food is important for fuelling your dance activity, but it should also be something that is enjoyed. The language you use to discuss food is also important. For example, rather than labelling food as 'good' and 'bad', or 'healthy' and 'unhealthy', we should aim to move away from these phrases by thinking along the lines of 'more nutritious' and 'less nutritious'. All food will provide us with fuel (calories), but some will provide us with more nutrients than others. Incorporating a wide range of foods within your diet will ensure your body receives the vitamins and minerals it requires. IADMS' recommendations for a dancer to include in their daily diet are shown in the accompanying illustration.

You can adjust this to take into account your individual needs. For example, if you have a very active day, you could increase the amount of carbohydrates, or if you are doing strength training and want to support muscle growth, you could increase the amount of protein. It is important not to eliminate any food groups, but rather to adjust the percentages sensibly.

All vitamins and minerals are important; however, research recommends that dancers should focus on the following to support training and recovery:

- Vitamin D due to the lack of sunlight exposure
- Magnesium to help with muscle recovery
- Vitamin C to support immune health
- Cod liver oil to assist with memory
- Vitamin B12 if you are vegan or vegetarian, as this is only available from animal sources

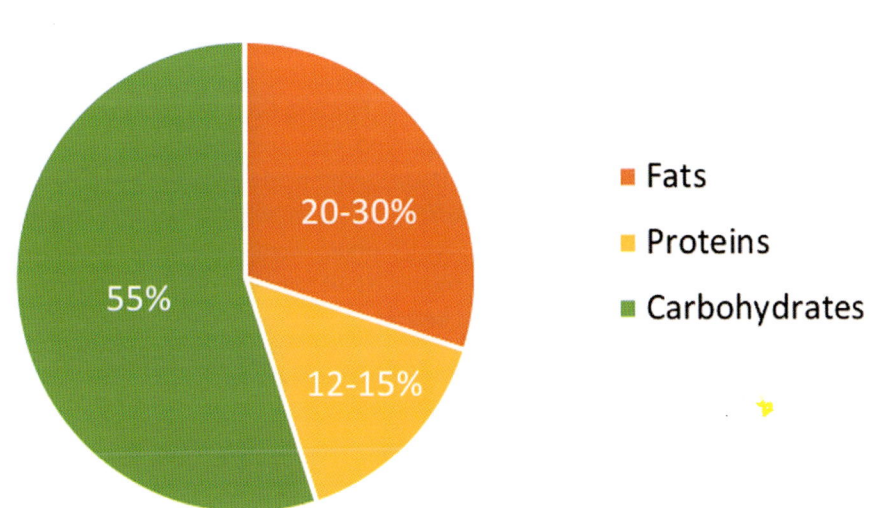

The recommended macronutrient split for carbohydrate, fat and protein from IADMS.

It is advised to seek these micronutrients from real food sources rather than supplements, but if you are unsure, then you should discuss this with a dietician. If you have any concerns about deficiencies, speak with your GP.

The body develops a lot of inflammation during exercise or injury; therefore, it has been proposed that anti-inflammatory foods can assist an efficient recovery. It can be helpful to include a selection of these foods throughout the day, these include (but are not limited to):

- tomatoes
- walnuts
- almonds
- olive oil
- tuna
- salmon
- cherries
- blueberries

How Much and How Often?

In order for you to be able to work out how much you need to eat, you need to be able to quantify how much energy you are expending each day. See this like a set of scales: the energy intake should match the energy expenditure. Eating too little throughout the week can lead to lack of focus, reduced recovery and fatigue. Anita Bean's *Sports Nutrition* book includes a simple way to work out your daily energy (calorie) requirements. In addition, you could use the IADMS nutrition resource paper available for free on their website.

Remember that this is an estimate and there may be some trial and error where you may need to eat slightly more or less to suit your energy requirements. If you need support with working out how much you need to eat or feel concerned that you may be becoming too fixated on the number of calories you are eating per day, speak to a dietician or your GP.

Once you know how much you need to eat, the next big question is how often should you be eating? There is no consensus whether it is better to eat little and often or have three main meals, but it is important you eat enough to fuel yourself for the day. Therefore, experiment with both and decide what works best for you.

TOP TIPS FOR PLANNING YOUR NUTRITION

- Aim to have your larger meals at least 2 hours before a class or performance.
- Have a snack or smaller meal 30 minutes before a class or performance.
- If you have finished an activity and will be active again within the next 6 hours, aim to eat within 45 minutes of finishing your activity, to allow your body enough time to replenish.
- Adapt your food planning around your schedule to avoid under-eating.
- Hydrate before, during and after activity.
- If you finish a class or performance late at night, aim to still include an evening meal but something that will be easier to digest, as you will be going to bed soon after.

Finding Reliable Information

It can sometimes feel difficult to find the right information when you are investigating nutrition. It is an evolving area of research and there are many conflicting views about what is required. It is recommended that you avoid seeking nutrition advice from magazines, social media, teachers or friends. Some more reliable sources of information would be:

- a dance-specialist dietician or nutritionist
- One Dance UK
- IADMS
- a book called *Nutrition for the Dancer* by Zerlina Mastin (Dance Books, 2009)

INJURY

Injury is something that the majority of dancers will encounter. While you cannot prevent injury altogether, you can learn to manage and reduce the risk.

Dance is a very demanding and challenging activity; therefore, it is to be expected that injury may occur due either to overuse or to a traumatic incident. However, an injury experience does not have to be a negative one. It can be an opportunity to reflect, understand your body and learn more about yourself.

Common Injuries

The most common injuries ballet dancers experience are in the foot, ankle, knee, hip and lower back. This is because these areas are used the most during training and, therefore, are more susceptible to injury. Some common injuries include:

- Posterior ankle impingement: a deep pain at the back of the ankle due to spending so much time on *demi pointe* or *en pointe*. The pain can build up over time.
- Lateral ankle sprain: when the ankle rolls outwards and the ligaments, tendons and sometimes bone on the outside of the ankle are damaged. This is usually caused by accidents such as tripping, falling or landing awkwardly.
- Shin splints: soreness or tenderness along the front of the shin, usually caused by poor technique, overtraining, calf tightness or lack of lower leg strength.
- Knee dislocation: your patella (knee cap) comes out of place, usually after landing awkwardly or receiving impact to the knee.
- Hamstring strain: the muscle fibres in the hamstring become damaged due to overstretching, often referred to as a pull or a tear.
- Labral tear: the ligament in the hip socket becomes damaged, usually caused by frequent high leg extensions with poor alignment or overuse.
- Pars defect: a fracture to the vertebrae causing sharp back pain, usually due to poor bone health alongside poor posture and repeated jumping or back-bending/arabesque.

It is vital to address injuries using a qualified and experienced practitioner to assist you with full recovery.

Addressing Early Warning Signs

Many of the injuries listed here could be avoided with early treatment and intervention.

MANAGING MINOR INJURY

In some cases, it may be appropriate for you to manage any aches or niggles yourself by:

- Adjusting your participation in class, e.g. stopping before jumps or doing a flat barre and centre.
- Reducing the number of classes you do in a week.
- Warming up and cooling down.
- Applying ice to any excessive swelling or for pain management.
- Getting a massage or applying self-massage to reduce any tension.
- Taping or strapping, if you know how to.

If you have an ache or niggle and you have tried the above but there is no improvement after 7 days, book in to see a physiotherapist to get some advice. You may need to seek support sooner if you have:

- sharp, shooting pains
- numbness or constant pins and needles
- loss of normal function or control of your limbs
- pain that disturbs your sleep
- any other symptoms that concern you

Finding the Right Practitioner

There are many different healthcare practitioners but working with a dance-specialist or, at the very least, sports and exercise specialist, can make the difference between having a successful recovery or an injury that continues to niggle and reoccur. When working with a practitioner you should view this as a partnership: the two of you working together and communicating openly. It is also important for you to share information between your dance teacher and your practitioner, to make sure everyone involved in your treatment is aware of your progress and working together.

THINGS TO ASK AND NOTE DOWN AT APPOINTMENTS

- Usually, how long does an injury like this take to heal?
- What do you hypothesize this injury to be?
- What classes can I do? Are there any I should avoid for the moment? (Bring your timetable.)
- What movements should I avoid? (Be prepared to demonstrate, explain or show videos.)
- What exercises should I be doing and how often?
- Are there any other strategies I could be incorporating, e.g. ice, heat, compression, taping?

Dancer: Regan Wilson.

Treatment can be expensive! It is good to see someone at least every six weeks for maintenance but if you have an injury, you may need to see them on a weekly basis. It is important to consider this within your budgeting and you may wish to purchase a health cash plan or private health insurance to help you cover the cost. Contact One Dance UK for further advice. If you cannot afford private health insurance and you wish to use NHS services, there are NHS Dance Injury clinics in London, Birmingham and Bath. This is a free dance-specialist service via the NHS and your GP can refer you. Visit the NIDMS website before your GP appointment.

Finally, it is important to not only find the right practitioner, but also to remain safe when attending a treatment session:

- Ensure your therapist is registered with either a professional association or a governing body. Note: all UK physiotherapists should be registered with the Chartered Society of Physiotherapists. Ask them who they are registered with and then check the directory on the relevant website.
- Use recommendations from trusted teachers, friends and peers.
- Tell someone the address of where you are going and what time you expect to be finished.
- If you feel unsafe or uncomfortable at any point during the treatment, do not be afraid to speak up, leave the location and call a friend or family member.

Recommended professional associations and governing bodies in the UK:

- One Dance UK – Healthcare Practitioners Directory

- British Association of Performing Arts Medicine (BAPAM) Directory of Practitioners
- The Sports Massage Association
- General Osteopathic Council
- The Chartered Society of Physiotherapy
- Sports and Exercise Nutrition Register
- UK Strength and Conditioning Association
- General Chiropractic Council
- Health Care Professionals Council

CONCLUSION

Throughout this chapter we have explored some of the key lifestyle considerations for a dancer in training that are equally applicable to professionals. The discussion has consistently highlighted two takeaway points:

- These are practices and habits that need to be implemented gradually and consistently.
- Our mental and physical health hold equal importance and we should share our time evenly when working on both areas of our well-being

During each section we have signposted you to different practitioners or organizations that can support your further with each topic. A summarized list of these resources has been highlighted below.

FURTHER RESOURCES

The following is a summary of recommended books to help you find what is most useful for your needs and interests:

Dance Medicine in Practice by Liane Simmel (Routledge 2014)	A complete guide, aimed at dancers and including deep core engagement, relaxing the lower back and scoliosis, shoulder placement strengthening, placement and muscle use during turn-out and high leg extensions *à la seconde*, alignment, pointework and depth of *plié*. Specific chapters focus on the spine, pelvis, hips, knees, feet, shoulder and arms. Each chapter includes diagrams, anatomy, pitfalls and how to avoid them, injury prevention tips, exercises and checklists for best dance technique.
Conditioning for Dancers by Tom Welsh (University Press of Florida 2009)	For dancers who want to take an active role in directing their own training and development. Comprehensive but concise. Focuses on avoiding injury, improving fitness, strength and flexibility, nutrition, and warm-up and cool-down. Includes a detailed catalogue of thirty exercises, including hip strengthening and stretching.
Anatomy, Dance Technique and Injury Prevention by Justin Howse and Moira McCormack (A&C Black 2009)	Takes an extensive look at anatomy and physiology before turning to injury prevention, causes, types and treatment. Also addresses adolescence and issues that dancers face, such as hypermobility, joint health, scoliosis, turnout and hip tension. Includes an extensive section on strengthening exercises, including pointework and foot injuries.

continued

Dynamic Alignment for Imagery by Eric Franklin (Human Kinetics 2012)	How to use image, touch and movement exercises to improve your coordination and alignment. Focus on relieving tension, enhancing the health of your spine and back, and preventing back injuries. Includes somatic techniques and imagery for finding neutral posture, placement.
Dance Science: Anatomy, Movement Analysis and Conditioning by Gayanne Grossman (Princeton Book Company 2015)	Takes a positive approach showing what a dancer can do to dance better, therefore, decreasing injury. The three sections provide a dance-specific, practical, hands-on approach to exercise for enhanced performance. Also a useful section on breathing.
IADMS Dance Teachers Bulletin (online, free)	Listed under the publications section of the website. Many short and very readable articles. Topics covered include conditioning for greater leg extension, supplemental training, pointework and turnout.

The following all have useful websites, and many have social media accounts, with lots of interesting content. These organizations tend to not repeat a resource that another organization has already published, so take your time to explore the many things each one has to offer:

National Institute of Dance Medicine and Science	Research and education Advice and information about healthcare NHS dance injury clinic information
One Dance UK – Healthier Dancer programme	Talks, events and conferences Advice, research and industry standards Health cash plan – Performance Optimization Package (POP) Healthcare practitioner's directory
British Association of Performing Arts Medicine (BAPAM)	Free initial appointment Online directory of healthcare practitioners Health advice and resources Events, education and training
Dance USA	Events and conferences Information sheets (free) Screening guidelines Advice, advocacy and industry standards
AusDance	Safe Dance factsheets (free)

International Association of Dance Medicine and Science (IADMS)	Resources IADMS Bulletin for Dancers and Teachers (free) Events and conferences Journal of Dance Medicine and Science (members only)
Healthy Dancer Canada	Conferences and workshops Resources for dancers (free)
Dance Science degrees	Trinity Laban Conservatoire of Music and Dance University of Bedfordshire University of Chichester University of Edinburgh University of Wolverhampton

Izabela Milewska and Paweł Koncewoj in *Century Rolls* (2012) by Ashley Page for Polish National Ballet.

CHAPTER 7

THE BALLET CHOREOGRAPHER'S CRAFT
Jennifer Jackson

Choreographers are the people who make the ballets for dancers to perform. They are integral to the development of our art form, expanding the vocabulary, the aesthetic and the forms that performance takes – now and into the future.

A glimpse at history tells us that the boundaries between practices and the contexts for showing choreographies are always shifting. When Feuillet was notating court dances in seventeenth-century France, choreography was seen as 'an arrangement of steps shared amongst a community of practitioners'.[69] The eighteenth-century dancing master was the person who both devised and taught the choreography as it moved between theatre and social settings. The nineteenth-century 'classics' were created under imperial and state patronage. By the twentieth century, the choreographer was seen as a modern artist, an individual creator and author of his or her own work. Today many choreographers make and attribute work 'in collaboration with the dancers'. We talk about dance-making in terms of architecture in space and time, movement material and relationships between choreographic objects. You are as likely to see dance performance in a gallery or a shopping mall as on a conventional stage.

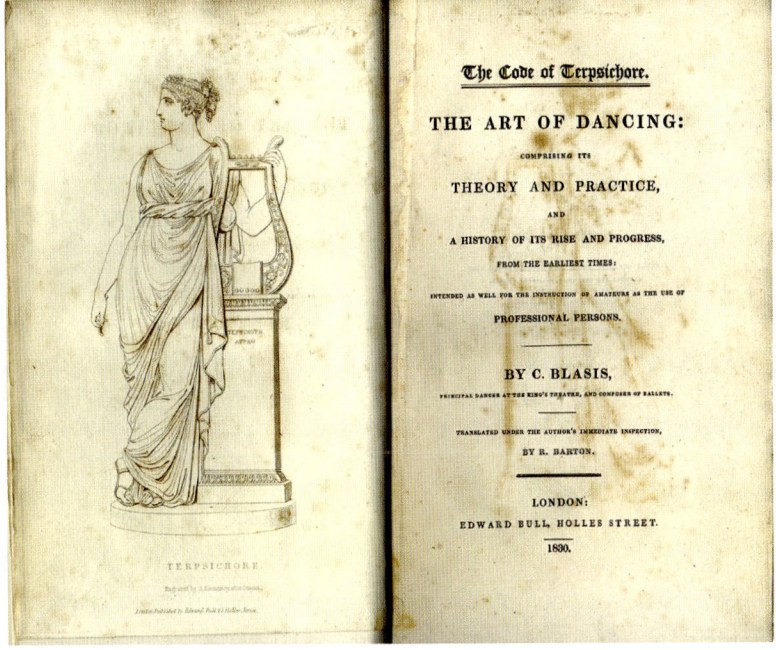

The title page of *The Code of Terpsichore* (published London: 1828 and 1830) by Carlo Blasis. Note the implicit fluidity between the roles of teacher, dancer and 'composer of ballets'.

Many ballet choreographers are also dancers. As far back as Marie Sallé, people have connected the impulse to dance and to make dances, drawing on the ballet tradition for their particular expression. The great pedagogue Carlo Blasis included material on 'The Composition of Ballets' in his writing. Choreographers such as Balanchine, Bournonville and de Valois were also teachers and their legacies are interwoven with ballet schooling. Today, choreographic study forms part of most vocational and academic dance courses. In 1926, the founder of The Royal Ballet, de Valois, called her school, The Academy of Choreographic Art; so at the beginning, choreography was at the heart of study at the Royal Ballet School. From 1999 to 2016, I worked there with Kate Flatt[70] to deliver a course of choreographic study, helping to forge some of the material for her book on choreographing dance for performance.

CHOREOGRAPHIC STUDY IN VOCATIONAL COURSES

But there are questions. You may be on track for a successful career as a ballet dancer. Why study choreography? Can choreography be taught? You might be able to teach someone how to write a dance, but does that make a choreographer? And many people say 'choreographers are born, not made'. Think for a moment... we might say that of *any* artist; the spark or desire to create is already there and unique to each person, but it needs to be ignited and shaped. Your own well of creativity may find its expression in many ways, including in choreography and your personal exploration of ballet as a performing art.

A course of study will not 'produce' a choreographer – neither will reading this chapter! But we can explore aspects of choreographic craft, as well as practical tools and frameworks for understanding what goes into creating dance; we can stimulate creative thinking and action around the elements, nurture confidence in the dance artist's creativity and provoke questions that will help you to think from the perspective of the choreographer. How do

I start? What is a dance made out of? Is there a craft I can practise? What skills and qualities do I need? How can my ballet training help me to make dances? How do I find and develop my artistic voice?

CHOREOGRAPHY AND CREATIVITY

Creativity in dance is most often a social endeavour and the inspired choreographer and dancers are mutually interdependent, perhaps more so than in any other art form. Arguably then, choreography should be intrinsic to all dance training.[71]

Choreographic study offers another perspective. It engages dancers in considering meaning and intention; this also relates to their growth as interpreters. It requires your 'serious play' within limitations, your choices and discernment. Choreographic and analytic tools can help you as a ballet dancer mature in your practice, and explore where you might lean into or away from tradition, to develop playful, combative, joyful relations with the form.[72]

SOURCES

This chapter draws on resources from my experience delivering choreographic courses and on interviews conducted in 2019 with six choreographers at different stages of their careers. These choreographers have been hugely generous in sharing their ideas about working practices, creating with ballet in different settings and what it is like to be the choreographer. The writing is structured so that their 'voices' take you, the reader, on the journey from getting started, through developing and refining the material in the studio, to finding a platform to show your choreography. If you are making your first dances, or you are already on the path of building a choreographic career, you can learn from their stories, their thinking, their

Ashley Page in rehearsal for *Century Rolls* (2012), Polish National Ballet.

processes and struggles to find a voice. You will also see the names of many other choreographers referenced as you read. Be curious about all these artists; research their work and consider their influence on the art form.

The choreographers (as they appear in the text) are:

Ashley Page, former director of Scottish Ballet, choreographs and directs internationally for ballet and contemporary companies, vocational schools, opera, musical theatre.

Cathy Marston, former director of Bern Ballett, choreographs internationally for ballet and contemporary companies.

Andrew McNicol, choreographs ballet internationally and founder of McNicol Collective.

Morgann Runacre Temple, filmmaker and choreographs for ballet companies and contemporary projects.

Georgie Rose, dancer, The Norwegian National Ballet, choreographs projects independently.

Aakash Odedra, Kathak dancer and choreographs for contemporary Kathak projects.

GETTING STARTED

The impulse to make dances and the inspiration and drive to continue is different for everyone.

Ashley Page was already dancing professionally with The Royal Ballet and featured in work by choreographers, including Kenneth MacMillan, Frederick Ashton and Glen Tetley, when he began making pieces. 'Kenneth [MacMillan] was a choreographer who invited you in to contribute a lot, so I started to feel: I'm making a lot of movement and maybe I should have a go at this'. But it was by chance that Ashley saw a television programme featuring contemporary choreographer, Richard Alston. It revealed vital aspects of craft that really fired his imagination: 'Listening to him opened up a whole new way of thinking. I'd never heard anyone talk about dance like that before, the whole thing about structure and form. I'd never really thought in those terms.... Before, in [my] early pieces, it was just about making movement, and trying to grapple after some sort of personal language'. So Ashley's journey of watching, analysing and influences began – and a life-long artistic friendship with Alston, who became a mentor and commissioned the early works which put him on the map.

Cathy Marston's journey also began as a dancer but choreography engaged her in a richer dynamic relationship with ballet. She had participated in choreographies at summer school and 'loved it'. Then, on joining The Royal Ballet School, her involvement in choreographic studies offered creative release that she didn't find in the 'regime' of daily technique class.

Andrew McNicol experienced a similar 'sense of freedom from the intensity of strict ballet training: choreography was a way to feel like I was breaking some rules'. Well before he knew what choreography was, Andrew was creating shows in the family garage with costumes, dance, music and sets – out of old wood. He 'fell in love with theatre and everything that makes it happen'.

Morgann Runacre Temple also started young. She was aged six or seven when she and her sister put on performances for her mum in the living room. She continued at secondary school and then, at vocational school, made dances with other trained

Morgann Runacre Temple in rehearsal with Demi Aldred (foreground).

dancers for the first time. She found inner motivation early: 'I was encouraged by the fact that, from a really young age, I found it the most fun thing that I could do. I remember taking it very seriously even when I was quite young.'

WHERE DOES AN IDEA FOR A DANCE COME FROM?

Choreography is about making decisions – or about objects placed in relation to each other so that that whole exceeds the sum of the parts – or about a continuity of connection between materials...[73]
Jonathan Burrows

The starting point for a dance can come from anywhere – a piece of music, an image, a text, a theory, movement research – and it's likely to link to an idea, experience or feeling that you personally want to find expression for and to communicate. This personal aspect is powerful and especially important for most makers.

Although young choreographer, Georgie Rose, acknowledges the joy she feels in developing the artistry to dance ballets that already exist, she says that 'creating was always the true method of expressing myself... In choreographing for me there is freedom, there is no right or wrong if it comes from something sincere in me. Of course it can be disliked but if its origin was honest, I'm at peace with my creation. This concept – my haven'.

Aakesh Odedra who trained in another classical dance form, South Asian Kathak dance, has also choreographed with ballet dancers. Beginning to make dances satisfied his desire to communicate. 'It was a way for me to be able to connect to people and allow my inner thoughts to externalize and convey a message that enables the external world to connect with the internal world'.

Consider the Context

Who are you working with and where is your work going to be seen? Often the context in which you are choreographing helps determine what you decide to do. The setting can be the element that

Final-year students in *Meadowdown* (2019) by Ashley Page for Images Ballet Company, London Studio Centre.

defines what music or dancers or story you choose as the focus. The performance 'event' will frame your dance and be part of the imaginative scope in which it is received. Place it in a particular space in the mind's eye. Be realistic about what you can achieve with the available resources, but parameters such as limited time, a given theme, making for an unusual space or to showcase a particular group of people, provide focus for your creative juices. After an intense period with little space between high-profile, well-resourced projects, Ashley made *Meadowdown* (2019) on a small budget for a specific number and gender of vocational dancers. He said 'that's quite good for you in a way, to solve this problem and make something interesting out of it'.

FIRST STEPS IN THE PROCESS

You have established the idea. The type of research you undertake and the amount of time spent preparing inside and outside the studio varies according to the nature of your project. Such factors as the numbers of dancers, subject matter, time available, the complexity of the music and scope, all have an influence on your approach. Choreographer Jonathan Burrows asks this excellent question: 'What is the right way to work for the thing that you want to do?'[74]

Cathy does meticulous preparation before making a narrative ballet with what she calls her 'masterplan': a spreadsheet with columns for scenario, story board, details of the set, music counts, highlighted bar numbers; tabs for characters or groups of characters; research of the narrative and related

Morgann Runacre Temple (centre) with Images Ballet Company in a workshop for her 2016 ballet based on Jane Glover's book *Mozart's Women*. Her 2018 ballet for Northern Ballet also titled *The Kingdom of Back* was based on the same theme. Dancers (left to right): Samantha Rodulfo, Rebecca McLauchlan, Hannah Smith and Jennifer Jackson (seated).

theory, and passages from the book made into lists of words. 'Usually we spend the first week or two transforming those words into movement phrases. I don't go in with any movement, but I go in with a load of other stuff. It's very useful for me as a document because being a choreographer is not just about making the steps; you've got the technical and publicity department wanting information, and they often want it before you've made the piece'. Her masterplan is a crucial reference for the whole production team and includes video links of scenes, which she clearly numbers and files every evening after rehearsal, so that everyone involved can access relevant material.

Morgann describes how her choreographic processes depend on the piece she is making:

'Sometimes I start with a kind of concept, or an idea, which has nothing to do with dance. For *Mozart's Women*, I did loads and loads of research. I'd read the Jane Glover book, then thought about [the women] as characters and how it could work as a piece. Then I went to the text, the letters that they [Mozart's family] had written and then the music. Getting into the movement was the last stage'. Her dance film *Tremble*, made for Scottish Ballet with Jess Wright, began with a music track by Anna Meredith that really excited them. 'We knew that we wanted to do something that was cumulative, we wanted to use lots of people and we knew the type of thing we wanted to make. We made sure we had a lot of material before we went into the room… we didn't have much time'. Another work, *Poppy Hotel,* began in the studio 'playing around… The music came much, much later, after I'd done loads of research in the studio by myself and with a couple of other people'.

WORKSHOP STRUCTURE

The 'open' culture of an exploratory choreographic 'workshop' is different from the ballet class with its more prescribed aims, and might be structured like this:

- Introducing the aim of the workshop: exploratory material around a theme; it could be an idea, e.g. a choreographic (or balletic) element or a process or method for making movement material.*
- Improvisation involving guided exploration of moving in relation to the given theme.
- A task or tasks drawing on improvised movement that establishes a framework for generating up to a minute of material.
- Developing and shaping set material, with attention to impulse and resolution, phrasing, structure, dynamics and spatial relationships.
- Sharing of developed work in the studio. Sense silence and stillness in the room before beginning, to raise awareness of the impulse and rhythmic life of shape and movement.
- Observing the material as a group and then reflecting, encouraging comment and discussion. This educates participants to look beyond technical virtuosity for quality and meaning.

*A series of workshops may focus on: points in the body and space; *en dehors/en dedans* and use of weight and gravity; phrasing; regular and irregular rhythm; stage space: directions and lines of travel; *épaulement* and spirals; duration and speed.

A moment caught in guided improvisation.

STUDIO PRACTICE: HOW DOES THE DANCE MATERIAL DEVELOP?

You may choose to develop the dance material in a number of different ways – for example, through instructing, improvising, directing, demonstrating, solo and collaborative research around movement tasks. Throughout the creative process, you are calibrating the relationship between how much preparation the work needs outside, and hands-on making inside the studio. In this, the most collaborative of arts, you are also evaluating and developing your working relationship with the people in the room.

Using Time Wisely

It is vital to make the most of your time with the creative team in the studio. Here are some of the strategies that these choreographers find make time in the studio worthwhile.

Very few choreographers devise all the movement before coming into the studio. Cathy agrees with a strategy suggested by contemporary and ballet choreographer Kim Brandstrup. He explained that he liked working with 'a room of people who were moving rather than a room of people who were

static'. Cathy finds that this approach gives you material to get going with. 'You can say OK – that slowed down, or can you do that on the floor? Or actually can we try something else?'

Ashley emphasizes attention to structure and not wasting time. 'Know who is on when, who dances with whom, all of that stuff. You've got an idea, even if that gets changed. In a room full of people and it's taking a bit longer than you expected, just do something and ask all to work on that – it gives you thinking time. Go with what you've got; if you don't have your first cast, work with the second and you might discover new things about them'.

He values working within time constraints. 'First night it has to be ready, you don't get a preview. There's something about the pressure of having a first night that makes you get on with it. You have your six weeks, or whatever, so many hours, you have to fight for your dancers quite often'. He describes a creation with San Francisco Ballet, where the dancers were so good, he 'wanted them all in it!' They inspired him to make an ambitious layered work, full of fresh invention, finished on the day that he was flying home. In this process he discovered how he likes to work: in short, intensive days with the pressure of deadlines.

Preparing for the Day

Andrew McNicol prepares thoroughly beforehand so that he can 'be free to respond and adapt in the studio'. He prefers to watch and lead work-shops ahead of time, getting to know the dancers so that, as he is 'imagining the work, it's with their strengths, qualities and personalities in mind'. He sometimes uses a colour palette to build a sense of how the world he wants to create, looks and feels. Using specific questions can help his thinking about structure and development, for example: 'What's the opening image, what changes and where do we end up? What's the through line? I don't have to have the answers to all these questions before, but might have a few ideas to try out to then discover or explore with the dancers. I often have a short move-ment phrase for day one, so I can put something out into the room quickly and get into a flow... then one thing suggests another...'

Although she adopts a few different modes of working, Morgann also begins with teaching some material, in order to give the dancers a feeling

Andrew McNicol researching in choreolab.

Improvising with phrase of ballet vocabulary; students at London Studio Centre in workshop with Jennifer Jackson.

for the language and to define boundaries for the movement exploration. 'I would always teach some phrases, even if it's really short, then work with tasks, often in twos, and then also make material on people, directing their movements.' More recently she has begun exploring improvisation, which she advises can be 'quite a hard tool, in terms of generating movement that needs to be set'.

IMPROVISATION

Improvisation is one of many ways to make and to perform dances. It includes: exploring movement within a given structure or task; responding to a stimulus with free invention; being in the moment and following the impulse to move. It can feel like flying. It's a way of generating lots of movement material that can be structured into a set piece.

The ballet choreographer William Forsythe developed a series of ground-breaking improvisation tools for dancers to explore form and dynamic range, and to break with habitual or trained movement.[75]

Finding material through improvisation and then deciding on the structure for that material is a way of choreographing that Burrows calls 'cut and paste'. Recreating improvised movement from video or memory is difficult and may involve loss of detail and complexity. In his chapter on Improvisation in *A Choreographer's Handbook* he writes: 'Many great pieces grow from processes which accept that what is lost leaves room for something else to arrive'.[76]

Using Improvisation

Georgie Rose is careful about how she uses improvisation. She defines a specific task and then strikes a balance between giving dancers space to feel free to make mistakes unobserved and supporting their blocks by offering challenges, a new step, thought or dynamic, to play with. Her aim

is to ensure that the dancers are not 'abandoned – like you merely left them to make your piece for you. You are guiding, stimulating and in a way choreographing the direction of their improvisation… changing dynamics, the music you play, the accents, the tempo and emotional background you want them to absorb.'

HOW CAN MY KNOWLEDGE OF BALLET HELP TO MAKE DANCES?

Ballet is 'a steadily expandable vocabulary of spectacular action, propelling unique and extreme capacities of the dancer's instrument…. Limits explored are not those of extreme emotion, but of expressive motion'.[77]
Lincoln Kirstein, co-founder New York City Ballet with George Balanchine

The ballet is created by the relation of each of the positions, or movements, to those which precede or follow it…. The steps which a dancer has learned… are, when separate, devoid of meaning, but they acquire value when they are coordinated in time and space, as parts of the continual rhythmic flow of the whole.[78]
George Balanchine

Training as a ballet dancer can be a huge asset, exposing you to the detail of particular movement language, its abstract or academic grammar and structures in space and time, as well as the experience of dancing in the form. Choreographic practice involves looking more deeply and freely from the perspective of creating with and beyond that language.

Georgie thinks her dancer training was essential preparation. 'Having a base of a vocabulary, and extensive knowledge of technique allows me to experiment and play in and with its yet unknown limits.' It has also given her an understanding of how to pace rehearsals and to manage the dancers' mental and physical fatigue when working at high intensity.

Ballet gives Morgann 'a lot of tools; an understanding of form, a starting point for movement in the body, a very clear movement language and also a verbal language – a way of talking about certain kinds of movement and qualities. It also gives me something to know where I am, in terms of communicating to other dancers. For example, it's a First, but it's like this!.... A kind of anchor point from which to be creative. And boundaries, because I get very stuck unless I have quite clear boundaries to start off with. So I think ballet training gives that safety net of knowing a little where you are and giving you a way to talk about things'.

Aakash Odedra echoes these thoughts. 'Classical discipline is very interesting because it helps you form a foundation that you can fall back on when you are in doubt. It's a constructed foundation – and then you have the ability or choice to deconstruct that foundation, whether it be the rhythmic aspect, expressive, acting or even just pure dance aspect, the technicality'.

Your Own Experience of the Vocabulary and Rules

It is not easy to make fresh choreography with ballet, a form that is so familiar and highly regulated. Part of your choreographic research is about developing the movement language to express your ideas, so finding your own inner connection with ballet as a form is vital for a sense of ownership and personal expression to develop. Get to know the rules intimately and give yourself permission to re-invent, to break and re-make.

As you read in Chapter 1, the geometric principles underpinning the technique and aesthetic are both rooted in nature, and universal and specific to the individual person. Ballet is a history of embodied knowledge and a 'vocabulary of human expression'. Your own practical knowledge of its principles develops through your experience of embodying the forms. In class you encounter its expressive dynamic range: research can start with your own body.

Morgann Runacre Temple developing choreography for Jacqueline Back, Rebecca McLauchlan and Demi Aldred as three women in Mozart's life in *The Kingdom of Back* (2016).

Creating with academic ballet vocabulary; Jennifer Jackson with dancers Samantha Rodulfo and Jaume Ruiz.

En place, *en dehors* and *en dedans*, which Roger Tully describes as the 'three great expressions in classical dance', are especially rich tools for exploring both your subjective relationship and the 'objective' form of the language and its expressive potential.

What if you look at these terms imaginatively, as concepts or states of being?

En place translates as 'in place' and evokes stillness, your physical centre, sense of self as a person, the aplomb (see Exploration in the box below and Chapter 1), poised in relationship to gravity, balance and the axis of vertical and horizontal planes.

Movement from the centre outwards (*en dehors*) and inwards (*en dedans*) engages the spiral musculature in the body and evokes many related ideas: opening and closing, expanding and contracting, sun and shade, light and dark, action and reflection; the sense of communication with an audience, how open or closed a particular movement shape 'feels' to perform.

Breath involves movement inwards and outwards and is often used to encourage individual expression. It can be a metaphor for phrasing an *enchaînement*, paying attention to where and how a line of movement begins and ends, its inward and outward flow and where the physical intensity or effort is directed.

WORKSHOP: *EN PLACE, EN DEHORS, EN DEDANS* AS TOOLS FOR DEVELOPING MOVEMENT EXPRESSION

Exploration – Sensing the Expressive Qualities of Movement and Shape

Stand in a relaxed but neutral pose – arms to the side of the body, feet parallel with heels touching. From centre and stillness, *en place*:

- Imagine the vertical plumb line (aplomb) reaching below the floor (like tap root) and through the body beyond the crown of your head.

Moving outwards, *en dehors*:

- Feeling the downward thrust of energy and upward flow through the vertical, simultaneously rotate the legs into turn out and (joining your hands at the navel) reach upwards past the nose so that the arms stretch above your head and open sideways until they reach a wide Second.
- Hold that shape for a few seconds, taking time to sense its character. Notice the physical sensation of the muscular activity and the feeling of 'being' in that still shape.
- Relax to neutral. Notice the different sensation and the feeling of being in a neutral place.
- Repeat the sequence a couple of times. Reflect on the feeling of *en dehors*. Make the shape again and intensify it, allowing the torso and legs to shift in response.

Moving inwards, *en dedans*:

- First move into the *en dehors* shape with arms to the side, then shift the feeling from being outwardly focused to being inwardly focused. Allow the legs and torso to respond to this feeling to make a new form. Notice the contrast in the physical sensation and the feeling of 'being' in the new still shape.

Creative Short Task
- Create four still shapes – two with a distinct outward feeling, *en dehors*, and two with a distinct inward feeling, *en dedans.*
- Improvise moving between these shapes in any order, slowly at first, observing the pathway of the limbs, torso and head during the transitions, and the expressive character of the still shapes. Experiment with shifting speed and quality, dynamics and directions in space.
- Expand the transitions between shapes with turning, jumping or travelling steps and use your exploration to make 30–45 seconds of solo material. Include at least two moments of stillness; clarify and focus the outward and inward character of the material.

Task Development
- Work in pairs or trios.
- Use the material to develop a conversational exchange between the dancers. Allow the material to be interrupted, repeated and copied between dancers. Clarify and focus, as above.
- Perform in silence and film your work.
- Observe and 'read' the relationships between the dancers that emerge in the choreographed movement.

Further Development
- Use these tools to analyse how the forms 'speak' back to you: for example, analyse found material in ballet class and develop qualities to infer meaning.
- Choose two pieces of music with a different character. Juxtapose your choreographed material with each piece, then choose the piece that feels most interesting to develop a considered relationship between movement and sound.

Cathy Marston in rehearsal with Les Grands Ballets Canadiens 2018.

WHAT ENVIRONMENT SUPPORTS THE DEVELOPMENT OF THE WORK?

When you are making a dance, conditions such as the broader social and cultural climate, the built environment and even the weather are the background to your work, rather than factors that you can influence. However, as the choreographer, you can affect and are responsible for many of the conditions inside the studio and for setting the tone of the working environment.

Cathy Marston sets out to engender a working atmosphere in the studio where everyone understands the shared goal of making a really good piece of work. Making work in places as diverse as Cuba, Denmark and San Francisco, she says, 'Every company is different, you have to feel the chemistry with the dancers; what do they need?'. Cultural factors, which are to do with company leadership and the broader political landscape, require a specific response, but she has practical ground rules that can be helpful in a range of situations: 'Concentration from the whole room, mobile phones silent and not looked at until the five-minute break, people standing up and starting the

rehearsal on time, and you have to find your way to make those needs felt. What I'm learning is, to ask what the work needs. Thinking of it personally is less helpful'.

Establishing good relationships with the dancers is a priority for Ashley Page. He uses specific strategies early in the process to build relations and the feeling of a 'company'. In his production of *On the Town* in 2019, he was choreographing with a mix of ballet and musical theatre dancers who were new to him. 'I made sure we all worked together on the first day, I had contact with them all for two hours and everyone had worked with me. It all clicked. It's amazing how quickly we got to know each other'.

Reflecting on this process, he suggested that his own choreography projects with a distinct cluster of like-minded dancers at The Royal Ballet in the 1990s had prepared him for 'the experience of looking after dancers' at Scottish Ballet from 2002 to 2012. He adds that choreographic practice is not just about creating interesting movement. It involves reading the different tensions between people in the cast. He values qualities in the choreographer that 'get the best out of people', including patience, caring and being approachable.

Ashley Page, director and choreographer, with the cast of *On the Town*, Japan 2019.

WHAT DO YOU LOOK FOR IN A DANCER?

Almost all choreographers involve dancers creatively in making movement material for their work. So, knowing how you want to work, what the work needs and what you want from your dancers will bring a clear focus into the studio.

Casting the right dancers for the work you want to make is important. Apart from general characteristics, such as strong technique, articulation, musicality and engagement, there are nuances in the dancer that will help develop a work. These choreographers highlight playfulness, generosity, sensitivity and a rigorous approach to movement. Chapter 9 also gives a good insight into whom you might want to invite into your rehearsal studio.

Cathy talks about dancers who offer 'more than', 'organized, thinking dancers, who get into the rehearsal and stand up'. 'That sounds really obvious' she says – but what a good tip, whichever side of the room you are! She gives an example of the detailed and imaginative thinking that makes a great dancer or collaborator: 'It's someone who will make connections between a scene that they've done on

day three, and ten days later they're doing another scene, but they can recall a little movement motif or how a thing worked. They stay organized with their material'. They understand what the character is wearing and replicate that in rehearsal. Tiny details matter.

Beyond dancing 'on the beat', Ashley values intelligence, the ability to understand phrasing, the way that the choreographer hears the music and why dance is constructed in a particular way. Speed, responsiveness, being unafraid to make mistakes and willing to enter into the creative flow, are also important. 'I like to work quickly. If I'm on a roll and someone says, Can I do that again? I'm – No, I need to keep going…. But also, I'm very open to suggestions. If they don't quite do what I'm after but it's more interesting, I'm very happy to go with that'.

Georgie feels strongly that 'pieces made from purely improvisation and movement direction can produce wonderful work'. But they are not the work of one choreographer and 'should be acknowledged as such: a choreographic collaboration'. She raises a good point. The role of the dancer, as a creative contributor in the highly collaborative process of making a ballet, is not always given recognition

Georgie Rose
in rehearsal.

in programmes and publicity. The debate about authorship, responsibility and ownership is on-going as choreographic methods cross fertilize between different dance genres. As a choreographer with responsibility for the choreographic structure of a work, you need to consider not only what is seen on stage, but the ethics in the highly collaborative process of making dance. What do you think?

WORKING WITH MUSIC

Dancing …is the art of composing steps with grace, precision and facility to the time and bars given in the music.

In place of writing steps to written airs, I composed… the dialogue of my ballet, and then I had music written to fit each phrase and each thought. [79]

Jean-Georges Noverre

Most ballet choreographers work with music in a considered way. The relationship between the music or soundscape and choreographed move-ment is normally the most fundamental for creating the world of the dance piece. Time spent preparing,

establishing and reflecting on this aspect is time well spent.

Detailed analysis of the music is a key tool, and every choreographer will refine their own system for understanding the music. Cathy can read music and, over the years of discovering what she needs, she devises her own notation, annotating the music score with 'little scribbles… and literally a dot and a dash for every note of the piece'. Although she may not refer to it in rehearsal, she has ensured through this deep analysis that she 'knows what the music is doing'.

Like many choreographers, Andrew might analyse the structure of an existing piece of music and use this to build a potential framework for the work with entrances and exits, solo and ensemble material, reflection and action. The music gives him 'a map, something tangible that helps navigate through the unknown' of the choreography. He can 'choose to follow this map or deliberately go against it'.

Using Counts

Using counts to understand rhythm and phrasing is useful for choreographer and dancers in the studio. They are often different from the way a musician counts music, but a ballet class accompanist will be familiar with the way dancers feel a phrase, often with the beginning of a counting pattern. In 1991, I choreographed Stravinsky's *Les Noces* in an educational setting for fifty recreational dancers aged between eleven and eighteen. Ballet musician Stephen Lade helped me to devise a counting system for the whole work. The counts were a framework for the different blocks of movement, like an app for locating where you are in time and space in relation to the whole. Even the youngest participants understood the complex score. It built the confidence that led to powerful performances and they grew to love the unfamiliar music.

Whilst counts are a very useful reference, they don't indicate aspects such as colour, texture, orchestration and flow. If used exclusively, they can mask the feeling and expressive qualities, and thus reduce the subtlety and richness of your response. Use them to analyse and communicate your understanding, but not as the only reference.

In ballet class the music normally aligns with movement quality to support the development of dancers' performing skills. As a choreographer you will experiment and explore different ways of aligning dance and music. Because of the close ties with musical beat and regular phrasing in ballet class, young ballet choreographers can feel it alien to break out of the pattern of response, which is engrained. Make friends with that feeling of alienation or discomfort – creating a dance is about going beyond what you know.

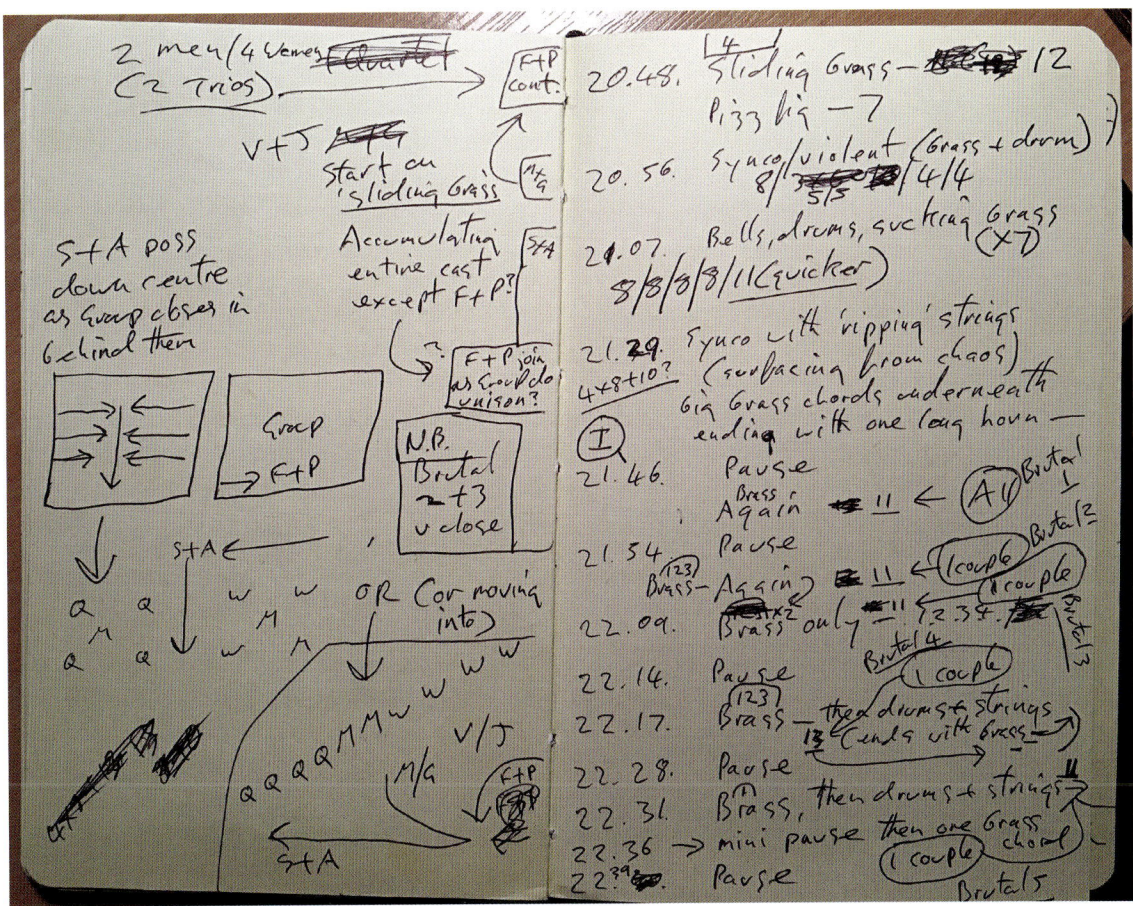

Pages from Ashley Page's notebook for *Guide to Strange Places* (2012) for San Francisco Ballet, showing his preparation for experimenting with alternative group patterns and detailed music analysis.

Aakash Odedra teaching a choreographic workshop for an adult summer school.

Working without Music

Dancing has a continuity of its own that need not be dependent upon either the rise and fall of sound or the pitch and cry of words. [80]
Merce Cunningham

Working away from the music and exploring movement in silence can sharpen your awareness of dynamics – the intensity of effort, accent, the impulse and resolution of a movement phrase. Play with these elements to develop and articulate the dance gestures. The clear focus on movement only can lead to new discovery when you return to relating to the music. Also try juxtaposing a completely different piece of music with your movement. The freshest ideas are (often!) accidental.

Develop your awareness, when watching dance, of how the music is used to express feeling and situation or to provoke you into responding. Make a list describing different music and dance relationships that choreographers use across dance genres; learning to articulate what you see can develop your own craft.

Contemporary dance and thinking offers plenty of ideas that can challenge traditional balletic methods and the resulting aesthetic of the dance. Merce Cunningham was revolutionary in the way he used chance methods to make decisions about the creation and performance of his dances. 'Objectivity' in the sense of shared rules and principles is built into ballet; try borrowing from other practices to find ways to refresh your palette of steps.

WORKSHOP: CHANCE OPERATIONS – PLAY WITH THE GRAMMATICAL STRUCTURE OF BALLET VOCABULARY

Exploring different ways of constructing material can lead to new discoveries about form and expression. What if you used the throw of a dice…

- Choose six fragments of movement material from different parts of your ballet class. Select fragments with contrasting dynamics – for example: a few bars of *frappé*, an *adagio* phrase, turns in open position, a final step and gesture from *grand allegro*, travelling *petit allegro* and *grand plié*.
- Number them from 1 to 6.
- Use a six-sided dice and throw four times to determine an order for the fragments.

- Write down the order and use this to make a sequence of the chosen steps.
- Respond to the challenges that the sequence proposes: be imaginative when you link each fragment, playing with the position in space, direction of travel and dynamics. Pay attention to the integrity of each fragment, its start and end point, and how to engineer the links in the *enchaînement*.
- Repeat this procedure again so that you have two different sequences. You might try using the Fifth Position to engineer the transitions.
- Observe the sequences in silence, reflecting, for example, on what and how the material 'speaks back' to you. Discuss the challenges in performing and the shifts in the movement's flow, phrasing, structure and musicality.
- As a development, choose a piece of music and shape your movement sequences to make a kind of dialogue.

ON COLLABORATION

This book is concerned primarily with what happens in the dance studio where the choreographed movement is explored and set, before the work is transferred to the performance space. As choreographer, you are at the centre of the collaborative relationships that make new work happen, working with people responsible for aural and visual setting, alongside publicity and programming, which prepares audiences to receive the work so that it communicates effectively. (Look at Chapter 9 to see the different people who may be involved in a creative team.)

How you work in a creative team will depend on the people and the project. Like any relationship, it involves sensitivity, exchange, boundaries, problems to solve, successes to enjoy. Much has been written about collaboration, and each journey will be unique; but reading about collaborative relationships, such as John-Steiner's *Creative Collaboration* (2000), gives an insight into how you might navigate the challenges. And follow Andrew's advice: 'Network – meet other artists, introduce yourself to people connected with the arts, that's how you hear about upcoming opportunities first or meet future collaborators.'

The financial and artistic risks of commissioning new music are huge – but opportunities at an early stage can lead to future creative possibilities.

Cathy Marston started working with composers at vocational school and now amongst her regular creative partners are Phillip Feeney and Terry Davis. With Feeney she works on making arrangements of specific music in order to indicate a location, emotional colour or time period. 'I like to suggest, rather than illustrate, scenically. It means that the music is taking a bit of the work from the set and costume design.' For example, with *Jane Eyre* (2016) for Northern Ballet Theatre, by anchoring the score in the music of Fanny Mendelsohn, she referenced the time when the Brontës were writing, as well as, on a more subtle level, pointing to the need for female artists to be heard.

Morgann Runacre Temple has developed a strong working relationship with sound designers, Tom Lane and Frank Moon; Jess Wright, with whom she regularly collaborates on dance films, is a colleague from her student days. Ashley Page's first major commission for The Royal Ballet involved a new score by Michael Nyman based on the film *The Draughtsman's Contract*, for which Nyman had written the music.

Many choreographers forge creative relationships with costume and scenic designers, who become integral to how their ideas grow and are realized. Ashley's fascination with what was happening in the production of contemporary dance introduced him to scenic and lighting designers Anthony

Mlindi Kulashe, Javier Torres and Antionette Brooks-Daw as Mozart, his father Leopold and his sister Nannerl in *The Kingdom of Back* (2018) for Northern Ballet by Morgann Runacre Temple, with sound design by Frank Moon, lighting by Alastair West and costumes by Kimie Nakano.

Images Ballet Company dancers in *The Kingdom of Back* (2016) by Morgann Runacre Temple, with sound design by Tom Lane, lighting by Christopher Nairne and costumes by Louie Whitemore.

MacDonald and Peter Mumford. They both became influential partners in many subsequent creative collaborations and opened doors to opportunities in other fields like opera and musical theatre. Looking outside the box he has built a reputation for fresh dynamic choreography, still closely linked with classical form.

OTHER STRATEGIES

Whilst there's no substitute for 'doing' choreography, many cite being in another choreographer's work as a useful learning experience. Watching and analysing ballets are also vital groundwork. Asked why he stood in the wings watching *The Sleeping Beauty*, Ashton said he was having a private lesson with Petipa! Choreographers make ballets in the shadow and light of their forebears. Fine artists refine their craft by copying the old masters. Igor Stravinsky's music and collaboration with Balanchine revolutionized ballet in the twentieth century and he is one on a long list of famous people who are credited with saying that great artists steal. What did he mean? Copying another artist's work and claiming it as your own makes it fake, but learning from other artists' work and their methods is part of the way that you develop your craft and find the platform for your work to communicate and to be seen.

NEW FROM OLD

Example of a choreographic study to develop learning in structure and vocabulary

Brief: Create a new study of up to one minute based on your re-working of a classical solo or *pas de deux* from ballet repertoire.

Process:

- Make a deep study of the choreography, analysing elements such as: spatial and musical structure, vocabulary, transitions between different sections, sense of journey, high points, theme, what is being expressed and how.
- Identify what interests you and use this to develop your study, choosing one of the following ideas:

  - Take one phrase or sequence of vocabulary and focus on developing it. Experiment with changing the direction of travel, location, scale, speed, pulse, intensity of effort. Reflect on how this changes what is expressed, and how you 'read' the choreography.
  - Take the theme and explore a new way of expressing this. Find an image or colour palette that evokes the theme. Improvise moving as if the air is the colour. Give the image and the colour a rhythm and texture.
  - Choose a phrase or quality that feels like the essence or heart of the solo, improvise with this; transpose specific movement between one space or body part to another.
  - Choose one section – fragment and re-combine the elements differently across the space and duration of the whole solo. Work the new transitions between sections and steps.

- Develop your choreography in silence: Make clear decisions about how you structure the material in space and in time. Work on the beginning and end of phrases and dynamics of movement. Clarify transitions between sections and steps. Include stillness as a visible action. Work all the material through in silence, making sure that the choices are clear.
- Develop a soundscape in response to the dance material: work with a musician or search for different music to juxtapose with the dance.
- Perform in studio. Reflect and invite feedback and discussion.

BEYOND BALLET

Looking outside ballet to other dance genres and art forms plays a vital role in nurturing your inner artist and craft. Ashley found inspiration in a different investigation of classicism. Seeing work 'coming from a more contemporary aesthetic', he realized 'the freedom of ideas that were being explored in a pure dance, abstract non-narrative approach to movement'.

Being 'hungry for different experiences' motivates Cathy to absorb as much as she can by seeing different companies, and attending exhibitions and concerts, alongside accessible internet research. Exposure to many different teaching styles and philosophies gave Andrew 'insight into different schools of thought and expanded [his] own thinking'. He advises other young makers to 'see from the perspective of the audience, go and watch as much theatre, dance as possible. Discover what works, what doesn't and why, so you can create what you want to see.'

How Do I Nurture My Artistic Voice?

The choreographic process invites research, exploration and discovery – going beyond what you already know about yourself and the tradition. In forging a place for their work to be seen, all artists must negotiate their own way between inner voice and outer industry demands.

Cathy appreciates a 'sense of slow burn' in her career and reflects on the resilience required: 'My experience is long and slow. Sometimes it can be difficult to see your colleagues suddenly get enormous opportunities very fast, but I'm happy with the journey that I've had because I've had time to discover myself along the way.... People ask me – how do I get opportunities? You have to keep putting yourself out there, no matter how awful that can feel sometimes. Develop a sense of self and at the same time listen to what people are saying – constant balancing act, how to just keep on your path and not shut out the world.'

Andrew recommends 'surrounding yourself with people you can trust and ask for honest feedback in the moment when you can really hear and receive it. Know that you can ask for what you want (you might just get it). Know that it's

Victoria Sibson as Bertha Mason and Javier Torres as Rochester in Cathy Marston's *Jane Eyre* (2016) for Northern Ballet, with costumes by Patrick Kinmonth, lighting by Alastair West and music by Philip Feeney.

Aakash Odedra directing dancers' workshop.

not always fair. Know that one teacher, school, company or organization is unlikely to give you everything you need or want... don't wait, go and create the opportunities.'

Aakash's advice to a choreographer is 'to really open yourself up to experiences and allow yourself to use that knowledge to find your own voice, in your own form or in different forms'.

THE CHOREOGRAPHER'S 'TOOL BOX'

Robert Cohan, Founding Artistic Director of The Place, is still making work in his nineties. At a choreography conference he talked about what a choreographer might need in their 'toolbox'. High on the list is the platform for showing your work. A vocational course will offer opportunities to practise making dances and then for seeing them on to the stage in performance. If you are in a company, working after hours may be the way to start. Ask your colleagues to join you and sign up for the choreographic showing. A deadline is a great motivator for seeing the process through. Make contact with the 'gatekeepers' – administrators, funders, local schools, community and business spaces – to get access to studio space, to develop and potentially perform your work. Look for festivals and umbrella organizations that provide performance venues and technical support. Every choreographer's journey is different.

Alongside the practicalities of suitable space, dancers, notebook, video, audio equipment, technical support, and access to facilities and refreshments, there are personal qualities. Choreography requires initiative, energy and commitment to follow through on, and feed, a process. It involves making decisions, being present to respond with intelligence and feeling to the evolving material or choreographic objects in relation to the overall vision and structure.

Start a journal for your project. Return to the ideas shared by choreographers in this chapter and jot down ten for your own toolbox. Allow the list to cross-fertilize into the areas of creation that aren't addressed. Research the resources included here and beyond, following your desire, interest and curiosity. Make a list of ideas or questions that you can use at different stages of the creation. Another of Jonathan Burrows' questions, 'What can you do, at this moment, in this process?',[81] can be an excellent way of focusing your creative energy and imagination to make the next choice. Andrew McNicol evokes a Buddhist saying 'see something as it is, not as you wish it to be' to encourage the creator to perceive what or who is in front of you and to work with that.

Be serious, be playful. Be yourself. Finding joy in what you do will nurture the creative spark, craft and courage to make your dances.

Cira Robinson and José Alves in Cathy Marston's *The Suit* for Ballet Black (2018).

CHAPTER 8

BALLET AND MUSIC
Jonathan Still

INTRODUCTION

Music is a term rather like 'driving'. We think we know exactly what we mean by it, but once we stop to consider all the things it involves, it turns out to be many things that seem unrelated to each other. Driving is the experience of being in a car, changing gear, being stuck in traffic or going full speed in the fast lane of a motorway. To drive, you need a car, but also a license, insurance, roadside recovery, an MOT, a parking permit, petrol or a charging point. You will also need maps. Some knowledge of how your car works is useful, but not essential, as long as you don't mind relying on others.

Researching music is a kind of journey, a listening expedition, perhaps. It helps to have maps and guidebooks, and to know where to go and what to see – unless, of course, you are happy to let algorithms, based on what you already listen to, determine your path. For public performances of choreography, music where both the composition and recording is out of copyright gives you the same freedom as driving around an empty supermarket carpark at night, but in any other conditions, using music is as subject to legal constraints as driving on a motorway. Understanding these legal aspects of music starts with knowing how it is made; the rights and roles of composers, publishers, performers, record companies and the limits of what you can do without permission. An understanding of meter, rhythm, and phrasing in music is the equivalent of basic car maintenance. You cannot really get through a ballet class without it. These three topics – researching ballet music, understanding copyright

and licensing, and the basics of meter, rhythm and phrasing – are the subject of this chapter.

RESEARCHING BALLET MUSIC

In his book on Tchaikovsky, Roland Wiley writes that 'ballet inspired by music is a twentieth-century conceit'.[82] At first glance, this seems extraordinary: surely, ballet is inspired by music? But this is Wiley's point. Tchaikovsky made such a difference to the credibility, quality and emotional expressivity of ballet music at the end of the nineteenth century that it is difficult to imagine that there was any other way to compose music for dance, or choreograph to music. As a result, histories of ballet music tend to tell the same story of evolutionary progress, where pre-Tchaikovsky composers, like Minkus (*Don Quixote*, *La Bayadère*) and Pugni (*Esmeralda*, *The Pharaoh's Daughter*) are the Neanderthals; progress begins with Adam (*Giselle*), improves with Delibes (*Coppélia*, *Sylvia*) and peaks with Tchaikovsky (*Swan Lake*, *The Sleeping Beauty*, *The Nutcracker*). After that, Stravinsky completely breaks the mould with his *Rite of Spring*.

It's a good story, but it's misleading. First, in their ballet careers, Minkus and Pugni would probably not have considered themselves 'composers' in the modern sense of artists struggling to express their inner world or stand out from the crowd as innovators. They wrote to a brief, and knew how to collaborate and fulfil expectations. Their role was nearer to what we now call a 'dance arranger' in musicals, someone who spends time with the choreographer in the studio to make sequences of music that fit closely with the steps, based on the main tunes and songs provided by a composer.[83] Second, while Tchaikovsky is rightly admired for his 'symphonic' approach to ballet music – developing dramatic tension through the repetition, variation, development and interweaving of musical themes – in other respects, he models his dance works on the examples provided by Minkus, Pugni and Johann Strauss, among others.

Not only that, *The Rite of Spring* certainly was mould-breaking, but that's not to say that no-one returned to writing music as they had done before. That includes Stravinsky himself, who afterwards wrote plenty of music in more conventional styles, celebrating the tango and ragtime styles popular at the time, as well as neo-classical works that borrowed dance forms and stylistic elements from seventeenth- and eighteenth-century composers, such as Pergolesi, Mozart, Bach and Lully.

Neoclassical elements also appear in Prokofiev's much later *Romeo and Juliet* (1935) and *Cinderella* (1945). Like Tchaikovsky before him, Prokofiev used the 'number opera' format associated with Mozart (i.e. each act is divided into several short 'numbers' that could be performed separately), a relatively simple musical language, and historical dance forms (e.g. gavotte, minuet and passepied) dressed in modern harmony. Almost a century after *The Rite of Spring*, Wayne McGregor's *Kairos* uses Max Richter's *Recomposed by Max Richter: Vivaldi – The Four Seasons* (2012). As the title suggests, this is a twenty-first-century composition based on music written nearly 300 years ago.

Musical Borrowing in Ballet

As these and several other examples demonstrate, borrowing, referencing, arranging and re-modelling old material have been part of the composer's toolbox for centuries. Around the time Adolphe Adam was writing *Giselle* (1841), composers at the Paris Opera would often drop in well-known tunes from existing popular songs, operas or operettas, to help the audience understand what was happening on stage. The French term for these musical quotations was *airs parlants* ('tunes that talk'). For a while, critics admired composers who were skilled at finding appropriate musical quotations to relay the action to an audience, but in time, they thought it greater proof of ingenuity when a composer invented all the tunes themselves. This is partly what makes *Giselle* stand out as a ballet score of that period. Rather than using *airs parlants*, Adam composed special musical themes for different characters, repeating, developing and varying them as the action progressed, thus creating a drama in the music, as well as on the stage, foreshadowing the symphonic approaches of Tchaikovsky and Prokofiev.

Works, Composers, Compilers and Arrangers

So far, this discussion has been about large-scale works written by one composer. This more or less defines what a musical work is: something large scale, written by a single composer who gets top billing on the programme. Music for ballet, by contrast, is often achieved through a messy mixture of collaboration, compilation, arrangement, orchestration and the available technology. Ballets like *Le Corsaire* or *Paquita* were compiled and overseen not by a composer, but by a 'ballet master', a role closer to our idea of artistic director and choreographer combined. This is similar to the way that some ballets are created today, as you will see in the case studies below.

THE PASTICCIO OPERA AND MUSIC FOR BALLET

The idea of the composer as someone who expresses their individuality in totally original works goes back to a nineteenth-century cult of the genius, and a belief in the importance of personal and artistic autonomy. It was not always like that. Many operas in the eighteenth century, for example, were composed in the form of a *pasticcio* (literally, a 'pie') – a collection of songs, arias and other music from several sources, arranged for a particular production. Guest artists would also bring along and interpolate their favourite solos, called 'suitcase arias', into whatever opera they had been hired to sing in. Similar practices have lasted much longer in ballet and, indeed, continue to the present day, alongside original works by individual composers.

The widespread belief amongst some critics and historians that musical works should, by definition, be the work of a single artist, coupled with a prejudice against those that aren't, may explain why so many ballets have been based on compilations of music by the same composer. Fokine's *Les Sylphides*; Jerome Robbins' *The Concert, Dances at a Gathering, In the Night* and *Other Dances*; Ashton's *A Month in the Country* – all of these use the music of Chopin, for example. They have the appearance of works, because there is only one named composer, even if, behind the scenes, an arranger may have skilfully woven together several pieces to make a coherent, full-length score. The conductor and composer John Lanchbery did that with *A Month in the Country*, Kurt-Heinz Stolze did it with the music of Tchaikovsky in John Cranko's ballet *Onegin*. A more recent example is Christopher Hampson's *The Snow Queen* for Scottish Ballet based on the music of Rimsky-Korsakov arranged by Richard Honner. A close relative of the single-composer ballet is the 'song book' ballet, such as Balanchine's *Who Cares?* (Hershey Kay's orchestrations of songs by George Gershwin), Twyla Tharp's *Nine Sinatra Songs* (Frank Sinatra), Christopher Bruce's *Rooster* (The Rolling Stones) and William Forsythe's *Blake Works* (James Blake).

Case Studies: Collaboration in Practice

Tchaikovsky and The Nutcracker *(1892)*

   No. 1: Gentle, mysterious music, 64 bars
   No. 2. Modulation, 8 bars
   No. 3: Noisy, joyful music for the entrance of the children, 24 bars.

   No. 4. Few bars of tremolo
   No. 5. March, 64 bars

This is how Petipa specified the opening music of Act 1 of *The Nutcracker*, from the end of the overture until the children's march. In addition to descriptions of mood and duration, he often asks for particular instrumentation or time signatures, or gives more fine-grained details of the interplay between dramatic action and music. Nonetheless, Tchaikovsky fulfils his brief in symphonic ways; listen to the way that the battle scene and transformation scene build in musical intensity in Act 1 of *Nutcracker* or, in *Swan Lake*, how the themes that open Act 2 are transformed into a dramatic extended finale.

Mthuthuzeli November and Isabela Coracy in Cathy Marston's *The Suit* for Ballet Black (2018).

Philip Feeney's The Suit *(2018) and*
The Cellist (2020) *for Cathy Marston*

Ballet choreographers in the twenty-first century often blur the boundaries between dance and theatre. Music technologies offer new ways of composing, performing or manipulating sound in real time. The roles of composer, sound artist, sound designer, music adviser or supervisor, arranger, orchestrator, dramaturg, scenarist and choreographer often overlap and interact, some choreographers creating scores for their own works. Sound designers might be employed to oversee the technical aspects of sound in a performance space, or their role could be to create a complex soundscape that involves a mixture of live and recorded material. Roles will vary from one project to another, depending on the individual participants, the other members of the team, the working practices and the nature of the project itself. Even if one person's name is given to simplify the credits, several people may have contributed to the score as it finally sounds. Behind the scenes, the contracts and royalty percentages might have been complex and difficult to negotiate.

In *The Suit,* created for Ballet Black, Cathy Marston uses eight different recorded tracks of pre-existing music played by the Kronos Quartet, and additional music by Philip Feeney. The credits are complex, as nearly every track is an arrangement of another work, so that for each there is a song title, a composer and an arranger.

The Suit is a collaboration with the dramaturg Edward Kemp, who has worked with Marston on many other ballets, including *The Cellist* for The Royal Ballet, based on the life of the cellist Jacqueline du Pré. For this, Philip Feeney created a full-length original composition, incorporating borrowings, arrangements and direct quotations from music strongly associated with du Pré's life and career. As with borrowings in French nineteenth-century ballet, these provide a way of underlining or signalling events to the audience through musical means.

Who can take credit for the musical structure – Marston? Feeney? Kemp? Elgar or the other composers featured in the score? All or none of the above?

Chroma *(Wayne McGregor, 2006)*
Giselle *(Akram Khan, 2016)*

If someone asked you who wrote the music for *Chroma*, what would you say? Joby Talbot? The White Stripes? It's complicated. Read the credits closely and you'll see that the ballet consists of

Wayne McGregor in rehearsal with Olivia Cowley of the Royal Ballet.

From audio transcription, to short score, to full score: three stages of the work of orchestrator Gavin Sutherland for Vincenzo Lamagna's music for Akram Khan's *Giselle.*

Joint enterprise: Vincenzo Lamagna, composer of Akram Khan's *Giselle*, with orchestrator and conductor Gavin Sutherland, Music Director of English National Ballet.

some sections entirely by Joby Talbot, whereas the White Stripes songs were composed by Jack White, arranged by Joby Talbot, and orchestrated by Christopher Austin. In turn, the songs came from an album *Aluminium*, which might be considered a kind of work itself – it was a project by the owner of XL Records, Richard Russell and Joby Talbot.

It is not unusual for composers to hire people to orchestrate their work, just as visual artists – Bridget Riley, for example – employ people to realize their artworks from detailed plans. Akram Khan's *Giselle* for English National Ballet was composed in close collaboration with Khan by Vincenzo Lamagna, partially drawing on elements of Adam's original music. It was orchestrated, however, by Gavin Sutherland.

COPYRIGHT AND LICENSING

In educational contexts, where the only audience will be other students and teachers, you can experiment with any music you like. However, if you ever want to put your work online, or have aspirations to choreograph professionally, an understanding of the principles and practice of musical copyright and licensing is essential.

WHAT ARE GRAND RIGHTS AND SYNC RIGHTS?

'Grand rights' are involved whenever music forms part of staged works, such as ballets, musicals, plays with incidental music, or operas; sync(hronization) rights are needed when music is used together with film. That means that if you want to use someone else's music in a video of your choreography that will be shared outside a personal or educational setting, then you will need to apply for both rights, as well as a licence to use the recording in this way.

Grand and sync rights have to be negotiated directly with publishers, though there can be advantages to approaching composers or record labels directly in the first instance. The more detail you supply about your project, the better: Who are you? What do you want to do? Who else is involved? Who is going to see your work, and where?

Copyright law and licensing agreements are modified in response to continuous, rapid changes in the technology and business models of the music industry. In an increasingly digital, online world, staying alert to these developments is as important for dancers and choreographers as any other aspect of their practice.

Music streaming services like Spotify or Apple Music make the playlist ballet seem an easy and attractive option: a musical universe at your fingertips. Bear in mind, however, that when you buy or stream an audio track, you do not 'own' the music outright. You are allowed to play the music at home, or in an educational context, and that's about it. To play it in public, you will need a venue license, and if you want to perform choreography to it, or film it, then you will need to get permission to do so, and pay the relevant fees. To do that, you will need to find out the name of the publisher and contact their rights department.

Every case will be slightly different, but here are some basic guidelines:

- In the EU, copyright in a composer's work lasts for seventy years after their death. This can be longer or shorter in other countries, or where a work belongs to an organization, rather than an individual or publisher.
- With songs that are collaborations between one or more songwriters and/or lyricists, copyright lasts until the last collaborator has been dead for more than seventy years.
- New arrangements of old works create new copyrights: so, for example, in the EU and US at least, John Lanchbery's (1923–2003) many scores for the Royal Ballet based on the work of long dead and out-of-copyright composers, such as Liszt (*Mayerling*), Mendelssohn (*The Dream*), Minkus (*Don Quixote* and *La Bayadère*) and Chopin (*A Month in the Country*) will be in copyright until 2073, possibly longer.
- If there is any chance that you are going to show your work in public or online in future, research the music rights implications of your choices as early as possible in the process.

METER, PHRASING AND RHYTHM

The Beat

The term 'beat' is often used to mean something like 'pulse' – a regularly occurring tick or accent that marks off units of time, or the rhythmic pattern of a

English National Ballet music director Gavin Sutherland explaining to first soloist James Streeter the vital importance of the upbeat for an orchestra (November 2016).

drum line in a song. In the past, however, if the beat in music was compared to the human heartbeat at all, it was not in the sense of pulse, but of systole and diastole, the contraction and relaxation of the heart as it pumps blood round the body. 'The beat' also meant, quite literally, the *movement* of a hand up and down as it indicated the passage of time: in other words, the beat isn't the resting or turning points at the top or bottom of the hand movement, but the movement itself.[84]

BEAT IMPLIES MOVEMENT

The concept of beat as movement is still evident in the idea of a conductor 'beating time,' and in the ballet term *battement,* which also refers to movement that goes from one position to another and back again. In French, *battement* also means an interval: the time available between two time points, not the points themselves. When teachers say 'fill out your music' or 'use all your music', this is roughly what they are referring to: move between the top and bottom of the beat, don't sit there.

Meter

This concept of beat as movement is also fundamental to meter, which, simply stated, means the division of a beat into two or three. Try it: keep in mind the contraction and relaxation of the heart muscles as you regularly lower (contraction phase) and raise (relaxation phase) your hand. That's duple meter – a *downbeat* and an *upbeat* of equal duration. Now make the downbeat twice as long as the upbeat: that's triple meter.

Another way to experience and understand meter is this: get a metronome or metronome app, and set the tempo at, let's say, 100 beats per minute (bpm). First, tilt your head from side to side every two clicks. After a while, tilt it every three clicks, then stop and listen. Now that tick will feel as if it is 'in three' (or a 'triple meter'). Of course, the tick is not in two or three, it's just a tick. But moving while you are listening profoundly affects your perception and cognition of music, particularly anything that involves the vestibular system, like bouncing, swaying or nodding. This is why 'listening to your music' is not always helpful, if by listening you mean standing still using your ears alone. Most often, you need to move in order to hear, even if it's just a nod of the head or a tap of the foot.

These definitions point at a difference between the counts that you use in class or rehearsal, and musical meter. Counts are literally just that: numbers that tell you when or where something happens, but not how. They may be aligned with perceived pulses in the music, but they do not have metrical accent: the differentiation between up and down beat, between tension and relaxation. Nor do they differentiate between duple and triple. You could say, roughly speaking, that counts are linear, whereas meter is

Beat as both pulse and movement: Gavin Sutherland conducting English National Ballet Philharmonic in a recording at Abbey Road studios for Akram Khan's *Giselle*. Note that Gavin and some players have headphones so that they can synchronize with a metronomic 'click track'.

cyclical. In music notation, each bar is a cycle of either two (with a time signature of 2/4 for example) or three (e.g. 3/4). There are endless combinations and elaborations of two and three, such as 6/8, which is a bar of two main beats, subdivided by three.

Phrasing and Melody

Phrases are often expressed in terms of quantity: an eight-count or eight-bar phrase, for example. But phrasing is about something more than this. A phrase in music is related to the length of a line in a song or poem: whatever you can comfortably sing in one or two breaths. To convey a phrase effectively requires a sense of overall shape, sometimes called rhythm, both in terms of dynamics (loud and soft) and timing. If you want to know what a melody sounds like without those qualities, perfect rhythm and pitch, but nothing else, search the web for 1990s ringtones. Since rhythm and timing are so crucial to musical performance in either music or dance, they are discussed in more detail below.

Rhythm

Although we use terms like meter, rhythm, timing, tempo and so on, as if they were separate things out there in the world, in practice, they are mutually involved in a way that is almost impossible to disentangle. If any term seems to capture all aspects of musical time together, it is rhythm. There are two main ways of understanding the term: one fuzzy and aspirational, the other more precise.

On the fuzzy side, philosophers, musicians, musicologists, artists and writers have been trying to define rhythm for centuries, and yet the term is still as broad and open to interpretation as the word 'love', perhaps even more so. Just think of some of the song lyrics that have the word 'rhythm' in them: *The Rhythm of Life, Rhythm is a Dancer, I Got Rhythm*. Rhythm in this sense is something like a life force, an energy, a way of moving, the shape and vitality of a movement over time.

The more precise definition of rhythm is when it is used as an abbreviation for 'rhythmic pattern' – a sequence of sounds of different durations. In this sense, you can talk about the 'rhythm of a step', meaning how the different components of a sequence of movements are timed in relation to a beat. Rhythmic patterns, by definition (because they are patterns), involve repetition.

It is helpful to keep both senses of the term in tension: to know and be able to execute the precise timing and rhythmic pattern of a step so securely that you can allow room for flexibility and change. Some people call this playing with the music or timing. When the fifteenth-century dancing master Domenico da Piacenza spoke of *misura* – the timing of steps to music, he used a phrase that captures both senses of *rhythm* very well: 'slowness compensated by quickness'.[85]

Timing and Tempo

Timing, like rhythm, has two main meanings: (1) being correctly in time with an external beat or being rhythmically precise and (2) speeding up/slowing down within that framework to give an expressive quality to music or movement. Tempo, although it is often expressed only as 'beats per minute' can also be used expressively. For example, *adagio* and *allegro* are both terms used in music, but they have richer meanings than merely 'slow' and 'fast'. *Adagio* literally means 'at ease' and *allegro* means 'happy' or 'cheerful'.

Thinking about tempo as a quality, rather than beats per minute, can enrich and enliven a performance. With reference to his *Adagio Hammerklavier*, the choreographer Hans van Manen has described how he perceives a difference between slow motion, based on 'total balance' and *adagio*, which is 'like a wheel that you push – and that moment where the wheel is still moving, just before it falls'.[86]

This last section aims to encourage you to think of beats, meter and rhythm not as 'music theory', but as expressive elements of music that are crucial both in choreography and class. Let the final word go to dance teacher Melanie Bales, emerita professor of dance at Ohio State University:

If the music selections are too similar in tempo or qualitative/dynamic range, the individual character inherent in each exercise or step

Lauretta Summerscales and Emilio Pavan in Hans van Manen's *Adagio Hammerklavier*, a study of slowness in music and movement.

cannot be revealed or practiced. When the rhythms and musicality are flat and metronomic, the experience edges toward workout furniture with a ballet veneer. No good teacher of ballet in any context will neglect music and phrasing – it is built into the lexicon and is part of what does the teaching.[87]

'That moment where the wheel is still moving, just before it falls.' Ken Sarahashi and Senri Kou in Hans van Manen's *Adagio Hammerklavier.*

The creative space – a dance studio.

CHAPTER 9

THE REHEARSAL STUDIO
Deirdre Chapman

In this chapter we look at key features of the studio and rehearsal process to try and understand what can make that period a magical, synergistic time. After reading, you should have a better understanding of all that goes on during the intense time spent preparing for performance: the external factors involved, the work in the studio, how 'attitude' influences product and how to make the most of the experience.

We will look at the following:

- External factors: how environment shapes the creative process and production:

  - The variables of performance schedules, budget and human resources.
  - How the balance of responsibilities shifts according to the context or scale of an organization or production.

- The work in the rehearsal studio – what happens 'in the room':

  - Various choreographic and creative processes.
  - How reconstructing a work differs from creating a new work.
  - Archival methods used for recording and remounting dance work.
  - The responsibilities of all those involved: dancers, creative team and support staff.

- Attitude and preparation: ways to be our 'best':

  - The qualities and attitudes: what choreographers, directors and rehearsal directors value and appreciate in their dancers.
  - What successful dancers working today do to prepare for various roles and what they most value.
  - What constitutes effective and intelligent practice.

Be the person people want to come back and work with.
William Tuckett, Choreographer (2018)

My personal journey started in Minneapolis when I was too small to even walk; watching company rehearsals and classes from behind the artistic director's chair at Minnesota Dance Theatre. I grew up dancing in the local *Nutcracker* performances in Minneapolis each year, eventually gaining my first job with San Francisco Ballet at the age of eighteen. Six years later I moved to Rambert Dance Company in London, and four years later I was a dancer with The Royal Ballet in Covent Garden. I danced there as a First Soloist for twelve years and continue to have a close working affiliation with the company. During my performing career, I had the privilege of working with more than thirty-five choreographers on new works, experiencing many varied processes. I have also been a part of the re-staging of a huge spectrum of both classical and contemporary works, and currently teach, coach, assist and re-stage both cutting-edge and heritage dance pieces.

Still life in the rehearsal studio.

My fascination with dance and our individual journeys develops apace. I am hugely grateful to the numerous choreographers, rehearsal directors and dancers, who responded to various questions about the 'rehearsal period'. In my search to answer a central question – What makes the time in the studio work best? – I include many of their thoughts about what they value in the studio, and the date of our communication.

THE PEOPLE WHO HELP TO BRING THE REHEARSAL STUDIO TO LIFE

Artistic Staff All the members of staff directly involved in working with dancers in the studio.

Choreologist A person who records movement using dance notation.

Coach An experienced staff member or dancer sharing knowledge of a role and helping a dancer to understand the intention and meaning of the choreography.

Creative Team The creative team is made up of anyone who contributes to the development of a new work, and/or re-staging an existing work, and may involve some or all of the following: choreographer, assistant to the choreographer, rehearsal director, composer, dramaturg, costume designer and lighting designer. Other roles of vital importance in bringing a work to the stage include: dancers, musicians, conductor, stage manager, wardrobe staff and technical staff.

Dramaturg In dance, a dramaturg is a person who advises on the thread of a narrative work. They help to determine what scenes are necessary in telling a story through dance and may play the role of a 'critical friend' during a process, helping to clarify how the work 'reads' to an audience.

Rehearsal Director or *Regisseur* This person may act as the assistant to a choreographer, direct rehearsals in the absence of the choreographer, and/or re-stage and coach choreographed works. Rehearsal directors are often left in charge of a new work after the *première*.

Rehearsal Period This is the allotted time in the studio and on stage before a 'first night', where the choreographer and dancers work together to create a ballet, or to re-stage an existing work. This period includes the rehearsal time on stage, and involves all members of the creative team in their various capacities. It finishes with the *première* of a new work, or the opening night of an existing work.

Repetiteur Often used interchangeably with rehearsal director, but a term for a person who is given the responsibility to re-stage and coach particular dances.

Scheduling Coordinator A person in charge of timetabling rehearsals, physiotherapy and costume fittings. In a large organization this is a designated role. In smaller organizations this responsibility is taken on by a rehearsal director, assistant to the choreographer, or dancer.

EXAMPLES OF COMPANY REPERTOIRE IN 2019

- San Francisco Ballet – over two weeks during spring 2019: overlapping repertoire of works by George Balanchine, Benjamin Millepied, David Dawson, Helgi Tomasson, Cathy Marston and Harald Lander; with *Sleeping Beauty* (Tomasson's version based on Petipa) performed two weeks later.
- Paris Opera – during the spring of 2019: overlapping repertoire of works by Paul Lightfoot/Sol Léon, Hans van Manen, Sidi Larbi Cherkaoui, Edouard Lock and Arthur Pita; a month earlier, they danced Nureyev's *Swan Lake*.
- The Royal Ballet – during the spring of 2019: overlapping repertoire in the main house of works by Frederick Ashton, Kenneth MacMillan, Carlos Acosta, Christopher Wheeldon, Liam Scarlett, Crystal Pite and Sidi Larbi Cherkaoui, and performances in the smaller Linbury Theatre of works by Aletta Collins, Kristen McNally, Goyo Montero, Juliano Nûnes, Calvin Richardson and Alexander Whitley.
- Ballet Black – rotating repertoire during 2019: works by Cathy Marston, Martin Lawrance, Mthuthuzeli November and Sophie Laplane.
- Rambert – rotating repertoire during 2019: works by Kim Brandstrup, Wayne McGregor, Sidi Larbi Cherkaoui, Marion Motin, Hofesh Shechter, Ben Duke and Merce Cunningham

The repertoires of The Royal Ballet, San Francisco Ballet and Paris Opera are advertised as a yearly season (autumn 2018 through summer 2019), whereas the repertoires of both Ballet Black and Rambert change on a gradual basis.

ENVIRONMENT: SCALE – PEOPLE – SCHEDULE

The size of an organization is a factor that affects the creative process and the time in the studio. It also affects the division of responsibilities between artistic staff and dancers. These responsibilities shift if you are working on an independent project, where there may be no permanent staff, as opposed to a large dance company with permanent staff and facilities.

Large-Scale Organizations: (Fifty+ Dancers)

These large-company environments have comprehensive resources to create or mount/re-stage a work(s). There are entire artistic and administrative teams, a technical department – including stage management and production staff, numerous wardrobe staff, music staff, a press department and additional support staff – all working toward the success of multiple productions over the course of a season. These organizations also have greater resources for body maintenance and health. A company class for warm-up and technique will always be provided, as well as 'state-of-the-art' physiotherapy, massage and specialist rehabilitation (usually including one, if not all, of the following: Pilates, gyrotonics and weight training).

Large ballet companies will either perform different programmes on alternate evenings or a cascading overlap of repertoire over several weeks/months. This mixed repertoire demands the maintenance of numerous ballets in performance, while completely different works are being rehearsed during the day. As a result, the timescale for the creation of new works shifts, as dancers are not available every day, all day, to work on a single piece. Scheduling for studio and dancer availability is complex; several casts will rehearse for a single work, and 'covers' are prepared in case of emergency. This constant juggling of repertoire and people demands that dancers and artistic staff are able to shift styles of movement almost instantaneously. In the period of time it takes to walk from one studio to another, you might move between working on contemporary work by artists such as McGregor or Cherkaoui, to classical repertoire like *Giselle* or *Swan Lake*.

Mid-Sized Organizations: (Twenty to Forty Dancers)

Most mid-sized companies have separate rehearsal and performance periods. These organizations will have designated rehearsal periods when they are only creating new work or rehearsing pre-existing works; then there will be scheduled performance weeks when the working timetable shifts to accommodate performances and/or touring.

Example of a daily schedule.

EXAMPLE OF SCHEDULE FOR A SOLOIST IN A LARGE SCALE COMPANY

TIME	REHEARSAL DAY	TECHNICAL DAY	PERFORMANCE DAY
10.00	CLASS (Choice of start time)	CLASS	
11.00	CLASS	Technical w/out and Make-up	
11.30		Stage rehearsal 11.30-14.30	CLASS (Choice of start time)
12.00	REHEARSALS 12.00-14.30 Ballet A: 10 corps de ballet and 4 covers.	Stage rehearsal	CLASS
13.00	Ballet B: Pas de deux rehearsal for New work (cover)		Hair/Make-up
14.00	Ballet C: Full length Classical work: solo variation rehearsal w/three casts.		Half hour call at 13.55
14.30	LUNCH	LUNCH	MATINEE 14.30-17.30 PERFORMANCE
15.30	REHEARSALS 15.30-18.30 New Ballet B: Soloists		
16.00	New Ballet B: Full cast	Further technical - in costume/no makeup 16.00-18.30	
17.00	5.15-6.30 ACT 1 – Full Length Classical work - full cast needed.		
17.30			Shower/dinner
18.00			
18.30	Rehearsals finish	Rehearsals finish	Prep for evening
19.00			Warm-up Half hour call at 18.55
19.30			EVENING 19.30-22.30 PERFORMANCE
22.30			Finish

In the US, most mid-sized companies have a theatre where they will be in residence, performing for a designated number of weeks of the year. Their rehearsal periods lead up to a block/series of consecutive performances, and then at the end of those performances, the company moves on to the learning of another work or series of works. Touring happens regionally, if at all.

In the UK, most mid-sized dance organizations do not have a singular resident theatre, but have a yearly touring programme that takes them all over the country, often performing a rotation of repertoire in multiple venues. The rehearsal periods for new works or the re-staging of older works take place in the interim periods between touring, and the repertoire tends to change gradually – one work being added and one dropped over a period of time, depending on the venue. Mid-sized companies in Europe are different in that they will often be the resident company in a small regional Opera House, and have a repertory schedule shared with the local Opera Company.

These organizations have physiotherapy and healthcare provision, although accessibility varies widely between them. In dance companies of this size a daily class is provided, and there are clear divisions of artistic, technical and supporting administrative staffing roles. These organizations will maintain most, if not all, of the following: press department, stage manager, music director or staff, technical department and wardrobe department, although these departments might comprise only one person in each, or even just one or two people performing multiple roles. Dancers in these organizations must be resilient and strong, and willing to be team players. There will be little or no hierarchy, and dancers must be happy to take on any category of roles.

Freelance/Independent Projects: (Number of Dancers Dependent on Project)

When working on an independent project, or in a very small company, dancers often take on additional responsibilities. These groups tend to focus on the preparation for a single evening of work, as opposed to a larger mixed repertoire. The funding for independent projects may be specifically for the creation and performance of an evening of works or a single work. Choreographers will work within a fixed, limited timescale, and with finite numbers of dancers hired for the project. Rehearsal periods will often happen in a variety of venues, depending on space availability. It is the individual dancer's responsibility to be physically and mentally ready to dance upon entering the studio for these projects, as a communal warm-up may or may not be offered. The choreographic/rehearsal process is time-pressured, intense and highly focused, although it may take place sporadically over a long period of time. The performance schedule will also be highly variable. One type of project may have a short, fixed period of performances, another may tour nationally or internationally over the course of a year or longer, with gaps in between performances and possible changes of cast.

Each individual's responsibility for the maintenance of these types of works is huge. Performances will usually run with no 'covers', and if an injury occurs, the work must be adapted or 'covered' by the existing dancers. Dancers invested and engaged in this type of work are able to adapt quickly and creatively when necessary. The longevity and success of a work may rely on their resilience and ability to 'think on their feet'.

Alongside this type of work is the additional personal administration demanded on the part of the dancers: managing taxes, contracts and, potentially, multiple commitments, while also auditioning/applying for future work. Freelance dancers must maintain their health and fitness independently between projects, and often end up developing a wide-ranging skill-set – for example, grant writing, teaching or leading on their own independent projects.

A YEAR IN THE MAKING

The Royal Ballet

- Roughly ninety-four dancers, including apprentice contracts.
- Permanent residence at the Royal Opera House, Covent Garden.
- Year-round contracts.
- Thirty-eight to forty performance weeks, with an additional overseas tour of two to four weeks.
- Ten to twelve programmes per year: on average, seven full-length ballets and four triple bills (an evening of three one-act works).
- Three to four new creations a year, which are choreographed while performing other works in the repertoire.
- The creative or re-staging period finishes with technical rehearsals on stage and imminent performances.
- Full time: artistic staff, choreologists, technical production team, wardrobe staff, music director and musicians, as well as on-going roster of guest-staffing, dependent on repertoire.
- In-house physiotherapy, including massage, physio, specialist rehab, Pilates, gyrotonics and strength training.
- Dancers become adept at adapting to a multitude of styles throughout the day and into the evening, sometimes rehearsing six to eight different works during the course of a week.
- Daily ballet class.
- Rehearsals possible 12.00–18.30, 12.00–17.30 on performance days.
- Five to six weeks paid holiday per year.

Rambert

- Twenty to twenty-two dancers.
- Permanent rehearsal studios, no resident theatre.
- Average twenty to twenty-five weeks of touring, both UK and internationally, per year.
- Rotating roster of about eight works over the course of a year; works performed for two to three years, sometimes with gaps of several months.
- Two to three creations a year during designated rehearsal periods.
- Daily class (variety of ballet and contemporary dance styles), later class on tour.
- Rehearsals possible 12.00–18.30 during rehearsal periods, two to three hours on performance days.
- Designated 'tech' weeks in vacant theatres for new work, as touring venues don't have the spare availability for complex technical rehearsals.
- Staffing includes rehearsal directors, stage manager, wardrobe manager and small technical team.
- Physio and massage available at specific times.

- Often gaps between the creative process and the technical/performance period.
- Works designed with technical parameters, which can adapt to a wide variety of stages.
- Dancers capable of adapting works to various spaces, and holding on to repertoire to rotate work seamlessly throughout the year.
- Six weeks paid holiday per year.

San Francisco Ballet

- Roughly seventy-five dancers.
- Permanent rehearsal studios, December–June residence at the San Francisco Opera House.
- Season of roughly fifteen performance weeks, national/international touring of two to four weeks.
- Average of eight programmes per year: three full-length ballets and five triple bills.
- Average of five to six creations a year during a designated summer/autumn rehearsal period.
- Creations are developed to the point of going on stage, shelved for several months and then quickly revived during the intensive winter/spring performance season.
- Dancers adept at quickly refreshing work to performance readiness.
- Full time: artistic staffing, technical production team, wardrobe staff and music director.
- In-house physio and massage.
- Daily ballet class.
- Rehearsals possible 12.00–18.30, less on performance days.
- Five to six weeks holiday per year, partially paid.

Ballet Black

- Seven to eight dancers.
- Permanent rehearsal studio, no resident theatre.
- Thirty to forty performances a year, nationally, with some international touring.
- All dancers participate in outreach/education work.
- Slowly rotating repertoire of around four to five works per year.
- Daily ballet class.
- Artistic director also functions as rehearsal director.
- Staff have multiple roles covering artistic, administrative, and technical duties.

Rambert Studios, London.

IN THE STUDIO

Regardless of the country, city or company, every dance studio is a familiar space for a dancer. Yet, depending on the production and people involved, even the same studio holds different experiences over a period of time for each individual.

PROCESS

A series of actions or steps taken in order to achieve a particular end.[88]

This term is used often in describing the journey that a creative team works through, from idea to rehearsals and eventual performance.

NEW WORK

Every choreographer has a different process. Some choreographers enter the studio with every step or movement choreographed already; others come into the studio with little more than an idea or theme that they want to explore. Most sit somewhere in between, and may even vary their creative

Marcelino Sambé and Francesca Hayward of The Royal Ballet in a workshop with choreographer Charlotte Edmonds.

process, depending on how many times they have worked with the dancers previously or how much time they have for a creation. The following descriptors highlight the different expectations of dancers' behaviour during a creative process and help us to understand how and why a process can vary so much in the studio.

Working Frameworks

Highly Directive

Some choreographers are highly directive in their work. They enter the studio knowing exactly what they want to do with the dancers in the room. In many cases, the choreographer may have developed specific material to the music before working with dancers and have a firm plan on how the material will be structured. This type of process can be very fast for the dancers, as it involves the choreographer doing nearly all their preparatory work in advance. Creating the material, structure and musicality of a piece becomes a matter of the choreographer 'teaching' the material. This happens much in the same way that dancers learn movement combinations in a technique class.

Expectations of dancers within this framework:

- Speed at learning and retaining material.
- Competence in the execution and articulation of a shared movement vocabulary.
- Ability to use own technical knowledge to help embed the demands of the choreography.

Dancers in ballet companies are often working within a shared 'classical' vocabulary, in which there are prescribed expectations guiding the execution and shape of certain movements. When this type of process happens in more contemporary settings, dancers may have been working with a choreographer for an extended period of time, thereby understanding that choreographer's particular movement vocabulary to the point that there is a shared movement knowledge-base.

Royal Ballet dancers, Joseph Sissens and Chisato Katsura of The Royal Ballet in rehearsal for *Yugen* (2018), choreography by Wayne McGregor.

Collaborative

These choreographers begin their creative process with thematic ideas and narrative concepts to help direct the development of choreography: ideas for parts of movement phrases only, as opposed to whole phrases or sections developed.

Expectations of dancers within this framework:

- Willingness to collaborate.
- Confidence in participating in a dialogue regarding movement development.
- Openness to revisions over a potentially long period of time.
- Mutual trust and respect for everyone present in the studio.

Trust above all. With trust, a dancer is allowed to fail, discover and grow in the studio.
Zenaida Yanowsky, Dancer (2018)

This is not a process to be rushed. Often a choreographer will allow time for material to settle on the dancers' bodies before revising the phrase or phrases further. These additional revisions are usually to tighten narrative or thematic intent, refine the underlying structure of the work or iron out moments that have not coalesced well.

These choreographers are receptive to input and ideas from the dancers they are working with and encourage dialogue, while still maintaining the ultimate vision of the work being created. When successful, this environment of trust creates an atmosphere of sharing that allows the choreographer to discover movement and ideas that they might otherwise have not come to alone. It also allows dancers to discover aspects of themselves, which they might otherwise have missed.

Choreographer Wayne McGregor with artists of The Royal Ballet.

Task-Orientated

These choreographers ask dancers to create much of the movement vocabulary for a work. They do this by using improvisatory exercises, and/or setting specific tasks through which the dancers develop material. In these situations, dancers have a large responsibility for developing movement. The choreographer will then cut and paste from the material developed to create an overall whole that is structurally and stylistically identifiable as their own. There is usually a lot of material thrown away in this type of process – in a sense like the editing of a film.

Expectations of dancers within this framework:

- A willingness to create material.
- A willingness to offer material without expectation of how it will or will not be used.
- Ability to retain a lot of material.

Synthesis

In practice, most choreographers' processes are something of a synthesis of the above styles. They will adapt material to the dancers they are working with, some even developing differing versions for different casts. They, ultimately, want the very best possible product to make it to the stage and are working within limited time-frames. Crucially, a choreographic process is affected by how well a choreographer knows the dancers on whom they are creating. Even if it is an integral part of their normal creative process, a choreographer will be more open to collaborating with dancers they have worked with previously.

Expectations of dancers in this framework:

- Adaptability.
- Sensitivity to what type of choreographer they are working with, and the time-constraints on the rehearsal period.

I expect dancers to be open, imaginative, constructive, generous and supportive; I most appreciate generosity, honesty and imagination.
David Nixon, Director and Choreographer (2018)

A dancer's personality determines in which of the above frameworks they feel most comfortable. Some dancers live for the rehearsal period; these individuals excel during a creative period, enjoy working with varied choreographers and love the process of learning work. The finessing of the subtle meaning in a single movement is fascinating and worth spending hours upon. Other dancers bide their time in the studio and only fully come to life on stage in performance. For these types of dancers the rehearsal hours can be painful and frustrating. The desire to be out on stage in front of an audience feels more important than the hours spent behind the scenes working on a piece.

RE-STAGING

A large proportion of the work within larger dance companies involves the remounting or re-staging of pre-existing works. The creative hours and money it takes to develop a work from scratch far exceeds the time and budget used to remount an existing work. Additionally, for both ballet and contemporary companies, there is a responsibility to maintain and present the heritage and historical legacy of their organizations in terms of repertoire choices. Companies revisit past works both to provide perspective or commentary on current works and to celebrate works that may have historical significance.

In every re-staging of a piece of dance there is an individual or artistic team with responsibility for the quality and interpretation of the work. While some living choreographers are intimately involved with remounting their work, the majority leave the re-staging to a team of associates that may include some of the following: an in-house or freelance rehearsal director, choreologist, *repetiteur*, members of the creative team and dancers from the original production. These individuals often play vital roles in the teaching and re-staging of works, both locally and internationally, and ensure that, regardless of the company, the work is presented to the highest possible standard.

Anna Rose O'Sullivan and artists of The Royal Ballet rehearsing for the re-staging of *Don Quixote*.

Factors that affect re-staging rehearsal time:

- Are the dancers familiar with a particular choreographer's work?
- Has the company previously worked with the choreographer?
- Has the work being re-staged been in the repertoire of the company over the last several years? (And, if so, how recently?)
- The strength of the relationship between the coach/rehearsal director and the dancer or dancers.

Variations in the Re-staging Process

Classical Repertoire

In larger ballet companies, the staging of classical works, such as *The Nutcracker*, *Sleeping Beauty*, *Swan Lake* and *Giselle*, are often considered part of the heritage repertoire of the company. This repertoire exists in related forms across the world, and is part of what may be called the classical ballet 'canon'. The quality of these productions, both in terms of staging and dancing, has a powerful effect on a company's reputation. While differences of style may exist between companies, the precision of these classical heritage works, and the demands for pure classical technique, enable these works to be assessed and compared around the world.

Because of the size of these large productions, teams of artistic staff work simultaneously to stage these ballets. Separate staff often coach principals, soloists and *corps de ballet*, and featured roles may be coached by individuals who have previously danced the roles, and/or have been involved in the production hundreds of times. These coaches have an in-depth knowledge of a work that can sometimes be the key to grasping the subtleties of a particular role. Their job is to help each dancer fully understand the choreographic intentions, while also finessing the technical execution. A constructive relationship is vital.

> *A mutual sense of respect and also a mutual passion for what we're doing in the studio.*
> Matthew Ball, Dancer (2018)

MULTIPLE ITERATIONS OF THE SAME BALLET

Let's look at a ballet such as *The Nutcracker* originally created in 1898.

In many dance companies this work is revived every year, and yet each rehearsal and performance is still a singular experience. Each revival of the same production involves some different dancers, differing points in an individual dancer's life and often different roles. All of these variables influence the energy and focus present in a given studio space, people's attitudes and, therefore, how effective, enjoyable and productive – or unproductive – a rehearsal process can be.

Marianela Nuñez and Vadim Muntagirov of The Royal Ballet, coached in rehearsal by Carlos Acosta and Alexander Agadzhanov for *Don Quixote*.

Neo-Classical Repertoire

Works such as *Apollo* (George Balanchine, 1928), *Symphonic Variations* (Frederick Ashton, 1946), *Song of the Earth* (Kenneth MacMillan, 1965) and *Dances at a Gathering* (Jerome Robbins, 1969) are examples of neo-classical repertoire by some of the great twentieth-century choreographers. These choreographers' works are looked after by a trust or foundation, which organizes staffing and takes responsibility for maintaining quality in every re-staging. It is crucial to a successful re-staging of any work that the new dancers learn to embody and understand the essence of a particular choreographer's style. The context and history of each piece is as important as the steps.

The re-staging of these neo-classical or abstract works involves teaching the choreography, and then facilitating the new dancers' abilities to integrate the movement into their bodies. Neo-classical work uses a base of shared classical vocabulary, which is extended and pushed further. A dancer's core classical technique generally allows them to pick up this type of material at great speed. At the same time, the dynamics and musicality are carefully explained and rehearsed in order to ensure a technically precise, accurate and stylistically authentic performance.

Modern Narrative Repertoire

Ballets such as *Onegin* (John Cranko, 1965), *Mayerling* (Kenneth MacMillan 1977), *Carmen* (Mats Ek, 1992), *Jane Eyre* (Cathy Marston, 2016) and *Giselle* (Akram Khan, 2016) are examples of modern narrative repertoire. The re-staging of this modern narrative work involves the additional translation of the narrative intention behind the choreography, and an understanding of how that intention helps the story progress. In all narrative work, dancers need to be well versed in the story and the characters involved. They need to understand how the choreographer has chosen to use those characters, and how each scene in the work contributes to the progression of the narrative.

Matthew Ball and Yasmine Naghdi of The Royal Ballet in rehearsal.

Re-staging these types of works needs time for the dancers to take ownership of their roles, to understand how to interact with the other characters and to learn how to develop the emotional authority to speak authentically to the audience. A constructive rehearsal director/coach/dancer relationship is vital for exploring the underlying subtleties in the characterizations.

Everyone in the room has to enter with empathy... and work with a sense of humanity.
William Tuckett, Choreographer (2018)

Contemporary Repertoire

Flight Pattern (Crystal Pite, 2017), *Rite of Spring* (Pina Bausch, 1975) or *Petit Mort* (Jiří Kylián, 1991) are examples of the influence of contemporary dance and thinking on the ballet stage. This genre/descriptor of work is large and variable. When re-staging contemporary works, the importance of the rehearsal director being able to articulate and translate an individual choreographer's movement vocabulary is crucial. In the twenty-first century, this movement vocabulary may be motivated by a variety of theories and techniques of the body, movement and relationships in space. Movement may come from unfamiliar cultural references, or be influenced by several different genres of dance. In this situation, dancers must be open to investigating and integrating unfamiliar processes of creating, developing and motivating movement. During the re-staging of one of these contemporary works, it becomes the rehearsal director's role to communicate those original ideas and intentions.

In smaller organizations, or when working on independent freelance projects, the re-staging process is by necessity highly collaborative. There is a much greater reliance on fellow dancers for feedback and teaching, and dancers must be willing to take on their own independent research to understand the background or details of a role. There may not have been a rehearsal director in charge of looking after the work when it was originally created, and re-staging a work likes this involves everyone's commitment and focus.

Systems for Recording/Archiving Work

- Benesh
- Labanotation
- Bespoke Systems
- Video archives

There is no standardized system for archiving dance. Both historical and current works are preserved through a combination of established and bespoke written notation systems and digital/video archives. Many works also rely on the embodied experience of the dancers involved. But while dancers will often remember their individual interpretation of a role, an authentic re-staging of a work several months, or even years, later is often dependent on the notation and notes written during its creation, as well as the digital records. A combined gathering of knowledge is often key, as the initial impetus or idea behind a movement may be forgotten or distorted when digital records are the only resource.

There are two types of commonly used written dance notation: Benesh and Labanotation. The use of these notation systems relies on an individual (or individuals) trained in one of them being present during a choreographic process. Without these specialist choreologists (or notators), the choreographer or their assistant, rehearsal directors, stage managers and/or dancers have to take on the responsibility of creating a record and archive of a work.

Notation provides an invaluable resource, even in the digital age, as notators or choreologists, often capture the initial choreographic essence of a work. For example, phrases of movement that are taught to help dancers understand a particular choreographer's movement vocabulary may be notated, even if not present in the final piece. Dancers inherently change or 'personalize' movement as it settles on their bodies. This 'personalization' is a natural part of the rehearsal process. But, in the 're-teaching' of a work, it is important to try and impart the 'essence' of the original choreography, so that the work doesn't gradually evolve further on every re-staging. Like a musical score, the notation captures the underlying structure of the work.

Page of Benesh movement notation for *Flight Pattern*, choreography Crystal Pite. Notated by Gregory Mislin.

Choreography © Pite 2017.
Notated by G. Mislin in BMN
Score owner The Royal Ballet

Benesh

Rudolph and Joan Benesh developed Benesh notation in the 1950s. In 1955, it was adopted by Ninette De Valois, the director of The Royal Ballet, to record and preserve its repertoire. The Royal Ballet currently employs two to three full-time choreologists to aid in the preservation of new work. They also assist in the re-staging of older works from the repertoire. This commitment to Benesh notation, prior to the advent of easily accessible video, has enabled accurate reconstructions of the works by such company choreographers as Frederick Ashton and Kenneth MacMillan. It also ensures that most current repertoire within The Royal Ballet continues to be notated.

Benesh records movements on a musical stave, positioning each part of the body in space at a moment in time in relation to those stave lines. The changing movements of the body are notated with the corresponding musical score below on the page, allowing for an accurate record of the desired musical relationship. Benesh also records the placement and movement of multiple people on the stage, the direction of travel, complex partnering, and the entrances and exits of dancers. All of these details, and more, will be present in a Benesh score.

Labanotation

Labanotation is another form of written notation for dance. This notation system was developed in the 1920s by Rudolf Laban. Like Benesh, Laban records the direction the dancer is facing, the level in relation to the ground of the body parts, the flow and direction of movement for the body and limbs, and the duration of a movement. Labanotation also incorporates the dynamics and intention of a movement. The notation is recorded vertically in time from the bottom of the page to the top, with bar markings and counts noted to the side of the notation (when necessary). The incorporation of dynamic markers has led to Labanotation often being used for the preservation of more contemporary works, where the motivation or intention may be as important as the actual movement. This notation system is also used for movement analysis in clinical settings.

Video

Video is increasingly used to aid in the archiving and preservation of work, especially for organizations with few resources and/or projects where a notator or assistant is unavailable. While every choreographer uses video differently, nearly all will make sure that several recordings of a work exist. Some choreographers use video as a part of their creative process – recording rehearsals to take home and analyse, coming back the following day with changes and revisions. This can be useful when a choreographer is working within a limited timeframe or has limited access to dancers.

When using video for archival purposes, it is important to record several versions of a work: several studio rehearsals, a rehearsal on stage and several performances, if possible. Some choreographers will even create archival 'tracks' for the various dancers in a project, and will film a work multiple times, recording each individual dancer's role.

RESPONSIBILITIES AND ATTITUDE

What makes the time in the studio work best?

Everyone needs a 'willingness to try, a good work ethic and a sense of humour'.
Jackie Barratt, long standing assistant to Christopher Wheeldon (2018)

Anna Rose O'Sullivan and Joseph Sissens of The Royal Ballet in rehearsal.

WHAT TO AVOID IN THE STUDIO

Factors that can lead to a negative atmosphere:

- An unsuccessful synergy between a dancer or dancers and the creative team.
- Personal issues outside the studio being brought into the room.
- Overwork or exhaustion on the part of either the choreographer or dancer(s).

Regardless of the scale or size of a project, when choreographers, rehearsal directors and dancers discuss their most difficult working environments in the studio they speak of individuals who, for one reason or another, metaphorically 'don't want to be in the room'. Sometimes being aware of potential pitfalls that can arise during the time in the studio is enough to cultivate a sensitivity to one another, and mitigate difficulties.

Characteristics of a Positive Studio Environment

- *Engagement*: In order to create or recreate a work successfully, all members of the team need to want to be involved. The end-product will not be a success without everyone doing their part to the best of their ability. For dancers, wanting to be involved means being open to the experience. This involves being active participants in the creative process of the choreographer. It means being open to feedback from rehearsal directors and coaches during the process of a re-staging and, above all, it means 'wanting to be in the room'.
- *Honesty*: When working intensely in a studio, the environment is, ideally, one of mutual respect between the creative team and the dancers. A rapport that is open, honest, supportive and collaborative has the best chance of success. Everyone in the room needs 'focus, clarity and diligence' (Sarah Lamb, Dancer 2018).

- *Humour*: A valued quality in the studio, which came up repeatedly in responses from choreographers, rehearsal directors and dancers, was a sense of humour. This is not humour in the sense of joking around constantly or finding everything funny; but being able to see the humour in a situation and being able to laugh at oneself.

The studio time for any work reflects its creative essence. The physical, intellectual and emotional effort invested then and there is carried forward on to the stage. The time in the studio pays off when it begins with a willingness to try, a willingness to take feedback and a willingness to engage. It is the responsibility of everyone – the choreographer, rehearsal director, coach, ballet master/mistress and dancers – to respect that communal effort, and to give their very best. Ultimately, you are working together.

An ability to enjoy work without that getting in the way of work.
William Tuckett, Choreographer (2018)

PERSONAL PREPARATION

Individual Homework

Every dancer has a responsibility to do a certain amount of independent performance preparation; this may take place before a creative project even begins. For example, prior to working with a new choreographer, you might do the following:

- Research new choreographers by watching clips of their past works on the internet.
- Look at who the choreographer has worked with in the past to gain insight into possible working styles.
- If the subject, theme or narrative topic is known for the new work, read the narrative story or thematic information.

For some, these preparation techniques help them to be ready for that important first experience with a choreographer in the studio. But

know what works for you as an individual and what makes you feel most confident. Some dancers, such as Sarah Lamb (2018), don't like to do any research in advance; they leave themselves as open as possible to ideas on the first day of creation, without any preconceptions of what a choreographer might desire. 'Inevitably one will have unconscious biases based on previous knowledge if one has already been acquainted with someone's work.'

Is There a Story?

If working on a narrative work, read the story associated with the work. In a full evening piece of narrative dance, it is imperative to understand the full story and the journey of the characters involved. The dance work will usually cut parts of the original narrative, but as the emotional progression of the story is portrayed through the dancing, it is necessary to understand the story you are telling.

Should I Use Video/Internet to Learn?

Digital content is now commonplace, and there are more and more recorded versions of interpretations of famous dance roles. It is possible to view a variation or an entire ballet on YouTube, and compare the various interpretations of different roles. In larger companies, comprehensive digital/video archives enable dancers to study multiple past performances. These ways of studying content can be exceptionally useful in observing what 'reads' to an audience, as well as gathering opinions on who has given a well thought-out interpretation to a role. However, overuse of video for learning can be a problem when dancers imitate the exact details of an interpretation. Take the time to understand the intention and motivation of the choreography for yourself.

Have I Prepared Myself Emotionally?

The integrity of any performance, narrative or abstract, relies on each dancer investing their time and thought into their individual interpretation. There may be psychological and emotional preparation for a particular role, if the subject matter is difficult. A full commitment to understanding the intention and motivation behind a work will allow the authenticity of a performance to come through.

Is My Body Prepared to be Dancing This Role?

Do I need to be working on any specific technique to help prepare myself for a role or specific work? Sometimes a choreographer demands an unfamiliar physicality, or style of movement, that you may need to take extra time to learn and practice to feel ready to rehearse. Is there another dancer or teacher who can

Claire Calvert of The Royal Ballet prepares her shoes for performance in a principal role.

help you develop these skills? Sometimes a role also demands incredible amounts of stamina, for which a dancer may need to do extra cross-training work, spending time in the gym with a specialist trainer.

Performance Preparation

Finally, there is the performance and the pre-show routine. A dancer's training, personal habits and personality will lead to different styles of personal preparation. The crucial moments before an actual performance are individual to each artist. Some of the factors that influence the pre-show routine include:

- Personal habits and needs – including diet, sleep, levels of anxiety.
- Types of work – repertory-based work, repetition of the same show for an extended period of time or improvisatory work.
- Company/organizational norms – touring or residential company schedules.

The pre-show routine often contains ritual elements. It is a period of sending a dancer into a state of 'readiness'. For some, preparation might take hours and include: sleep, meditation, food, make-up, hair and a thorough warm-up. For others, the pre-show routine might involve dinner at the pub, a quick coffee and some chocolate.

As one ages, this pre-show routine changes. In general, as dancers age their habits before a show become more entrenched, and the recovery time needed after a performance increases. Dancers acknowledge that their warm-up varies, depending on what they are performing. A major role involves far more focus and a longer warm-up/preparation period.

Union or organizational rules also affect pre-show time. Most companies limit the number of hours dancers work in the lead up to an evening performance, giving dancers time before a performance to rest, eat and prepare. In some companies, an evening warm-up is provided before the show, and may even be mandatory. Others provide only a morning class and rehearsals during the day before the performance. Within an independent project, a dancer may only be obliged to be at the theatre for 'the half hour'; the

responsibility of being ready for the show rests solely on their shoulders. Regardless of circumstance, each dancer must make sure they are ready and warm for what they need to be doing on stage.

Touring schedules will also differ from the time-table that is run at the home base. Generally, dancers will start slightly later in the day on tour, as the stage is often the only space available for class and rehearsals. But, if a company is doing a series of single performances in multiple venues, the travelling, 'get in' – which includes the technical focusing and preparation of the stage – staging and dress run, and the performance itself, may all happen in one day. This type of timetable doesn't allow for much rest. Dancers must be in control of their own self-management.

Viewed from the wings, third-year students of Images Ballet Company in the 'dress run' on tour.

Dancers in the wings preparing for their entrance.

USEFUL TERMS FOR THE STAGE

Half Hour: 35min before a performance for UK companies; 30min in the US. Everyone involved in the performance is expected to be in the theatre.

Beginners: This is the call 5min before the curtain rises on a performance.

The Five: This is the 'five-minute call' – 10min before curtain up.

Stage Right, Left, Upstage, Downstage: Directions in relation to the dancer when facing the audience. (*See* Dancer's Square in Chapter 1.)

Proscenium Arch: The frame at the front of the stage that marks the boundary between the back-stage performance area and the auditorium.

Tabs: The curtain at the front of the stage that can be drawn at the beginning and end of the performance.

Flats: These are hard, high walls, which frame out the stage and create the wings for the dancers.

Wings: The space between the flats for entering and exiting the stage.

Prompt Side: This is dependent on the theatre, and refers to where the stage manager is placed in the wings on the side of stage.

OP: The opposite side of stage to the prompt side.

Lighting Bars: These are the long bars that hang at the top of the stage space and carry lights. They can be lowered to alter the positioning of the lights.

Lighting Booms: These are the towers of lights that stand in the wings.

FINAL THOUGHTS

The studio period is multifaceted, taking the dancers and creative/artistic team through an evolving process of gestation and development. It may be days, weeks, months or years, depending on the project. Our closer examination of studio time highlights the importance of being aware of each project's collaborative aspect – large or small.

Choreographers, rehearsal staff, dancers and all members of a creative team, generally share the desire to make the most of these special hours in the studio. While external factors may sometimes cause distractions, the studio provides focused time to fully develop a new work or to recreate the essence of an existing work, the end goal being a successful performance on stage. These hours of emotion, passion, levity, sweat and effort hold the potential to produce the magic and brilliance that the dancers, creative team, staff and audience all crave.

Anita Feerick: third-year ballet student at London Studio Centre.

CONCLUSION: FROM STUDIO TO STAGE
Nicholas Minns

It is unlikely when you start ballet classes that you are thinking exactly where they might lead. While there is in training a great value for both body and mind, ballet is a performing art and to realize its full potential it needs to be performed. If you have arrived at this page after reading all the preceding chapters, you will have taken a vicarious journey from the studio to the stage – advice on all aspects of a dancer's education, a broad range of ideas on the art and technique of a professional dancer, and an introduction to music and the craft of choreography. There's a lot to think about; as the late Roger Tully used to say, 'Ballet is a "happening", not a "doing", but a lot has to be done before it can happen'.[89]

Ballet derives from a court environment, designed on a grand scale to impress, and the form is, in many ways, a display that moves out from the stage toward the audience. This seems a long way from barre work in a studio setting, but it is worth remembering that the ballet technique itself is conceived as a movement outwards (*en dehors*) from the dancer's centre, a physiological place that derives from the Fifth Position. *En dehors* and its converse, *en dedans*, can be understood as paths of energy spiralling through a dancer's body; from the dynamic point where they converge derive all the exercises of academic ballet. The search for, and subsequent use of, such a centre is equally a search for freedom within the technique, which can only be acquired through an inner mastery of sensation in the body. The sensation of this centre will be different for each dancer and, because it is internal and essentially hidden, it cannot be seen reflected in a

studio mirror. But it can be nurtured through diligent practise of the technical principles outlined in this book, and guided by a knowledgeable teacher.

The form of what we call 'classical ballet' developed in the flow of the French, Danish and Italian schools that converged in Russia in the late-nineteenth century. The era that produced such ballets as *Swan Lake*, *The Sleeping Beauty* and *The Nutcracker* – the 'classics' that are still seen in various adaptations today – coincided with the contribution of great teachers. But that accumulated classical tradition soon found itself transformed in early twentieth-century Europe by Diaghilev's Ballets Russes. With graduates of the St. Petersburg (Mariinsky) school, including Nijinsky, Karsavina, Fokine and Pavlova, Diaghilev demonstrated that radical dance innovations could spring from classical ballet traditions. Many more dance artists, including Balanchine, had left Russia and Chapter 2 brings the reader to the mid-twentieth century when their influence in the West led to a re-vitalization of ballet and its formal establishment in schools and companies worldwide.

The genealogy of ballet is like a family tree, where the union of choreographic styles and influences produces new generations of dance. Isadora Duncan's performances in St. Petersburg, for example, may well have influenced the plasticity Fokine employed in his choreography. In this light, a ballet like his *Les Sylphides* can be understood as a synthesis of ballet technique and a contemporary flow of movement that in turn illustrates how the dance form is constantly evolving. You only have to look at works by Ashton and Sir Kenneth MacMillan for The Royal Ballet, Maurice Béjart for his Ballets du 20ème Siècle, John Cranko for Stuttgart Ballet, Jiří Kylián for Nederlands Dance Theatre, William Forsythe for Frankfurter Ballett, Mats Ek for the Royal Swedish Ballet and John Neumeier for Hamburg Ballet to see, in Europe alone, the many permutations of ballet technique and form in the latter half of the twentieth century.

New expressive forms of dance have also given birth to various contemporary techniques. In the US, Martha Graham was a major influence on choreography of emotional depth, while one of her dancers, Merce Cunningham, left to start his own company and his idiosyncratic style. Both Graham and Cunningham developed techniques that are every bit as monolithic as ballet; you cannot perform their works authentically unless you have been immersed in their technical underpinnings.

Although Cunningham came from Graham, he transformed her influence into a technique that, while uncompromisingly contemporary, can look surprisingly classical. When he first came to London with his company in 1964, the dance critic Alexander Bland declared, 'Here is heart-warming proof that [ballet] is an art with a future, opening up ranges of possibilities which stretch out of sight; it ought to be celebrated with champagne in every dancing academy in the land'.[90] Perhaps what Bland recognized was Cunningham's use of the dynamic centre of the body; his technique was designed to allow his dancers to move in any direction at any speed at any moment.

Studying at New York's Juilliard School at around the same time was a young German dancer by the name of Pina Bausch, who was to return to Essen to work as a soloist with an advocate of German Expressionism, the choreographer Kurt Jooss. She later founded her own company and developed the major strand of Tanztheater (Dance Theatre). Bausch was interested less in how her dancers moved than in what moved them, but they were trained in ballet technique; it was her choreographic imagery, music, sets and costumes that transformed the way her dancers appeared. Her admirers and disciples are legion and have spread the vocabulary and form of Dance Theatre throughout the world.

The range of styles within established ballet companies can also be very broad, as can be seen in the Royal Ballet where Wayne McGregor has been the resident choreographer for the past fourteen years. There are also companies that maintain training in ballet technique but have no traditionally 'classical' repertoire. At the same time Bausch was developing the form of Dance Theatre in Germany, Forsythe at Ballett Frankfurt began experimenting with ballet's choreographic lexicon. His focus was on what the ballet-trained body can do *beyond* academic ballet. Another contemporary choreographic direction is an increasing integration of different techniques and cultural influences into the ballet tradition, of which the choreography of Sidi Larbi Cherkaoui, Twyla Tharp, Crystal Pite and Akram Khan are representative examples.

While the development of ballet continues, there is a corresponding interest in reconstructing the past, rather like the historically informed performance of classical music. In recent years, Alexei Ratmansky, the Russian choreographer and artist in residence at American Ballet Theater, has reconstructed, among other works, *The Sleeping Beauty*, *Swan Lake* and *Giselle* from existing notation created by the dancer Vladimir Stepanov as a reminder of how Petipa and Ivanov used the ballet vocabulary to create them. While these reconstructions reflect the level of academic training at the time, they also demonstrate the integral relationship of choreography and mime to music.

For a ballet-trained dancer emerging into such a multifaceted dance world, the principles and advice in this book are invaluable, for in the postgraduation process of professional auditions and company apprenticeships, you must be open and able to embark on any number of permutations of classical ballet technique. Having the confidence of a dynamic centre will be vital. Maintaining it leads you back into the studio, to those same exercises with which you began, with that same inner awareness constantly filtered through both your love of dancing and your ongoing performing experience. This continuous process is your individual path as a dance artist between the studio and the stage.

KEY TERMS AND CONCEPTS

A comprehensive glossary of ballet terms is available in books, and abbreviated versions in online dictionaries, for example:

Richard Glasstone *Classical Ballet Terms: an Illustrated Dictionary*, 3rd edn (Dance Books, 2013)

Gail Grant *Technical Manual and Dictionary of Classical Ballet* (Dover Publications, 1982)

Rhonda Ryman *Dictionary of Classical Ballet Terminology*, 3rd edn (Royal Academy of Dance, 2007)

American Ballet Theatre Online Dictionary www.abt.org/explore/learn/ballet-dictionary/

Technical manuals are broader in scope and include theory, diagrams/photographs, advice for the teaching of ballet and terminology. Two highly influential and important texts about the Vaganova and Cecchetti methods continue to be widely used today (*see* Chapter 2).

It is worth considering the meaning of the following terms that you will encounter in your learning.

WHAT IS GOOD PRACTICE?

Good 'Good ballet' accords with the natural laws of the physics of movement. It is both technically and aesthetically functional; technical function serves to realize aesthetic form.

'Good practice' relates to the idea of diligent, accurate application and effort in class; involves integrating reflective and embodied knowledge, to develop understanding of the principles as you experience them, and awareness of your own and the wider 'dance'; recognizes that learning to dance involves the whole person, engaging all spheres of experience (physical, intellectual, emotional and spiritual).

Correct Applying ballet technique in an appropriate way, that is 'in harmony with the physical laws of motion'.[91] Ballet vocabulary is articulated with attention to the fundamental principles of alignment in the body posture and placement in movement, and with appropriate dynamic.

Susie Crow adds that correct practice involves:

Accurate execution of what is asked, attending to the details specified. Attention to such details, which may be new, unusual or even uncomfortable, is part of the dancer extending themself, their knowledge and understanding, and a feature of the developing artist.[92]

Truthful Being attentive to the experience of your own body dancing in relation to the physical laws and aesthetic principles; for example, recognizing the feeling of your weight distributed around the line of the aplomb.

NOTE These ideas don't mean that there is one 'right' way of performing or exploring. Ballerina/Director Maina Gielgud commented on the importance of being open to different approaches:

I worked with so many teachers as a student and it helped me tremendously because I didn't have this sort of blocked thinking, that there was only one way.[93]

'What is Good Practice' is adapted from Alvarez, I. and Jackson, J. *OER* Online Educational Resource) *Contexts, Culture and Creativity: Enriching E-learning in Dance Project* (University of Surrey, 2012)

En dehors (tr. to the outside) Direction of a movement outward from the centre; also expression in classical ballet.

En dedans (tr. to the inside) Direction of a movement inward to the centre; also expression in classical ballet.

En place (tr. in place) The physical centre or axis point of the body in relation to gravity, and feeling of being centred; stillness, where connection between spheres of experience can be registered.

Aplomb Fundamental to the concept of verticality, also referred to as the dancer's axis; 'the plumb line used by architects and builders to establish vertical upright over the centre of gravity'.[94] Derives from French *aplomb* (sixteenth century) and the phrase *à plomb* 'poised upright, balanced', literally 'on the plumb line'. Infers poise and assurance.

Dynamic The quality of effort and intensity in movement or action.

Dynamic of Opposition Attention to oppositional pull between 'points' in the body; sustaining balance, shape and releasing movement. For example, the downward thrust through the heel and foot, gives the upward lift through the hip joint in the opposite direction, as experienced when the two legs pass equally across the vertical in Fifth Position, creating the potential for movement in all directions (front, side and back) and the spring action into the air.

Épaulement (tr. shouldering) Initiated in the thoracic spine and the back, the rotation of the upper torso and shoulders in opposition to a stable pelvis. Functions to activate the inner spiral musculature around the aplomb and to enhance individual expression. Encourages somatic awareness of the oppositional forces in the whole body posture; for example, in Fifth, from the left shoulder to the right hip, and the hip through to the heel of the corresponding turned-out foot.

Proprioception (also known as kinaesthesia) Perception or sensory awareness of the body's position and movement, including (in dance) orientation of the body in space and in relation to other objects. Registered by receptors in the muscles, tendons and joints, active in approaches to improving posture, alignment and flow.

Somatic (in dance) Related to the body as perceived from within. A somatic approach involves considering 'my' practice from the first-person perspective and attending to the inner sensation of the mechanical and aesthetic functioning or feeling of the body's movement in forms.

SUPPLIERS

There are hundreds of Dancewear and *Pointe* Shoes suppliers, catering to diverse taste and needs.

In the UK, the following brands are popular, and you can find expert guidance in the essential task of fitting *pointe* shoes correctly in stores such as Freed of London.

Freed
Porselli
Gaynor Minden
Bloch
Capezio
Russian Pointe
Suffolk

RECOMMENDED READING

References to the sources are included in the Endnotes and are noted with a superscript number.

The recommended readings below are annotated briefly as a guide to their content.

Arkin, L. & Smith, M. National dance in the romantic ballet. In L. Garafola (ed.), *Rethinking the Sylph: New Perspectives on the Romantic Ballet* (Wesleyan University Press, 1997), pp. 11–68

This chapter, and Smith's later book *Ballet and Opera in the Age of Giselle* (Princeton University Press, 2000) are must-reads for anyone interested in ballet music of this period.

Burrows, J. *A Choreographer's Handbook* (Routledge, 2010)

Full of thoughtful ideas and practical tips.

Flatt, K. *Choreography, Creating and Developing Dance for Performance* (The Crowood Press, 2019)

Comprehensive and user friendly, covers everything from first ideas to realising the work on stage.

Forsythe, W. *Improvisation Technologies: A Tool for the Analytical Dance Eye* (ZKM, Centre for Art and Media Karlsruhe, 1999; 2nd edn 2003)

Developed between 1995 and 1999 by the influential and important choreographer as a tool for dancers to explore the spatial and temporal geometries of ballet form.

Homans, J. *Apollo's Angels: A History of Ballet* (Granta Publications, 2010)

Comprehensive and inspiring history of the art form

Jackson, J. My dance and the ideal body: looking at ballet practice from the inside out. *Research in Dance Education* (2005, Vol 6, no1/2. pp. 25–40)

Reflects on individual agency and the place of somatic approaches in learning in ballet.

John-Steiner, V. *Creative Collaboration* (Oxford University Press, 2000)

Inspiring account of creative exchanges, including between dance and music.

Jordan, S. Choreographers and Musicians in Collaboration, from the Twentieth to the Twenty-First Century. In N. Donin (ed.), *The Oxford Handbook of Creative Process in Music* (Oxford University Press, 2018)

A recent and wide-ranging overview of trends in collaboration in music and dance in the last 100 years or so, from the author of *Moving Music* (Dance Books, 2000), the key textbook on this subject.

Joseph, C. M. *Stravinsky and Balanchine – a Journey of Invention* (Yale University Press, 2002)

Excellent read and analysis of their artistic practices.

Krasnow, D. & Wilmerding, M. V. *Motor Learning and Control for Dance* (Human Kinetics, 2015)

Provides information on how new skills can be developed through knowledge of motor behaviour.

Naughtin, M. *Ballet Music: A Handbook* (Rowman & Littlefield, 2014)

The best reference book available for musical details of complex ballets like *Le Corsaire, Paquita* and different versions of *Swan Lake,* from the music librarian of San Francisco Ballet.

Newman, B. *Grace Under Pressure: Passing Dance Through Time* (Dance Books, 2004)

Inspiring reading; brings the work and wisdom of dancers, teachers and choreographers vividly to the page.

Pakes, A. Dance works, concepts and historiography. In (G. Morris and L. Nicholas, eds) *Rethinking Dance History: Issues and Methodologies*, 2nd edn (Routledge, 2018), pp. 56–68

This brief but accessible article covers some of the important philosophical and historical background to the notion of the 'work' in both music and dance.

Paskevska, A. *Ballet Beyond Tradition: The Role of Movement Concepts in Ballet Technique* (Routledge, 2005)

Excellent ideas about how concepts in Limon technique enhance ballet technique, including oppositional forces, suspension, release.

Tully, R. *The Song Sings the Bird: a Manual on the Teaching of Classical Dance* (Gremese, 2011)

Thought-provoking introduction to the classical principles in ballet and detailed descriptions of the fundamental barre exercises.

Whitley, A., Brooker, S. & Miller, C. *Look Before You Leap: an Advice and Rights Guide for Choreographers*, 2nd edn (DanceUK, 2012)

A standard text on music rights for choreography.

WEB-LINKS

On Healthy Dance

Royal Ballet School: www.royalballetschool.org.uk

See within the site for information on 'Healthy Dancer' programme.

IADMS: www.iadms.org

IADMS provides a platform for international networking between dance medical practitioners, dance educators and dance scientists. An excellent site for research: past and current.

On Music and Ballet Repertoire

- www.abt.org/explore/learn/repertory-archive/ American Ballet Theatre
- www.frederickashton.org.uk/ballets.html Ballets of Frederick Ashton
- www.jirikylian.com/creations/theatre/ Ballets of Jiří Kylián
- www.kennethmacmillan.com/az-of-ballets Ballets of Kenneth MacMillan
- www.nycballet.com/Discover/The-Repertory. aspx New York City Ballet repertory
- http://musicsalesclassical.com/listen/dance Dance music ideas from Music Sales
- www.boosey.com/pages/dance Dance music ideas from Boosey & Hawkes

On Copyright and Licensing

- www.prsformusic.com/licences General information on music licensing from PRS for Music.
- www.prsformusic.com/royalties/theatre-royalties-and-grand-rights Explanation of the difference between grand and small rights licensing.
- www.boosey.com/pages/dance/DanceLicensingInfo Music publishers Boosey & Hawkes special information on licensing music for dance.

ENDNOTES

1   Olsen, S. *The Golden Section: Nature's Greatest Secret.* (Wooden Books, 2009)
2   Hemenway, P. *The Secret Code* (Evergreen, 2008)
3   Guest, I. *The Dancer's Heritage: A Short History of Ballet* (The Dancing Times, 1979)
4   Au, S. *Ballet and Modern Dance* (Thames and Hudson, 1988)
5   Tully, R. *The Song Sings The Bird* (Gremese, 2011), p. 17
6   Jackson, J. My dance and the ideal body: looking at ballet practice from the inside out. *Research in Dance Education* (2005, 6(1–2), pp. 25–40)
7   Homans, J. *Apollo's Angels: A History of Ballet* (Granta Publications, 2010)
8   Smith-Autard, J. *The Art of Dance in Education*, 2nd edn (Bloomsbury, 2002)
9   Guest, I. *The Dancer's Heritage* (Dance Books, 1988)
10 Nevile, J. Early dance manuals. In Marion Kant (ed.), *The Cambridge Companion to Ballet* (Cambridge University Press, 2007), pp. 12, 17, 174
11 Jaffé, N. A. *Folk Dance of Europe* (Folk Dance Enterprises, 1990), pp. 172–4, 284
12 Oreglia, G. *The Commedia dell'Arte* (Hill and Wang, 1968)
13 Nevile, Early dance manuals, p. 10
14 Kirstein, L. *Four Centuries of Ballet* (Dover, 1984)
15 Homans, J. *Apollo's Angels* (Granta, 2010), p. 9
16 McGowan, M. *The Court Ballets of Louis XIII* (V&A Museum, 1985)
17 Cordova, S. D. Romantic Ballet in France: 1830–1850. In Kant, *The Cambridge Companion to Ballet*
18 McKenzie, A. unpublished notes to the author (2012)
19 Bruhn, E. & Moore, L. *Bournonville and Ballet Technique* (Adam & Charles Black, 1961)
20 Roslavleva, N. *Era of the Russian Ballet* (Victor Gollancz, 1966), p. 18
21 Roslavleva, *Era of the Russian Ballet*
22 Homans, *Apollo's Angels*, p. 249
23 Homans, *Apollo's Angels*, p. 251
24 Garafola, L. Russian ballet in the age of Petipa. In Kant (ed.), *The Cambridge Companion to Ballet* (2007), p. 152
25 Guest, *The Dancer's Heritage*, p. 29
26 Slonimsky, Y. Cradle of the Russian ballet. In A. Haskell & M. Clarke (eds), *Ballet Annual 1961* (Adam & Charles Black, 1960), p. 132
27 Meisner, N. *Marius Petipa* (Oxford University Press, 2019)
28 Quoted in Roslavleva, *Era of the Russian Ballet*, p. 66
29 Meisner, *Marius Petipa*
30 Garafola, Russian ballet in the age of Petipa, p. 151
31 Legat, N. *The Story of the Russian School* (British-Continental Press, 1932), p. 33
32 Legat, *The Story of the Russian School,* p. 32
33 Legat, *The Story of the Russian School,* p. 25
34 Wood, M. *Historical Dances* (Dance Books, 1982)
35 Ralph, R. *The Life and Works of John Weaver* (Dance Books, 1985)
36 Kirstein, L. *Four Centuries of Ballet* (Dover, 1984), p. 95
37 Clarke, M. & Crisp, C. *The History of Dance* (Orbis, 1981)
38 De Valois, N. Future of the ballet. In *Dancing Times* February 1926, pp. 589–591
39 Macaulay, A. *International Dictionary, Vol. 1* (St. James' Press, 1992), p. 55
40 Frederick Ashton writing to Richard Glasstone (1984).
41 Macaulay, *International Dictionary, Vol. 1*
42 Bland, A. *The Royal Ballet* (Threshold, 1981), p. 46
43 Quoted in Bland, *The Royal Ballet*, p. 6
44 Moore, L. *Echoes of American Ballet* (Dance Horizons, 1976)
45 Moore, *Echoes of American Ballet*
46 Pritchard, J. *Anna Pavlova, Twentieth Century Ballerina* (Booth-Clibborn, 2012)
47 Craine, D. & Mackrell, J. *Oxford Dictionary of Dance* (Oxford University Press, 2004)
48 De Mille, A. *The Book of the Dance* (Paul Hamlyn, 1963), p. 66
49 Joseph, C. M. *Stravinsky's Ballets* (Yale University Press, 2011)
50 Craine & Mackrell, *Oxford Dictionary of Dance*
51 Au, S. *Ballet and Modern Dance* (Thames & Hudson, 2002), p. 146
52 Ashton, F. at Lecture Demonstration led by Nicola Katrak in Eye, Suffolk, 1985
53 Tully, R. *The Song Sings the Bird* (Gremese, 2011), p. 11
54 Tully, *The Song Sings the Bird*, p. 22
55 Interview and email correspondence: Jennifer Jackson with Zoe Arshamian (2020), Francesca Hayward (2020) and William Bracewell (2019).

56 Skoog, M. *One Dance UK* Article, *How to Succeed in Today's Market* (2018) www.onedanceuk.org/wp-content/uploads/2018/10/ODUK_Issue_5_Full_Digi.pdf

57 Bourne, M. *Telegraph* www.telegraph.co.uk/news/celebritynews/11913635/Is-traditional-ballet-facing-its-swansong.html (2015, October 6)

58 McGregor, W. *The Talks* (2016) https://the-talks.com/interview/wayne-mcgregor/

59 Anna Paskevska's excellent book, *Ballet Beyond Traditon* (2005), explores how concepts from Limon enhance practice in classical ballet.

60 Tully, R. unpublished interview with the Editor, Jennifer Jackson (2012)

61 Bläsing, B., Puttke, M. & Schack, T. *The Neurocognition of Dance, Mind, Movement and Motor Skills Mind, Movement and Motor Skills* (Psychology Press, 2010), ch. 8

62 Fairchild, R. DanceSPIRIT www.dancespirit.com/robbie-fairchild-letter-to-teenage-self-2640876493.html?rebelltitem=1#rebelltitem1 (2019, October 7)

63 Fitt, S. *Dance Kinesiology*, 2nd edn (Schrimer Books, 1996), p. 304

64 Redding, E. Dancers: Fit Bodies? (keynote speaker) *International Symposium on Performance Science* (Vienna, Austria 2013)

65 Krasnow, D. Chatfield, S. *et al.* Imagery and conditioning practices for dancers. *Dance Research Journal* (1997), Vol. 29, No. 1 (Spring)

66 Stahl, J. Baryshnikov's advice to grads: be generous enough to let yourself fail. *Dance Magazine* (2019, May 16)

67 Bussell, D. Modern ballet dancers need many more tricks up their sleeves. *Telegraph* (2016, July 15)

68 McGregor cited in Welbye, H. *Q&A: Choreographer Wayne McGregor* (2014) https://theartsdesk.com/dance/theartsdesk-qa-choreographer-wayne-mcgregor

69 Foster, S. *Choreographing Empathy: Kinaesthesia in Performance* (Routledge, 2011) p. 38

70 Flatt, K. *Choreography, Creating and Developing Dance for Performance* (The Crowood Press, 2019)

71 Professor Christopher Bannerman in Brown, G. (ed.), *A Focus on Creativity: Proceedings of Two Seminars Exploring Creativity in Ballet Education and Training* (Royal Ballet School, 2015) p. 18

72 Jackson, J. in Brown, *A Focus on Creativity*, p. 22

73 Burrows, J. *A Choreographer's Handbook* (Routledge, 2010), p. 24

74 Burrows, *A Choreographer's Handbook*, p. 25

75 Forsythe, W. *Improvisation Technologies: A Tool for the Analytical Dance Eye* ZKM (Centre for Art and Media Karlsruhe, 1999, 2nd edn 2003)

76 Burrows, *A Choreographer's Handbook*, p. 26

77 Cited in Copeland, R. & Cohen, M. (eds) *What is Dance?* (OUP, 1983), p. 243

78 Balanchine, G. Notes on choreography. *Dance Index* (4/February–March 1945), pp. 22, 31

79 From *Lettres sur la Danse, les Ballets and les Arts*, (St Petersburg 1803) translated by Beaumont, C. W. *Letters on Dancing and Ballets* (C. W Beaumont, 1951) p. 3

80 https://www.brainyquote.com/quotes/merce_cunningham_802808

81 Burrows, *A Choreographer's Handbook*, p. 25

82 Wiley, R. J. *Tchaikovsky* (OUP, 2009), p. 135

83 Suskin, S. *The Sound of Broadway Music: A Book of Orchestrators and Orchestrations* (OUP, 2011) pp. 193–202

84 Grant, R. M. *Beating Time and Measuring Music in the Early Modern Era* (OUP, 2014) pp. 43–62

85 Baxandall, M. *Painting and Experience in Fifteenth Century Italy: A Primer in the Social History of Pictorial Style*, 2nd edn (OUP, 1988), p. 78

86 Anderson, Z. *The Ballet Lover's Companion* (Yale University Press, 2015), p. 249

87 Bales, M. Ballet for the post-Judson dancer. In *The Body Eclectic: Evolving Practices in Dance Training* (University of Illinois Press, 2008), p. 74

88 collinsdictionary.com

89 An expression Tully used in class, and referenced in *The Song Sings the Bird*, (Gremese 2011) p. 12

90 Bland, A. *Observer of the Dance 1958–1982* (Dance Books Ltd, 1985), p. 65

91 Paskevska, A. *Ballet Beyond Tradition* (Routledge 2005), p. 7

92 Crow, S. Correspondence with the Editor, Jennifer Jackson (2020)

93 Gielgud, M. In Newman, B. *Grace under Pressure: Passing Dance through Time* (Dance Books 2004), p. 143

94 Tully, R. *The Song Sings the Bird*, (Gremese 2011) p. 17

INDEX